Praise for
An Athlete's Guide To Winning
in Sports and Life
by Olympian Jonathan Edwards

"This is an important book for every athlete, parent and coach with big dreams. This book should be by your side on your entire journey. I highly recommend it."

Ruben Gonzalez - Olympian (The world's only four decade Winter Olympian) - www.FourWinterGames.com

"For years, Jonathan described me as 'Pierre Inc.' because of my business like approach to the sport of bobsled and my ability to compete at the highest level. It was an approach that led me to one **Olympic gold medal** *as well as an Olympic silver medal in addition to eleven World Cup overall titles over a lengthy career. The concepts that Jonathan outlines in his book, "An Athlete's Guide To Winning In Sports and Life" are the same one's that I used to have Olympic success and are what I teach to athlete's looking for success no matter what the sport. I recommend every athlete, parent and coach should read this book and get to know these concepts if they want to be successful."*

Pierre Lueders - Olympic Gold & Silver medalist, 11x World Cup Overall Champion, and 2x World Champion, along with dozens of world cup medals.

*"As someone who has worked closely with the Napoleon Hill Foundation spreading the word of the most famous self-help book of all time, "***Think And Grow Rich***" I know a thing or two about success. I've also been part of 50 books on the topic and speak worldwide. I can tell you that "An Athlete's Guide To Winning In Sports and Life" by Jonathan Edwards is a MUST READ for anyone who is serious about being successful in sports and life at any level. I highly recommend it."*

Greg Reid - www.KeynoteSpeaker.tv . Speaker and author featured in over 50 books, 28 bestsellers in 45 languages.

As the world's leading expert in sponsorship for athletes we work with athletes at all levels across all sports including World Champions and Olympians, as well as global brands and athletic organizations. So we know a thing or two about what it takes to succeed in high level sports. Jonathan Edwards' book, "An Athlete's Guide To Winning In Sports and Life" is a must read for ANY athlete, parent or coach who is looking to have success at the highest level. I highly recommend it!"

Vickie Saunders - Owner - The Sponsorship Consultants http://www.thesponsorshipconsultants.com/

"As I wrote to Jonathan after I read this great collection of success strategies, 'Where has this book been all my life?!'"

As a bit of backstory, I've known Jonathan ever since he was training for the 2002 Olympics, and during that time found myself extremely impressed with his personal drive and ability to overcome seemingly insurmountable obstacles. In "Young Athlete's Guide To Winning In Sports And Life, Jonathan becomes your personal mentor, as he clearly outlines the principles, strategies, and habits exhibited by all successful people. I loved this book — don't make me come over there, get yourself a copy NOW!"

Charles Staley - Trainer of Olympians, and multiple MMA and NCAA Champions in numerous sports. Top Fitness Coach, Presenter, and Author

When teams or organizations order this book in bulk, we use this page to showcase their logo. To inquire about bulk book purchases please email hello@athletespecific.com

This page is blank.
Not sure why it's blank. The publisher told us to leave it blank, and to leave a little something on the page so that the printer didn't confuse it as a blank page.

So here's a little "something".

An Athlete's Guide To Winning in Sports and Life

I'd like to congratulate you for purchasing this book.
To get your free chapter on Long Term Athlete Development please go
to www.AthleteSpecific.com/book-bonus and download the chapter.

And if you'd like to take what you've learned in this book to the next
level. Please go to
http://athletespecific.com/high-performance-course-athletes/
When you are there, apply the coupon "YouAreAwesome" and receive
$100 off your purchase.

An Athlete's Guide To Winning in Sports and Life

First Edition

Jonathan Edwards - Olympian

Oly Press

ISBN-13: 978-0-9997630-0-1

Dedication

To the teammates, competitors, coaches, doctors, support staff, friends, family, and to Mom and Dad, who told me I could make my athletic dreams come true.

And those who told me I couldn't.

And to those who will tell you that you can.

And to those who will tell you that you can't.

This book is dedicated to them all.

Contents

Section 2: Preparing For Game Day

Section 3: Train. Recover. Compete. Recover. Repeat.

Section 5: Get Results. Review Those Results. Keep The Lessons. Try Again.

Foreword

So, I wrote a book.

I didn't think that the book would be a long book, but as I started to compile articles and emails I had written over the years on topics I'd covered with every parent, athlete and coach I'd come in contact with, I quickly realized this wasn't going to be a "Hi, how 'ya doin'" book, but that it was going to be an "important" book.

Like most coaches, I have moments where I think, "Sheesh, if you (the athlete) just understood THIS you'd GET IT!." That is what this book is about.

The world of sports from youth to college age is muddy. There are plenty of people today lamenting the fact that sports is 'broken' and that it needs to be fixed. That there is too much of an emphasis on winning and not enough on development. These arguments place the blame outside of us, the athlete. Complaining about the way things are and not about what we can do to change the outcome. This is no different than blaming the weather, or the traffic, or your equipment.

While I agree that certain things could change, it does nothing to help you right now. This book is meant to fix that.

I want this book to be a resource for you. A special one. While it is written to the athlete, a parent or coach will benefit from owning this book because they will hear me talking to the athlete. With that knowledge they can then pass on this info to the athletes they coach and love.

This book should be beat up. Dog eared. Frayed at the edges, because it's meant to be referred to again and again. It should be in your gym bag to read on the bus to a game, or before practice. A friend of mine actually laminated the cover of his copy so it survived the trip to the weight room every day. When he was tired, or worn our, or just wanted some inspiration he read the book or listened to the audio version.

When you have a challenge, you should pick up the book and look through the table of contents and find the chapter that applies to your challenge and read it again. And again. And each chapter also has a corresponding video over at www.AthleteSpecific.com so be sure to watch that as well.

I want you to be awesome. I want you to know that you can do this. Because if little 'ol me. The only child of two musicians can go on and become an Olympian as well as a Division One recruit in a completely different sport, than you can to. Believe it because it's true. You can do this.

When you have a second. Send me an email. I love hearing stories of of athletes who my writing touches. Tell me who you are. Where you are. And what's your sport. I read all my emails and I'll send you a note back. Send it to coachedwards@athletespecific.com.

I believe in you.

Sincerely,

Jonathan Edwards - Olympian
coachedwards@athletespecific.com

Introduction

There are no limits.

"Our deepest fear is not that we are inadequate. Our deepest fear is that we are powerful beyond measure. It is our light, not our darkness that most frightens us. We ask ourselves, Who am I to be brilliant, gorgeous, talented, fabulous? Actually, who are you not to be?

Marianne Williamson
from her book <u>A Return To Love</u>

First and foremost I want to thank you for picking up this book. Many of the athletes I work with won't read anything past a textbook that they have been assigned to read for school, so I appreciate that you are here.

This may be a really big read for you, and you may be thinking "I'm never going to get through this whole book, but I guarantee that if you read this entire book, you will reach your athletic goals faster than you ever thought possible..

I wish I had a book like this when I was starting out in sports. Although, I'm not sure if I would have had the guts to read it. There's so much to learn when it comes to sports and our focus tends to be on the easy things. Either the ball is at your feet, the puck is on your stick, you're lifting weights...or you're not. It's an on/off switch of training/no training, doing/no doing.

Then there is the whole idea of looking at those around you to see what it is you should be doing or not doing. An environment of constant self-comparison is a recipe for disaster and I want to help you so you know what it is you should focus on and what you should not!

What If

What if I told you that there was an activity you could be involved with where you could spend your time doing something that you really enjoyed. Would you be interested?

What if I told you that you might get in pretty good shape too? You might even get really buff. It would be hard work at times and you're not going to like everything about it or all of the people involved while you do it, but it would teach you about hard work, dedication and time management. You'd also learn about healthy eating, visualization, meditation and maybe even some spirituality? (But in a cool way, not some woo-woo sort of way?)

What if I told you that by doing this activity, that you'd probably be introduced to after school, you may get a chance to travel around the United States and Canada. Maybe even the world! You'll get to meet really cool people who are high achievers. Some own their own companies and others are the top performers in other companies earning hundreds of thousands and even millions of dollars a year or more.

And what if I told you that if you spent enough time and got really good at this activity that there might be a chance you could get to hang out with movie stars, actors and actresses and even other professional athletes? Sound good?

And finally, what if I told you that even if you ended up not liking this activity after a while you would still get to keep all of the cool characteristics you developed while you were doing it. Attributes like grit and determination. Working well with others. An ability to teach and to figure things out on your own and in a team setting. All of those skills and attributes would stay with you. Pretty cool, huh?

Well those are just some of the attributes you will develop as you continue with the sport, or sports, that you love. And this book is in your hands to help you do that.

What You Will Hear

In the sports world today you will often hear people talk about how crazy sports has become. You will probably hear your parents, or other parents talk about how kids don't have any free time because they are playing so much. Or that there are so many tournaments and showcases an other opportunities to compete. Or that it's all just so demanding and not "fun" anymore like it was when they were young.

You'll hear people talk about how kids used to just play outside for hours and hours and you had to call them in for dinner. Those same people will rant about evaluations and the cost of equipment and tournaments, too.

The truth is, it's different today than it was years ago and that requires a new way of thinking. Today's sports aren't good or bad or harder or more difficult than they were years ago, they are what they are and this book will help you navigate the current landscape of sports, and most importantly, how to win.

Stop Chasing Fun. Understand Enjoyment

A common mistake of athletes (and parents) around you is that sports should be "fun." Countless studies have been done that interview kids in sports and everyone of them will tell you that the number one reason they play is that sports is fun.

Well...what else is "fun"? How about this for a list:

Xbox. Eating pizza. Playing games and watching movies. Going on a road trip. Hanging out with friends. Graffitiing a wall. Watching "fail" videos. Watching cat videos. Watching fail videos of cats. Watching videos of the Kardashians. (That was fun until people realized just how stupid it really was.)

The bottom line is that "fun" has a lot of definitions. If you ask one hundred people what is "fun" you'll get a hundred different answers.

The problem with the word "fun" is that when something isn't "fun" anymore then what do you do? You quit! When something isn't fun you just stop and find something else to do and replace it. It's usually an even exchange. "This thing stopped being fun so I replaced it with this other thing that is also fun." While you might be bummed for a nano-second you quickly forget that thing you just gave up. It's almost like apps on your phone. "Well, this game bores me so I'm going to swipe over here and play that game." You don't get sad by shutting down the app, you just leave and head to the next one.

I want to encourage you to stop using the word "fun" to describe your sport experience. Why? Because there are going to be times when sports isn't fun. (Although I argue in Chapter 10 that your beliefs can change that in a heartbeat.)

No, sports isn't always fun. But overall sports are "enjoyable." I want you to replace the word "fun" with the word enjoyable. While the word "fun" and "enjoyable" can sometimes be interchanged the word "fun" has an aspect of amusement to it. The word "fun" can mean "to have a good time" or to "be entertained". It's a distraction from something else. But in the definition of the word "enjoyable" there is an aspect of satisfaction to it. There are benefits to having an enjoyable experience even when it's difficult.

I remember playing lacrosse when I was young in an absolute downpour. The field was so muddy that pigs would have liked to play on the field we were on. At one point I got so much mud in my eye that the referee had to stop the game while I flushed out my eyes. Was it fun? Not particularly. Was it enjoyable? Heck yeah! We even lost!

Another time I almost got frostbite on my hands while competing in Switzerland. It was bitterly cold and our start house had no heat. My fingers were in so much pain that it took hours for them to warm back up. Fun? Not really. Enjoyable? You bet. I was training to go the Olympics on the side of an Alp in Switzerland! It was one of the best experiences of my life.

When you talk about sports being fun you open yourself up for quitting very easily, so stop calling sports "fun" right now. If something isn't fun the people around you will wonder why you don't quit. But when you talk about your situation as being enjoyable, you can be working your butt off in the hot or the cold and still be having fun. Make sense?

I find it interesting that people will come home from a practice or a game and think, "Well that wasn't much fun. Maybe I should do something else." Yet I never hear people say that about math! If you came home from school and said, "You know Mom, Dad, math just isn't much fun anymore. I think I'm going to quit." Your parents would have said, "Suck it up Princess. You need math for college so get back in there and tough it out!" You may even spend money on tutoring or extra help. You may take a different class to get caught up. But you wouldn't even consider quitting because it's a law that you complete it and it's just not an option for you.

But so many people will just quit sports because it isn't fun. If you are seeking only fun in sports you will quickly be disappointed. Why? Because you will run into a coach or teammates who want you to do more be more and have more. They are going to make you work and work hard. Why? Because sports is tough and the goal is to win. If you aren't winning now you're going to need to work harder. Is that going to be fun? Not all the time. But is it going to be enjoyable? You bet.

People Love To Tell You The Odds

People are quick to spew statistics to completely demoralize you like: only 3-5% of high school athletes get to play sports in college. Or that the odds of getting a scholarship is really small and you shouldn't "get your hopes up". Or my favourite, "Only three men in the whole country make the Olympic team every four years!" (Haha. Did that one.)

What all of those comments are basically saying is, "You are crazy to think that little ol' you has a chance to become anything in this world." I hate those people. (Hate is a strong word, I know, but if there is one thing I can't stand it's when older folks do what they can to stifle a young athlete's dreams because they don't want them to be disappointed if they don't make it.)

Listen, I know what you're trying to do and I want to tell you before I go on that if you can shut out the negative thinking of those unmotivated people who come around you and spew that crap, you have a huge advantage. See, those same people will go buy a lottery ticket after work tomorrow hoping that they will somehow win a game that has even worse odds than what it is you are trying to do!

The world is full of negative thinking and you will end up hearing some of the worst of it. It won't be a matter of "if" you hear it but "when" and the odds are you've already heard some of it. This book is designed to give you a plan to reach your goals and not just "hope" for them. I'm going to give you hope by giving you the tools to navigate this crazy world of sports. Whether your goal is to play in college, get a scholarship, compete professionally, or compete at the Olympic games I'm going to help you create a plan to do so and to insulate you from the people who are more than willing to say that you can't. When you have a plan you have armour against the dream-stealers. Consider it your force field of confidence. When you have a plan, you have confidence. And when you have confidence you can make ANYTHING happen.

You Can Be Awesome

You have in your hand something that I wished I had as an athlete growing up. You see, you are probably a thousand times better than I was at your age. As the son of two musicians, I didn't grow up in a household that was surrounded by sports. As an only child, I didn't have any older brothers or sisters whose footsteps I could follow, or who could wrestle with me or play sports with me. There was no one to toughen me up athletically. No. My Mom was an Opera singer and my Dad was an Organist and Music Director.

While my Mom will attribute my athletic success to her brief stint as a high school soccer player, and the most famous "sport" photo of my Dad is him holding a baseball bat upside down, understand that I didn't come from athletic genes.

However, I did have an "interest" in sports and I vividly remember that day in third grade losing every event in the Sports Day at the Nash School in South Weymouth, Massachusetts. I also remember getting my butt kicked. literally, by our schoolyard bully Michael that same day after school; he's in prison now for other things, but that's another story not worth telling. I loved Sports Day...but I hated getting my butt kicked.

I would play street hockey for hours with my friend Wayne in his driveway. I'd then go home and we would throw tennis balls on the roof of my house for even more hours with the lacrosse stick hoping it would hit the peak of the house just right so it would take a funny bounce and I would have to make some daring catch in the yard to get it. (No wonder I became a goalie.)

In fifth grade I started to play soccer, hockey, and lacrosse and after a slow, unathletic start, got pretty good at all of them, becoming an

All-American in lacrosse and an Olympian in the sport of luge (wut?!). While I bumbled along like most kids, I didn't really have a "plan"; or not one that was particularly laid out. My success in sports was fueled by my interest in the sports I played and my enjoyment in figuring them out. Along the way I had some good coaches and some really bad ones, too. I was just really interested in solving the challenge that sports provided. The love of the games helped me reach some pretty cool heights, like going to the Olympics and becoming a recruit to play at a Division One school in the NCAA.

Sports Is Different Now. But The Same.

I know that the world around sports is a lot different now than it was back when I competed. There are a lot more kids involved in sports, and since 2000 the business of training and coaching youth sports has exploded into a multi-billion dollar industry. I know because I have had my own strength and conditioning business and I've helped others market and grow their businesses by helping young athletes get better. We have more resources now than ever before to play, compete, and get better. Whether it's a piece of equipment, a tournament, or a training facility, there are more opportunities than ever to participate and improve and more people who have the money to take advantage of all of those resources. It feels like a buffet in Las Vegas. The offerings are endless and it all looks so good, but not all of it is good for you.

I still feel that something is missing in today's athletic environment. Sure, there are lots of tips and tricks and techniques available. You can go buy a new piece of equipment to help you improve your game. You can go buy the latest Under Armour mouthpiece that will supposedly help you breathe better, or you can go out this afternoon and join a gym to try and get bigger, faster, stronger. But what is missing is a plan, the glue, the stuff that holds all of these techniques together. What people are missing is the overall philosophy of thinking that helps athletes make great decisions at all stages of their career. While people are happy to complain about the environment of sports today and how it should change, I'd rather focus on you, the athlete, and what you need to do to navigate your current sports situation. People can complain all they want about how sports shouldn't be professional so early. How kids are playing too much, too soon. How it's all too much. But while those people complain, your love of your sport will carry you through all of that. Odds are the sport you participate in isn't going to change fast enough for you to reap those benefits, I'd rather help you get through it all successfully, now. If you want to help change it later, go right ahead.

I wasn't very good at sports when I was young even though I loved to play and could have played for hours. No one taught me about rest and recovery, which is essential to becoming an awesome athlete. The approach I took, and that you are probably taking, is "more" must be better. More games, more training, more equipment, more gear, more tournaments. Get seen, get a scholarship, and hopefully make the team. But what no one talks about, until this book, is how it all fits together and how YOU fit into the entire picture. That's what this book is all about.

I've been a student of sports training and tactics for thirty years now and what I'm laying out in this book is more than just psychology and mindset. It's an overall approach to your athletic career that will take you from the beginning, all the way through to your highest athletic result. Whether you're just trying to make the high school varsity, or play professionally, this book will help you.

This book is here to help you become awesome at your sport. I want you to be awesome, probably more than you want it for yourself. Whether you picked this book up on your own or someone who loves you gave it to you as a gift. I want you to know that I believe in you! Let me say that again I believe in YOU!.

"Why do you believe in me? You don't even know me?" You might ask yourself. Here is why I believe in you: I didn't have a person in my life like me when I was young, and I made it all the way to the Olympics; I only wish I knew then what I know now because I would have avoided so many pitfalls and training mistakes and probably extended my career a long way. If you desire to be your best. I can teach you how to achieve your best. Understand, I am in your corner and I have your back on this stuff. So let's get started.

Don't Cut Corners

You know how when you run laps with your teammates some of them will cut corners. They won't run the whole distance, they slack off the pace, and then coast along. They are the ones who only run hard when the coach is looking. You might even find yourself cutting corners sometimes. The athletes who don't finish their lap all the way, will not get past the first chapter of this book. Don't let that be you! Your goal is to read this book as fast as possible. Start at the beginning and cruise through it. Don't skip pages and don't cut out chapters. Every page of this book is designed to help you understand everything you need to know to reach your goals so leave no page unread. In a few pages I'll share with you tips I learned when I went to Stanford University, about faster reading, reading comprehension AND critical thinking. These are techniques you will be able to apply to your schooling and everyday life.

Unapologetically Obsessed

When you decide that you want to get really, really good at your sport, you will immediately want to do more than other athletes around you. You're going to want to get to practice early and to stay late too. You're going to want to ask more questions of your coach, and of other coaches too. You're going to want to miss a party to study the film of your last game. And you're going to want to be more meticulous (look it up) in how you care for your equipment.

That's just a partial list of some of the things you're going to want to do when you become obsessed with your sport.

People marvel at athletes who train and compete at a high level. They look in awe at their dedication to their craft. The general public can't comprehend the amount of work, and time, and commitment to their obsession with the detail that surrounds their training. To their level of "compete" when they get out on the field of play.

When should you adopt that level of obsession? How about now? How about last week, or last month, or last year? The sooner the better, really.

How "obsessed" should you be with your sport? That is completely up to you, but let me ask you, if you had to go to a surgeon tomorrow for surgery, how obsessed would you want him to be? The truth is, only you know how obsessed you need to be about your sport. Obsession is completely personal because your obsession satisfies a need inside you and no one else. To the outsider, they may think that what you do is out of the ordinary but that's perfectly fine. They aren't living your dream, you are. And that is why it is so important to be:

"Unapologetically Obsessed"

You don't have to apologize to anyone for what is perceived as your "obsession" with your sport. Your goals are yours and yours alone and how you make them happen is up to you. Only you know what will satisfy you when it comes to your effort. I know countless athletes who share the same story: of returning to the friends or family members who gave them a hard time for all of the time they put into their sport, but who were so proud of them for going for their goals. It's odd really. The same people who were doing their best to pull them away from their training and competing were the most proud of them when they came back. If only those people had been more supportive! Who knows where you can end up!

How This Book Is Organized

I've divided this book into five main sections:

Intro: The Introduction (that you're reading right now)
1.   Your Approach To Your Sport
2.   Train. Recover. Compete. Recover. Repeat.
3.   Game Day
4.   Get Results. Review. Keep The Lessons. Try Again.

In the **Introduction** I want to inspire you to go after everything you want in sport. There is more opportunity now for you to succeed than ever before. And while it may seem there is more competition I don't want you to focus on that. People will get injured, get tired, or quit, but you will persevere in the face of everything that can and will come against you.

In **Section Two: Your Approach To Your Sport** I want to give the mindset you need to navigate the sports path that you are on so you can win. It doesn't really matter if you're in high school or you are a pro trying to extend your career, the attitude you have in your head is what will take you further. One of my favourite quotes by **Ralph Waldo Emerson reads, "What lies behind us and what lies before us are small matters compared to what lies within us. And when we bring what is within us out into the world, miracles happen."** You are bringing what is inside you to this world of sports and it will be awesome. In this section I'm going to give you an overall framework for how to think about training and competing and how to take advantage of all of the opportunities training and competing will provide you.

In **Section Three: Train. Recover. Compete. Recover. Repeat.**, we'll discuss your training and preparation for Game Day. I use the term Game Day because I think it's appropriate to the largest number of athletes. Even if you're a skier or a figure skater or a Nascar driver you can relate to the term Game Day as the day when it's all gonna go down and you get to showcase your talents in comparison to your competitors.

In **Section Four: Game Day**, we'll discuss how to be prepared and how to execute on your best Gameday experience so you have your best result. No matter how much work you do in Section Three, it doesn't really matter if you can't put in a good result on Game Day and I'll reveal how to do that.

In **Section Five: Get Results. Review. Keep The Lessons. Try Again**. we'll discuss how to look at your Game Day results without losing your mind. Whether your Game Day results are good or bad, I'll help you evaluate your results so you can keep improving while making you bulletproof to the inevitable ups and downs of competition.

Finally, in **Section Six: Ongoing Thoughts And Considerations**, I'll cover topics that every great athlete needs to be thinking of consistently. The topics in this section could be sprinkled throughout the book, however, I felt they deserved their own section because of their importance.

How To Attack This Book

*"Before anything else, preparation
is the key to success."*

Alexander Graham Bell
Inventor of the telephone, the metal detector,
the wheat husker and the hydrofoil boat.

Just like you make a game plan for every competitive situation you are in, I wanted to give you a game plan for how to read this book so that you get the most out of it and win. When I wrote this book people asked me questions like, "Why is it so long? Nobody is going to read it." And, "Why is the Table of Contents so long?" or, "Does every chapter need to have a Conclusion AND a Summary?" The answer was, "Yes". And here's why: I attended Stanford University for a Summer after I competed in the Olympics and one of the reasons I wanted to go there was to learn how really smart people think. So, that summer I signed up for a Faster Reading course which was one of the best investments I have ever made in my life.

In that course I learned how to read a nonfiction book. Books like the one you have in your hand. It also applied to school text books as well. I am sharing with you what i learned there. Would you like to read a book faster? Would you like to retain more of what you learn? Did you think that reading a book about how to win at sports would help you with your grades? Well, here it is. A step-by-step approach to reading that will change your life:

Step 1) Read the table of contents first.

Read the Section Headings and then go back and read the subheadings. This will give you an overview of the entire book and how it's laid out. Just like scouting out a course before you run it, you'll be faster if you do and slower if you don't.

Step 2) Read the Introduction.

This is where I'm going to lay out for you my approach to this whole process and why it will help you. Don't just rush into the book. By listening to what it is I'm going to tell you, you will have an understanding of what's to come.

Step 3) Read the Conclusion at the End of the Book.

You know that old saying, "Don't spoil the story by reading the end first!" That's bad advice when it comes to reading non-fiction or any story where you want to recall and remember what's in it. It's great when you're watching a movie and you want to get surprised at the ending. You don't want a "surprise" ending at the end of your athletic story do you? When you are reading a nonfiction book like this one you want to read the end first to see what the outcome is. You will get the idea of how this all fits together, so you have a framework for understanding my vision for you, and where I'm going to lead you. So read the last chapter and then...

Step 4) Read the whole book.

Now that you have an understanding of how the book is laid out, where it's going, and how it's going to get there, you are going to have better retention of the entire contents. By understanding what is coming next and how it all fits together you will better understand all of the concepts and how it all fits together. This will increase your retention and it will help you understand all of the concepts involved. Be sure to apply this approach to each chapter as well. Read the opening, then read the Conclusion and Summary and then go back and read the chapter from beginning to end. This is powerful stuff so don't discount the method. You will read faster and retain more.

The sooner you understand these concepts the sooner your game will improve.

Own This Book

If this book was loaned to you by someone, do yourself a favor and get online and buy your own copy. This book is meant to be written in and marked up. I want you to always have a copy nearby at all times and I want you to take this copy and mark it up. Dog ear it. Take notes.

Journal in it. This shouldn't be a nice and tidy looking thing on your bookshelf...it should be in your bag, beat up and read through multiple times so you can refer to it again and again.

I Love You

I spoke to a group of high school athletes once and told them that I loved them. I wanted them to know that I believed in what it was they were doing and that they could make their dreams come true. At the end of that talk, an athlete came up to me in tears and said, "You know, my father has never told me that he loves me." I was shocked, but it made me realize that there are probably more athletes who grow up in environments like that. I don't know if that's you, but I want you to know that I believe in you, and I want you to know that I love you. Yes...I love you. We all need someone in our life who tells us they love us and I hope that you have that someone in your life. I know that it's quite possible that you don't have someone who is super-supportive of you or your efforts and want you to know that I love you. It's quite possible that you are not in a place where you feel a lot of love directed at you, or to what you're trying to get done. So understand this, I'm on your side. I want you to win. I want you to take all of what you've learned in this crazy sports scene and to take it with you for the rest of your life.

I Want To Hear From You

When you have a moment, send me a note at coachedwards@ athletespecific.com I want to know who you are and what you're doing. What sports are you involved in and what are your goals. Shoot me an email and tell me your story as it's the "juice" that keeps me going. I respond to all my emails. :)

Pay It Forward

Finally, share this with someone who you know, like and trust. This book is fast becoming the most shared, gifted and otherwise referred to book of it's kind and that starts with you. So take a picture of you with the book and post it to Facebook, share it on Twitter, Pin it, Instagram it. You name it. I sure would appreciate it.

You Can't Lose

I wish you success and happiness and don't forget...whether you win or lose in your sport, reach your dreams, or fall flat on your face, the lessons you will learn along the way will serve you for the rest of your life in ANY activity you choose. Work, school, life, or relationships, they will all be affected for the better. You will take these lessons with you your whole life.

I believe in you.

Jonathan Edwards - Olympian

Section One

Your Approach To Your Sport

"For every athlete there is a shift. For some it happens very early and for others it comes much later. It's a shift where things start to get serious. Not so serious that the whole thing becomes drudgery. Just a shift from, "hey this is fun and entertaining", to "I want to be really good at this someday."

Jonathan Edwards
Olympian, Speaker, Author, www.AthleteSpecific.com

Chapter 1

Understanding The Big Picture

"You can't connect the dots looking forward; you can only connect them looking backwards. So you have to trust that the dots will somehow connect in your future. You have to trust in something - your gut, destiny, life, karma, whatever. This approach has never let me down, and it has made all the difference in my life."

Steve Jobs
Creator of Apple

You've probably been doing this "sports" thing for a while now. Whether you specialize in one sport or you still do a couple of sports and you're getting serious, you probably have been doing things a certain way, up until now. You're looking to take things to the next level. You have talent, and a passion for your sport and you'd like to be better and maybe even get to play in college or go to the Olympics some day. You may even want to play professionally.

Whatever your sport, and whatever your goals, I want to help you with a new approach to how you...well...approach things. Many athletes bumble along from training session to training session. From competitive event to competitive event. They wolf down some fast food on the way to another practice session in the hopes of getting better because that's what everyone else around them is doing. We are going to help you with an approach that is athlete specific and that is designed for you in mind.

"Hoping for the best, prepared for the worst, and unsurprised by anything in between"

- Maya Angelou
from her book **I Know Why The Caged Bird Sings**

How You Want It To Go

If you've been playing sports for any length of time you probably realize that it's not a straight uphill path. But while you may read this and think, "Yeah, totally, I know it's not a straight path." In your heart and in your head, you really wish it was.

Not only that, your parents and your coaches wish it was, too. But the truth is that your athletic path is going to look something like a Stock Exchange graph.

How It's Going To Go

The reality is your path to athletic success is going to be riddled with ups and downs, plateaus and troughs. It's going to be a wild ride...if you let it become wild. The truth is that while it will be filled with ups and downs like a roller coaster it doesn't have to feel like a roller coaster.

Riding The Roller Coaster

Have you ever been on a roller coaster? (For those of you who haven't been on one, think of riding in a car on a twisty road where you are the passenger. Like riding along with your grandmother who grew up in the country and has bad eyesight. She's all over the road and you have no control!) Do you remember what it was like? It was probably pretty scary if the ride had some speed to it. Now after you rode the coaster, did you do it again? Some people would say, "No way! I'm not going on that thing again." But others jump back on the ride and find that it wasn't nearly as scary as it was the first time around.

Why is that?

The reason it isn't as scary as it was the first time is because now you have an idea of what's going to happen. You know where the curves are and you know what's up ahead. When you know what's up ahead you are more prepared and when that coaster goes way up high you know that eventually it's going to settle back down. When the track gets twisty you know that it has to straighten out eventually.

Each time you get on that coaster the excitement is there but the feeling of being out of control goes away. Eventually, you'd have no tension riding that roller coaster because you would know exactly what was coming. In fact, you'd probably get bored and find something else to do because that roller coaster didn't excite you at all.

Sports is just like a roller coaster. It has it's ups and downs, it's twisty parts and it's straight parts. It goes fast at times and it slows down at other times. Lots of people start the ride but will get so freaked out about the ups and downs and the twists and turns that many will quit. They say things like, "Get me off this thing! I didn't know it was going to be like this! This is not what was advertised!"

Parents watching start to scream, "They shouldn't put my kid through this! They should ban roller coasters! They should be flatter and less twisty! There shouldn't be as may roller coasters!" While others get excited that their kids made it to the end safely and ask, "Can my kid do it again, this time a little faster?"

I want to help you understand the roller coaster you're about to ride on and I'll give you one of the biggest lessons I will give you in this book. Are you ready? Here it is:

"No one is riding the same roller coaster."

While I can tell you about the ups and downs and the twists and turns, you're going to find out that everyone is having a different ride. You may have a twin brother or sister competing alongside of you and I can guarantee you that they won't have the same experience that you will have. While it looks like the same ride, It's all different.

But what I'm going to help you with is how to navigate this journey. How to prepare for the ups and inevitable downs. How to win and how to lose. We'll cover topics like how to watch your mindset and what to eat. How to sleep better and how to find your next best coach. We are going to cover a lot in this book and your homework is to read it all. But before you start, just know this...

You Can't Lose (Really)

In the world of sports we win or lose, everyday. Sports are designed to have people who win and people who do not. It's actually why we practice and why we compete. We go out every day to challenge ourselves. My favourite quote that I've created to explain this is:

"An athlete puts themselves in a position to be embarrassed every day and promises to themselves to never let it happen again."

Jonathan Edwards
Olympian, Speaker, Author

You are designed to seek challenges. As human beings we are so advanced mentally that we put ourselves in challenging situations just to see what happens. We climb mountains and jump out of hot air balloons. We say things like, "Well, jumping out of a perfectly good plane with a parachute is getting boring, how about we create some wings and fly a bit?" That's how wingsuits were born and those are pretty cool.

We have looked at gravity and said, "Pfft. Whatever. How high can I jump?" At some point I bet two cavemen said, "First one to that rock wins." (What their prize was, I'm not sure.) Challenge and competition is in our blood. It's who we are and it stimulates growth in us that makes us better. The challenge is what makes it fun. Without challenge we are bored out of our minds!

Along this journey you will grow as a person. When and if you transition out of your athletic journey, whenever that may be, you will be physically, mentally, and emotionally stronger than you would have been had you not taken this challenge. You are embarking on a journey where you can't see the end when you start. Like climbing a mountain, you know it's a big mountain and you can't see the top but you know the top is up there somewhere so you keep finding a way to move upwards and know that eventually you'll get there. And whether you reach the top or not, the views along the way will be fantastic. While it may sound a little cheesy, the path to the top of the mountain is ultimately what changes you. It's not the view from the top but who you had to become along the way that's what lasts with you forever.

You will win and you will lose and you will grow. When you miss a question on a math test no one ever says, "Well, that's horrible. I guess I shouldn't have bothered." No, you buckle down and refocus. You figure out what you missed and then come back and try it again. "A new question please." you say. And you move on.

Get Your Hopes Up

If you're like most athletes, you've come from parents who love you and want the best for you. (I know, I know, that's not always true and I'll cover that in the section on Parents) Many parents take that love and try to wrap their athlete in, what I call, "Love Bubble Wrap". Part of their "love" equation is to keep you from being disappointed. They don't want you to get your hopes up because they think that if something goes wrong you'll get disappointed because your hopes were so high. Like if you were climbing a ladder. If falling off the ladder means being disappointed then falling from a lower rung must be better than falling off from way up high.

If this is you, I'm encouraging you to get your hopes up. Let them soar as high as they will take you. Understand that up until now you've probably been protected too much. Let loose. Don't be afraid to get your hopes up and to be disappointed. I want you to be disappointed every once in awhile. Why? Because when you get disappointed and then overcome that disappointment you will be stronger. You will be more committed and you will continue to work harder. If you never get your hopes up, and you never get disappointed, you will end up quitting when disappointment finally comes because it will come in a big, big way. You want to get used to the feeling of being disappointed but you don't want to stay in that feeling. You want to feel the feeling, understand there is something for you to work on in order to get a better result, and then work to get better. It's that simple.

When you get comfortable with being disappointed and then workthrough that feeling and improve yourself then the whole world opens up to you. The world is full of people who don't want to be disappointed and they end up doing absolutely nothing with their life. They get started on something and along the way they just quit. They give up. It's all too hard for them and that's going to benefit you because you aren't a quitter. You understand that disappointment is just a temporary feeling as you work towards becoming better and better.

My friend Ruben Gonzalez is the world's only athlete to compete in Olympic Games spanning over forty YEARS. He also has the nickname of "Bulldog". Why do people call him Bulldog? Because he won't quit. While people around him get disappointed with their results and then give up, Ruben just powers on. He feels that feeling of disappointment every day and then keeps going. He's like the Energizer Bunny crossed with a Bulldog. He keeps going and going and while people around him give up, he ends up winning just out of attrition!

Fall In Love With The Work...
Not The Result

"I fell in love with the work. And the work was joyful and it was difficult, and interesting; and that was my focus."

Jerry Seinfeld,
Creator of the insanely popular TV Series "Seinfeld" based on his stand-up comedy act. It is estimated that Jerry earns $36 Million dollars a year in royalties from a show that ran for just nine seasons.

Only four years into my Olympic career I had the opportunity to sit in a CBS production truck that was airing the sliding events at the Winter Olympic Games. It was in that truck that I learned one of the most valuable lessons of my athletic lifetime that I have carried with me still to this day.

It was obvious to me that the people in the truck were working in some crazy-paced-New-York-rush-hour style to get the footage from that day's race packaged and ready to go for prime time TV coverage. And while everyone was hustling to get the show edited the producer said something that I've never forgotten. He said, "We are going to bust our butts to get this show done but will probably get bumped for the soap opera story from figure skating today."

Disappointed, I asked, "Why's that?" And he said, "Because our TV ratings are driven by the viewer who really loves the soap opera crap and who would rather see the fluff-story than the real glory. <u>If we didn't love our work here that would get really frustrating.</u> We'll pull an eighteen hour day only to see the work we put together never make it on TV."

That has always stuck with me. **The idea that if you can fall in**

love with the work you do everyday you'll never have a bad day.

As an athlete you are going to put in a lot of work. You are going to miss going out to the movies with your friends and maybe a couple birthday parties. You're going to spend extra hours in the weightroom and in the gym. You'll spend hours and hours pouring over video footage of games and events to help you get an edge. You are going to do all that AND you're going to lose probably more often than you win. All of these activities are the "work" that you will need to put in to have successful competitive events and your results in those events will determine how far you go in your sport.

For most athletes however, they fall in love with the results of their work and not the work itself. They get completely wrapped up in only the results of their games and their competitions. Good result? Good day. Bad result? Bad day. Bad life, actually.

For many professional athletes who retire, they are often quoted as saying that what they miss most is not the competition but the good times in the locker room. The time spent in the gym and on the practice field. This is where the real work happens and it is ultimately what the athlete misses most.

But just like those guys and gals in the production truck that day at the Olympics, if you can fall in love with the work you put in every day, you won't worry too much about the result. You will also have confidence knowing that if you put in your best effort you have already won. You will withstand the inevitable ups and downs that you will face in a sport that is incredibly unpredictable and you will have a long and very healthy athletic career.

No Drama

We will cover this in more detail in later chapters, but I want to touch on it now.

Avoid "drama." Of all sorts.

We live in a drama filled world and it sucks the energy right out of us. People don't think it does and that they are "used to it" but it does drain your energy. People love drama and they secretly crave it, and they like to create it. They like it in their TV shows, their relationships, their movies, their music. Don't let that be you. In my company we have a "no drama" rule. Years ago we had an employee who was having trouble in her relationship with her boyfriend and every day it was some new dramatic story that she would just have to share with her coworkers. It got to the point where it was sucking everyone into this drama-filled environment that was affecting everyone's performance. Eventually we had to let this person go because of performance issues and when we did everyone's performance improved.

The world of sports and athletics is stressful enough mentally, emotionally and physically that you don't need to add to that stress. In fact, everything you do outside of your sport needs to be an oasis that allows you to recover mentally, emotionally and physically so that you can come back and give it your best performance. Period.

Create a rule in your life that you won't let drama poison it. You won't talk about it, or talk about other people's drama. There is no room for it in your performance-filled life. Why would you want to fill your thoughts with drama when you can fill it with all of the positive thoughts that come from all the good things going on in your life?

There will be people who are in your life now, or who will come into your life, who will have lots of drama to share. They may be parents, coaches, friends or teammates and they will be full of drama. Give them a hug (it doesn't have to be a real hug it can be a virtual hug) and send them on their way. Trust me on this...no drama. Ever.

Be So Damned Good
They Have To Pick You

Your goal as an athlete is to be so damned good that the powers who decide have no choice but to pick you for the team. Your performance has to be so good that there is no question that you are number one. Your Physical Ability, your Technical Ability, and your Tactical Ability should all be so good, so above everyone else, that there is no choice but to put you on the team, in the competition, etc. It should be a no brainer. You need to strive for total, competitive, domination.

In 1992 I was on the US National Luge Team in the sport of Mens Doubles. Leading up to the 1992 Olympic Trials my partner Mark Grimmette and I had been the fastest US doubles team. Overall we were sixth in the world and we were the fastest US team on the Olympic track in LaPlagne, France, site of the Luge competition for the Albertville games.

While we had already proven ourselves on the Olympic track

as the fastest US team, that wasn't going to have any bearing on our placement on the Olympic team because the selection process was going to come down to an Olympic Trials race on our local track in Lake Placid, NY. This would be similar to a bunch of golfers who all play on the same course at home, but they were competing to be on a team that was going to compete somewhere else. They've had hundreds, maybe thousands of rounds on that home course and could do it blindfolded. But that home course is much different compared to the courses around the world and it would be as though the golfers could play that home course using only their short irons as opposed to the European courses where you need to use the whole bag.

That was us in Europe. Mark and I had developed an ability to negotiate foreign tracks quickly and we were so good at it that it almost seemed unfair to have to race back in Lake Placid where we would all be extremely close on a track that wasn't very similar to the Olympic track. In an extremely tight race (where the three US sleds were a total of .08 seconds apart) Mark and I finished third. And while we still had an opportunity to make the Olympic team on a coach's pick, ultimately, we were left off the team.

I don't remember crying so hard in my life and remember vividly when the announcement was made and it wasn't our name on the roster. We went through all of the stages of grieving. There was denial as we couldn't believe that we weren't on that team. Then there was absolute anger over the decision. "How could they!" we thought. Then bargaining. Then depression and ultimately...acceptance.

In the acceptance stage we vowed that for the next Olympic team we would be so good that they had to pick us. We would work on our starts, and our sled, and our mental preparation, so that next time, we would race ourselves onto the team. (In a bit of "we told you so" they ultimately revamped the selection process with the US Olympic Committee so that the next Olympic team was picked on the results a team had during the World Cup season and not from one Olympic trials event.)

The following year, Mark and I were back on the national team and were excited to get back to the Olympic track that we were so painfully left off. With the full Olympic field there Mark and I won our first world cup medal, a silver. Beating our long-time idols by two thousandths (.002) of a second. It was bittersweet because one could only think, "What if we had gone to the Olympics? Would we have won the silver medal?"

That year we won three world cup medals and finished fourth overall in the World standings and were on our way to solidifying ourselves as the best sled on the US team. We ended up racing onto the 1994 Olympic team in our last race of the fall world cup season and ultimately finished fourth at the Olympics. Ultimately, the bottom line was that we got so damned good that they had no choice but to pick us and that is the position I wish for every athlete.

Now, I fully understand that there will be times when you are on the bubble and you need to rely on a coach's decision to pick you. However, I see too many athletes in those positions who feel slighted when the coach doesn't pick them. They feel like the coach has something out for them or that they just don't like you for some reason. Athletes like this who are always in these positions need to work smarter, unfortunately. I say unfortunately because it will feel like a bad thing to them, a challenge, a burden to be shaken. It's not that at all.

When an athlete doesn't make a team, or doesn't get the chance to compete in the big game (or any other event for that matter) it's a time for feedback. A time for reflection. For evaluation. For planning and attacking with a new plan. It's a time to look back on what worked and what didn't. A time to accept new approaches to training, technology, equipment, coaching, etc. It's a time for learning and for growth. For reflection and contemplations. It's a positive time and not a negative one. There is no good or bad...only learning.

Conclusion

When you understand that your path to success if going to be full of ups and downs you will start to remove some of the unnecessary emotion that can really affect you as an athlete. It's going to be a roller coaster and if you can be prepared for that, you will be better for it. Know that no matter if you have good results or bad results, who you become along this journey is going to stick with you forever in all of your future pursuits. You can't lose. So if you know you can't lose feel free to get your hopes up. Dream big dreams and know that others along the way will quit or won't even try. And finally, eliminate all drama from your life. Friends, family and coworkers will want to share their drama with you. Be a drama-free zone and decide that your goal is to be so good at your sport that you dominate your competition and leave no choice but for the coaches (or judges) to choose you as their number one choice.

Most stress comes from when you're on the bubble. Do your best to keep yourself from being in that situation.

Watch This Video

**www.AthleteSpecific.com/
be-so-damned-good-they-have-to-pick-you**

Take Action With These Steps

- Have there been times when you underestimated or overestimated the difficulty of a situation and it caught you off guard? How can you prepare yourself for future situations that will be similar?

- What are some of the beliefs you have about future competitions that may be setting you up for failure by underestimating/overestimating their difficulty?

- If you stop thinking about wins and losses, making the team or not making the team, what are some of the other benefits you will reap by being on this journey?

- Get your hopes up! What are your true hopes and dreams for your athletic future? Don't hold back. Get your notebook and write them down now.

- Fall in love with the work and not the results. Make a list of all of the activities you love while training to be better in your sport. It could be the car ride with a parent to getting all muddy and sweaty on the field. List it all.

- Eliminate the drama from your life. Make a list of all of the people, places and things in your life that cause drama. How can you reduce or eliminate those things?

- Be so good they have to pick you. Who do you need to become to be unbeatable? To be the best?

Chapter 2
Your Job As An Athlete

No matter what the sport, an athlete has only **two** jobs to complete. Most athletes get really confused thinking that they need to focus on working harder on...well...everything, and that putting in more time and more effort is the answer. But for what? What is it that you are exactly trying to accomplish? That is always the question.

You might say, "Well, I'm trying to make the team!" or "Get to the Olympics" or "Play professionally someday."

That would be a mistake. All of those thoughts are valid but they are not your real goal. Those are byproducts of a bigger goal which I will explain in a moment. For now, understand this core topic: **Your job as an athlete is to withstand challenges, and to take advantage of opportunity.** Let me say that again:

"Your job as an athlete is to withstand challenges and to take advantage of opportunities"

Jonathan Edwards,
Olympian, Speaker, Author

That's it.

What Do Challenges Look Like?

Challenges can come in many forms. Some of those challenges occur on the field of play and some happen off the field of play. What's the difference?

Some obvious "challenges" that you might recognize would be a football player getting tackled by another player. A hockey player might be trying to stop an offensive player with the puck trying to get around him for a shot at goal. Goalies are constantly being challenged by opposing shooters. An archer might be challenged by the wind and the weather as would a skier or a track athlete running against the wind.

In individual sports where there is not a competitor on the field per se, they can still be challenged. Take for example an X Game athlete in skateboarding or snowboarding. Any athlete who throws down a more complex trick with more flips or more rotations is effectively challenging the rest of the competitors. In order to withstand that challenge every athlete would need to either copy the new trick or come up with something even more complex.

Some Challenges Aren't On The Field of Play!

I know a track athlete who had challenges that came not from an opponent on the field but from the politics in an organization that didn't want him there. In the end this athlete decided to compete for another COUNTRY! To withstand the challenges and reach his dream it meant competing against the flag he was born under and completely switching gears. This may be an extreme example for you but it is testament to the fact that every challenge has an answer if you just look for it.

What Do Opportunities Look Like?

Everyday that you are participating in your sport you are presented with challenges as well as given opportunities to take advantage of. Either you can withstand the challenges and take advantage of the opportunities, or you can't. Let me explain:

Over the years I have worked with a lot of athletes from a number of sports. Many of them in the sport of lacrosse, soccer, football and hockey. Lacrosse is a pretty interesting example because you have this stick in your hands that isn't like a hockey stick that you would use primarily on one side of your body. A hockey stick has a curve and you mainly use it on one side of your body or the other . You are either a lefty shot or a righty shot. But many lacrosse athletes get to a point where they have a good side and a not-so-good side. There is a mental block that says they are just like a hockey player who has one strong hand and that's it. Now there is nothing about the lacrosse stick that makes it one-handed, and there is nothing on their body that restricts them to being one-handed. But an athlete will say, "I'm only righty. I'm not going to use my left hand."

Well, what happens in the game when you have opportunities to use your left hand but can't, or worse, won't. Let's say a defender plays you a certain way so that you can't use your right hand and your only opportunity there is to go left-handed? You've just missed an opportunity to take advantage of the defender.

Basically what happens in this situation is an athlete says to their sport, "Here I am! Now give me opportunities." That's not how it works. In a game like lacrosse, like any team sport, the games are fluid. They change every day. No two games are the same. Some days there are opportunities that suit the athlete as they are now, and other days there aren't.

Let me give you another example. Mikaela Shiffrin is the top US Skier currently and one of the best in the world. Google her name and learn more about this amazing athlete and I highly recommend following her on Instagram too. She competes in the slalom where the gates are placed very close together, and the Giant Slalom where they are placed a little further apart. What I love about the sport of skiing is that every run is different and every hill is different. You must become a very technically proficient skier to win these races and she is winning them with ease.

Why? Because she has come to the race with the biggest set of athletic tools to take advantage of the most opportunities the course gives her. If she came to the hill and said, "I'm really good at left-handed turns on flatter slopes." but the course was really steep and had mostly difficult right-hand turns, she wouldn't have a chance to win because she is basically saying, "Um...I need this course to adjust to me. I'm not going to adjust to it."

The whole point of athletic events is that they are a set of challenges and opportunities. The athletes who are able to defend themselves from the harshest challenges, and who can take advantage of the most opportunities, wins.

Think of Lebron James for a moment in the sport of basketball. What kind of athlete would he be if he could only shoot the basketball from ten feet away from the basket. Not very good. Why? Because teams would just defend him close to the basket and make him shoot from outside. The reason he is such a valuable athlete is because he can shoot from all over the floor. If you try to defend him from one place on the floor he will drive around you and shoot from someplace else.

This is how you need to view your game and yourself as an athlete. How can you take advantage of more opportunities. How can you withstand those challenges coming against you. When you narrow down your focus and realize that the better you are at those two things, the more valuable an athlete you will become, the more goals you will attain.

Identify Your Challenges
And Opportunities

Take a moment and consider the challenges you face in your sport as well as the opportunities your sport asks you to take advantage of. Write them in the boxes below and keep in mind, sometimes the challenges and opportunities you face don't always come on the field of play. They can be political challenges or strategic opportunities that don't always involve your physical abilities. Fill in the boxes below:

Challenges:

The challenges I face in my sport are:	What I am looking to improve so I can withstand these challenges:

Opportunities:

The opportunities I want to take advantage are:	What I will work on so I can take advantage of more opportunities:

Conclusion

As an athlete you have only two jobs that you are preparing for: withstand challenges and take advantage of opportunities. Those challenges and opportunities can happen on the field of play or they may be off the field. Either way if you focus on improving yourself to be able to do those two things then your athletic career should be a breeze. Ignore them at your peril.

Watch This Video:

www.AthleteSpecific.com/
challenges-and-opportunities

Take Action With These Steps:

- What are the challenges you are currently facing that are giving you difficulties? What can you do to overcome them?

- What opportunities are you not able to take advantage of currently? What can you improve to take advantage of more opportunities?

- Some of the challenges you may be facing may come off the field of play. What are some of the challenges that you might be facing off the field of play?

Chapter 3
Decide What You Want...Now

*"The only person you are destined to become
is the one you decide to be."*

Ralph Waldo Emerson
(1803-1882) was an American essayist, lecturer, and poet who led the
transcendentalist movement of the mid-19th century

My Favourite Quote

*"Until one is committed, there is hesitancy, the chance to draw
back, always ineffectiveness. Concerning all acts of initiative
(and creation), there is one elementary truth that ignorance
of which kills countless ideas and splendid plans: that the
moment one definitely commits oneself, then Providence
moves too. All sorts of things occur to help one that would
never otherwise have occurred. A whole stream of events
issues from the decision, raising in one's favor all manner of
unforeseen incidents and meetings and material assistance,
which no man could have dreamed would have come his way.
Whatever you can do, or dream you can do, begin it. Boldness
has genius, power, and magic in it.
Begin it now."*

William Hutchinson Murray
(Scottish Mountaineer and Writer 1913-1996)

I have always loved the quote above. Read it again and let it sink in. (You can also grab a cool version of this quote by going to www. AthleteSpecific.com and downloading a free wall poster.

There was a point in my high-school lacrosse career where I

definitely told myself that I wanted to play lacrosse in college. I'm not sure when it happened but I decided, and acted early enough that that small decision could have an effect on how I thought about training every day and was able to have a significant affect on my outcome. Many athletes, never really put it out there and say, "I want to be an All-American", or "I want to play in college." or, "I will be an Olympian." They just wait, hoping for enough victories to pile up that it might just happen. You may have probably said something like that to yourself even though it may be in casual, quiet conversation with yourself.

But did you really feel it? I mean really feeeeeeeel it.

I said it to myself for lacrosse, but I actually messed it up on the way to the Olympics and it probably bit me in the butt. (More on that in a moment.)

You see, there was a day when I thought about playing lacrosse in college and I could really feel it. I can't point a specific "day" when it clicked, but there was definitely a time when I started to really act on those thoughts. I could see myself playing and I could feel the field. I could see myself in the stadium, and imagine the equipment I would be wearing. What that did for me was give me something really concrete to shoot for. I had this anchor in my head and in my body that I could see, me, playing at that level. But without *deciding* that I wanted to make it happen, it never would have happened.

When I had my first real shot to go to the Olympics, I didn't really do that. I was just on the "path" to get there. Everyday it was more of the same training and the same racing and the same "stuff" that put you on track to go to the Olympics. It was fairly mundane and I was just going through the motions. They were BIG motions, mind you, but I didn't really know what being committed really meant. In lacrosse it wasn't the same. There were a lot of directions you could go and by declaring that I wanted to play lacrosse in college it really focused and refined my training and my approach daily, but when I was training for the Olympics it was obvious and it lulled me to sleep a bit. While I was on the fastest team on the US squad, not declaring that we would be on that Olympic team came back to haunt us when we lost the close race at the Olympic Trials. We didn't own it, and deciding what you want and declaring it really helps you own it.

Why You Won't Decide What You Want

So why won't you decide what you want? Well, for one thing, when you decide what you want you are instantly identifying what you DON'T want and that can be hard. By deciding what you want and therefore what you don't want you are now opening yourself up for disappointment. "What if you go for it and don't make it?!" Or what if you miss out on something else?

This is a very common error and it's not just something that happens to athletes. Most people don't go for anything in their life for fear that they might make a fool of themselves or miss out on something else. The ironic thing about that is they can't even define what that "something else" is! Don't think about what you will lose by defining what you want, think of all the great things you will get by achieving what you want. This will provide all sorts of added energy to make your dreams come true.

Another reason you won't define what you want is that you may feel pressure if people know what you are trying to accomplish. This may open you up to all sorts of criticism that you really don't want to deal with or are unprepared to deal with. If that's the case, don't tell anyone. We'll cover more of that decision later, but for now, keep your thoughts, hopes and dreams to yourself and let the idea of what you want to grow.

Take a moment and write down what you really, truly want. Don't worry, it's just you and me. Grab a pen and write it down in the box below. Magic happens when you write it down. Go ahead...

What I really want to have happen is...

```
All- American
```

Did you write it down? Seriously? Go get a pen and write it down! I'll wait.

Ok, good. How'd that feel? Does it seem more real now that you wrote it down? Stare at it for a minute or two and it will start to sink in.

What Will Happen Once You Decide

Just like the quote at the beginning of the chapter says, when you are committed (or made the decision) "providence" moves too. What the heck is "providence" you ask? It's not the town in Rhode Island where Brown University is located. It is a concept that tells us that when you decide on what you want, all of these things, people, ideas and forces that you can't currently see or comprehend will start to come out of the woodwork to help you make that dream of yours a reality.

The sooner you decide on what you want the sooner "providence" will start to move, and the sooner those things start to move the sooner you will see progress toward what you want. It's a strange concept, and a little hard to explain, but it's the truth and the sooner you decide the sooner it will start to make things happen.

You Don't Need To Worry
About The "How"

You are an incredibly smart, soon to be very driven, athlete. I know that because you are reading this book and you are really looking to take your performance to another level. But I want to give you a warning: When you start setting goals you're going to start to ask, "Well, how am I going to make this all happen?" Some of your goals might be pretty lofty and right now you just can't see how you are going to put together all the pieces. Heck, you can't even see all the pieces right now anyway. Just know that when you are given a dream of achieving something great and you have it in your heart to continue, you don't need to know all of the "how's" yet. They will come.

This is where many good athletes get stuck. This is the point where dreams die because athletes get overwhelmed by all of the ideas that need to come together to make it happen. This is just like climbing up a mountain. You can ask, "What does it look like at the top of the mountain?" I don't know yet but I just know it's going to be awesome. "Well how are you going to get there?" I can't see the whole path but I know that the trailhead is right there so I'm going to start there.

You just need to get started and you just need to focus on the part of the path that you can see. Know that the path leads to the top of the mountain and that the view is going to be incredible once you get there. Along the way the path will twist and turn and you'll get a taste of the view when the forest opens up a bit and you can start to see the horizon.

Interested vs. Committed

When I was ten years old I spent my summer at Camp Dudley in upstate New York. It was here that I got my first taste of the sport of luge. It was fun. It was interesting. I enjoyed it. But I was also interested in other things. Luge was interesting to me, but I wasn't really committed to taking it anywhere.

Five years later I had the chance to try luge again. Same camp. Same hill. Same sleds. But this time, luge was also an opportunity to compete in the Olympic games. Now THAT sounded cool!

The first time I tried luge, it was fun. I learned how to drive a sled. I learned how to lie flat on the sled. I was interested. But NOW I was committed. I wasn't going to have the chance to go to the Olympics for soccer, or hockey, or lacrosse. I was now committed to luge because the path it would take me on led to the Olympics.

Most athletes get introduced to sports and they get interested. It's fun! They may be with their friends or they make new friends. They like the gear and the stuff. The grass or the court. They might really like their coach. All of these things are interesting, but they aren't committed.

Transitioning From Interested To Committed

That first time I tried luge the idea of going to the Olympics was too big. It was too far away. Or perhaps I just didn't understand that it was possible. For many athletes they can't dream of being in the Olympics, or playing professionally. They are just having fun and they are along for the ride. They go to practice, they play the games, they ride the buses. It's all just fun at that point.

But along the way the dream grows. It's now in sight. What seemed so far away that it couldn't be seen is now a glimpse out there in the distance. But the bottom line is that it has now taken hold of you. It goes from a "no way" to a "hey, that's possible".

It's important to understand where you are in this process. If you're reading this and you think what I'm saying is cool and all but you can't see it happening for you yet, that's fine. Just keep plugging away. It will come.

As you have more victories in your sporting life...more successes... more evidence that you can do this...you will start to see that goal on the horizon. It will become clearer and clearer. When this happens, you have reached a sweet spot in your athletic life. It is at this point that everything will shift. Like a scale that finally shifts when there is enough weight on one side, you too will feel a shift inside you that makes everything you do now make more sense. That advice you got from your coach will now stick. The food you eat will now take you to your goal or away from it. You will want to get more sleep. You will listen to music that inspires you OR you may even turn off your music and listen to positive coaching advice in your phone instead of some crappy Drake song. (Was that my outside voice that said, "crappy Drake song?")

Coaching Interested Athletes vs. Committed Athletes

As an athlete I think it's important that you understand just how frustrating it is to coach kids who are interested vs. kids who are committed. Years ago I coached a group of very talented lacrosse players. There were just under twenty kids in the group and of that talented group I'd say half of them were *incredibly* talented. Overall ninety percent of them were motivated kids who wanted to get better.

But there was ONE kid…

This kid drove me absolutely nuts. He thought he was talented… but really…he was just interested. He wasn't committed. As a coach I would tell him what to do and how to do it. I would let him know that what he was doing was good but if he made a tweak here and a tweak there he'd be doing even better. He would talk a good game and tell me that he wanted to play lacrosse in college, but in reality, he would miss his chance.

This kid was interested. Sure, he wanted things to happen, he could see the goal on the horizon, but even with all of that he was still just interested.

This athlete would show up late to practice or miss practice entirely. His equipment was a mess. He'd sometimes forget a glove, or BOTH gloves. He even ran over his own stick with his car in the parking lot! He wasn't committed, he was interested.

On the other hand I had a group of five boys who have all gone on to play in college. These guys were great because you could tell them something and they would apply it. They were committed. As a coach you could work with them because they would try something and then provide feedback on what they just tried. They would ask questions like, "Coach I just tried that but it didn't work like I thought it would. What do I need to do differently?"

Now THIS is coaching. THIS is an athlete who wants to get better and who works in harmony with his coach to work and collaborate and to try and get better. When an athlete is committed it creates a synergistic relationship and now, NOW everything is working to that common goal. The athlete is committed and the words of the coach fall on fertile soil like a seed ready to grow.

When you are committed, everything you do takes you to your

goal or away from it. It's black or white. But when you're interested everything is grey. You don't know what will help and what won't. It's all...interesting.

Being Committed To The Right Goal

I had the opportunity to coach an athlete who was committed, but it was to the wrong goal. Instead of focusing on being the best in her sport she was only focused on being the best of the girls that were around her. This girl had so much talent. She was mentally tough. Physically tough. And spiritually tough. She had all the tools. But the goal on her horizon was not the right goal.

You can focus on the wrong goal and still have success, but it's a false success. This is especially true for athletes who are only focused on being the best on their team. They think they are doing all the right things but then they go to compete outside of their team and they realize they are the Cream of the Crap. They aren't good at all.

This is the challenge of staying focused on the right goal. There is a saying that if you shoot for the moon and miss, you'll still be one of the stars. Make sure your goal is a Moon Shot goal and not a star goal. You can be committed to being a star and still be interested in that moon shot but we want you to be committed to that Moon Shot.

The Perfect Athletic Career

Imagine, if you will, that you can see ten years down the road. You've competed in every competition you could and you've made every practice. You did your best on every rep and were coached to improve on every missed detail.

You were well rested for every training session and ate all the right foods. You drank the right amount of fluids and mentally you had a positive expectation going into every practice and every competitive event. Along the way you made the most of every opportunity you ever had.

Where do you think you would end up?

Most athletes think of all of their opportunities to train and compete like they are adding bricks to a lego house. Or perhaps like they are shoveling dirt onto an ever larger pile. You need to look at every opportunity that you have to play your sport, not just as an "add", but as an opportunity to remain perfect. Training and competing then are not additional items on a list like taking out the trash or doing the dishes, they are opportunities to remain perfect in the path that is laid out before you. Let me explain:

If you have an opportunity to practice today, but you call in sick, you miss an opportunity to improve that is never to be regained again. The opportunity was there and you chose against it and now it has passed. The same holds true if you miss a game or decide to watch some ridiculous "fail" video on YouTube instead of watching footage of people .

Sometimes the decisions may not seem like they are fully yours but in reality they really are. If you get injured, or you are left off of a team, this may seem like it was outside of your control but in reality, your decisions, or lack thereof led to those missed opportunities. (More on that in the Chapter 4: 100% Responsibility.)

Many athletes who have long, successful careers will be caught saying, "I never imagined I would play this long." I always think to myself, "What if they not only imagined it, but planned for it too?" Would they have taken things more seriously at a younger age to improve even more and not miss any opportunities to be great?

"But Coach, what if by taking it more seriously they burned themselves out and didn't play that long?" you ask.

I don't buy it. When you truly enjoy what you do, and you take advantage of every opportunity you have to train, compete, and recover so that you can improve and train, compete and recover again, you break records. I can guarantee you that every one of those athletes looks back and wonders, "What if I had eaten better and slept more? What if I had taken better care of my body? What if...?"

You have the opportunity now to plan and set goals for an amazing career that will last as long as it can possibly take you. Every day you will have decisions that will take you closer to your goal or further away from it. But you will only know how those decisions will affect you if you are not afraid to set goals and keep them in front of you. We will cover that more in Chapter 14.

It's Never Good Or Bad
It's Just Feedback

"I never hit a shot, even in practice, without having a very sharp, in focus picture of it in my head. It's like a color movie. First I 'see' the ball where I want it to finish, nice and high and sitting up high on the bright green grass. Then the scene quickly changes and I 'see' the ball going there: its path, trajectory, and shape, even its behavior on landing."

Jack Nicklaus,
regarded as one of the greatest golfers of all time with 18 major championships, 19 second-place and 9 third-place finishes.

Jack Nicklaus is considered one of the greatest golfers of all time. Odds are, if you are a young athlete, you've never heard of him. He's the guy with all the records that all the other golfers are trying to chase. Ricky Fowler, Dustin Johnson, Jordan Spieth? They all look to Jack Nicklaus as the best who has ever lived. People thought Tiger Woods might be able to catch his records but then...well...Tiger got a little distracted.

Jack tells a great story about how he never took a golf shot without first having a picture in his mind of where he wanted the ball to go. The reason being, he wanted to have great feedback. Each time he took a shot and the ball didn't go where he thought it would go he would now have feedback from the club, into his hands, and into his brain that he could then process and make improvements on.

Jack was incredibly curious. Each shot he took he would try to put the ball in a certain spot, and when it didn't go there he would ask himself, "Why did that just happen?" With that one question, combined with a ton of ambition, he became one of the greatest golfers in history.

What do you do? When you take a shot, lift a weight, run, sprint, lift, throw....whatever it is that you do in your sport...what do you ask yourself?

Most athletes don't think too much when they practice or play. They take a shot and miss and say to themselves, "I suck!" Instead of thinking critically and thinking first, "This is what I wanted to have happen." and then asking, "Why did I just get that result?"

Many athletes think, "Why did that happen to me?!" instead of asking, "How did I just make that happen?" And then the follow up question, "What can I do to improve on that?"

Conclusion

When you actually decide what it is you really, really want in any area of your life your brain immediately starts to notice previously unseen things to make it happen. You may be working your tail off and training hard, but when you actually decide now that's when the magic starts to show up. It may be a new coach, or a piece of equipment. It could be a new teammate or a break on a class that allows you more time to practice. Whatever they may be, you won't notice them until you decide what it is you really want.

When you set a goal...maybe it's to become an All-american or an Olympian or to play professionally, then everything you do, or don't do, will be held against that goal. And everything you do, or don't do, will take you towards that goal or away from it. Until you decide what you really want, and then set the goal to attain it, you are just a rudderless ship bobbing in the ocean. Set the goal and you will have direction.

Watch this Video:
www.AthleteSpecific.com/
decide-what-you-want

Take Action With These Steps:

- Be confident and decide what you really want. That feeling in your heart? Yeah...that's it. Write down what you want. Now.

- When you decide, people, ideas, solutions and other mysterious "things" will show up to help you reach your goal.

- Be committed to what you want and know that when you are committed all coaching inputs and other directions will have impactful meaning. Otherwise they are just noise.

- Coaches love athletes who are committed vs. interested. What they say then has incredible meaning to you. Otherwise they are just yelling at you.

- Take a moment to think of the perfect athletic career for you. See yourself making all of the practices and all of the games. Getting all of the rest and eating all the right foods. How would you perform?

Chapter 4
100% Responsibility

"You must take personal responsibility. You cannot change the circumstances, the seasons, or the wind, but you can change yourself."

Jim Rohn
(1930-2009) American entrepreneur,
author, and motivational speaker.

What if I told you that you are 100% responsible for everything that happens, or has happened to you, in your sport and in your life. From here on out, you control it all. Would you believe me? Probably not. But you would be doing yourself a disservice. You see, when you take 100% responsibility for everything that you do from here on out, and you take responsibility for everything that has happened up until now, you will have ultimate control over your actions and therefore your results. Many athletes feel helpless, like they are along for a roller coaster ride that has a bunch of ups and downs. It feels fun, sometimes, but they can't really control it and therefore don't take any responsibility.

The truth is your experience in your sport is more like a Formula 1 car race. You are picking a course to ride on. You've got the car, the team of people who support you, and it's up to you to put it all together and race. Just like the Jack Nicklaus story in the previous chapter you can take responsibility for everything you do, and when you do you will get the best feedback possible.

Take 100% Responsibility For Everything

Have you ever had a bad performance and blamed the referee, or the weather or maybe even your equipment? How about your teammates? Or your coach?

It's pretty easy to do and pretty common to do it, but I want you to stop blaming anything other than yourself. Now.

Taking 100% Responsibility for the outcome of your actions is uncommon practice. People love to blame everything but themselves. Why? Because if they place blame on something other than themselves then they don't have to feel bad about themselves. They can actually feel good by thinking, "Hey, that wasn't my fault." I'm sure you don't ever do that.

Think of the last time you were late for an appointment. You probably said something like, "Sorry I'm late coach. The traffic was horrible." What you should have said was, "Sorry coach, I didn't look at the weather last night to see that is was going to snow/rain today and warn my ride that we should leave early because traffic volume would be heavier today than on other days. I would have woken up earlier and had all of my gear ready to go."

To become an elite athlete that's pretty much how you have to look at things. You need to take responsibility for everything. The more you can do to take responsibility the more control you have. As an athlete, taking 100% responsibility can really empower you and get you closer to your goals faster than you ever thought possible.

When we blame something or someone outside of ourselves we immediately give up any chance of improving our own situation and that is what we really need to have happen. In order to have better results we need to change ourselves. Why do we need to change ourselves? Well, for one thing, you need to change yourself because your current self hasn't reached those dreams you've set for yourself now has it? Sure, you've got a long road ahead of you and you have some time, but your body hasn't caught up to your brain yet. If you were perfect you'd already be succeeding at the highest level, right? But since you aren't getting those results that you wanted yet, you must need to change something and that something is...you guessed it...you!

When I competed in the sport of luge, our races were timed to the thousandth of a second. That's .001 on the clock. A blink of an eye takes longer than that. A small fart is an eternity compared to .001. It was not uncommon for us to win or lose by hundreths if not thousands of a second. When I finished fourth at the Olympics we beat our fellow American teammates by .005 of a second. That's the equivalent of racing just under two miles at an average of fifty miles an hour and one sled beating the next by less than one inch in distance.

The first thing an athlete who takes 100% responsibility does is looks back on that race and thinks, "Where did I lose that time?"

Well the truth is that there are hundreds of places you could lose that time. It could be a wrinkle in your suit. A bad start. A drop of a foot. Too early an entrance or too late an entrance into one of the fifteen curves on the track.. Your steels could be too hot or too cold. It can go on and on and on. The bottom line, however, is that you have a hundred opportunities for incremental improvements which add up to massive improvements.

But what would happen if you looked back at the clock and thought, "My coach didn't set up my sled right. It's not my fault." or "The weather was bad, I'm no good in this weather. I can't control that." When you put that out there and place blame on something other than yourself you immediately lose all control and therefore all ability to improve. When you blame the weather, or your equipment, or the alignment of the stars you lose the opportunity to learn and that's what's most important. As an athlete we are in a constant state of learning, adjusting and progressing. Learning, adjusting and progressing. No learning? No adjusting and no progressing. In fact, you'll go backwards because the athletes around you who are taking 100% Responsibility will blow right by you.

When we take responsibility and we learn ways to fix past errors, we are now empowered to improve because we have the tools to improve on our next performance which is what we really need to have happen.

Be Really Honest With Yourself And Others

Here's a common example in a team sport. Let's say you're on a hockey team and your team is down by a goal with a minute left in the third period. The pace of the game is fast and furious and your team is tired. In a last ditch effort to extract the puck from the opposing team one of your players hooks and trips one of their players and the ref calls the penalty.

What happens next?

Well, there are probably a bunch of people in the stands yelling,

"The Ref sucks! Boooo". "How could you call that!", "That's a crappy call ref! You lost us the game!" You'd probably agree with me that those are some pretty common complaints at the end of a game like that. But can you see what's wrong when that is the main response to that play? It puts the direction of the blame on someone else. In this case it's the referee who made the call. But what happens if people walk away thinking that the only reason they lost was because of the ref?

There's no learning! The team misses out on an incredible opportunity to improve but yet everyone walks away thinking the ref was the jerk who lost the game for them.

Let's take the same situation and look at it in a different way. Same play. Same call by the ref. What if, instead of blaming the refs, the questions and answers started to fly like this:

"Why did the ref make the call? Well Jimmy didn't move his feet on the play. Why didn't Jimmy move his feet on the play? He was tired. Why was he tired? Well, he works really hard in the gym and on the ice. He's doing all the things the coaches ask him to do. Maybe our strength and conditioning program hasn't adequately prepared a guy like him for a third-period situation like that. How could we have avoided that situation? The coach could have had another player out there who had played less minutes. Jimmy needs to work on his maximal strength and his endurance so he has more gas in the tank at the end of the third. (And I could go on and on.)

So what's happened now? Instead of losing an opportunity to learn and improve there are now hundreds of opportunities to learn and improve. But so far, I've only talked about the decision of the coach, and Jimmy. That may not affect the athlete sitting on the bench who may not have been on the ice at the time the play happened. And they might, wrongly, be thinking about the decision of the ref, and the coach, and Jimmy's bad play. But what they should be thinking about is the hundreds of plays they were involved in PRIOR to that play.

The goalie can be thinking about the save earlier in the game that he missed or the loose rebound he was unable to control that led to the goal in the second period. The fourth line guy, who really wants more ice time, needs to think about the check he missed in the first period. The face off guy who lost forty percent of his faceoffs needs to be thinking about why he lost those forty percent and how to win more. When the whole team does this, it goes from one or two guys looking for ways to improve to the entire team looking for ways to improve. The improvement ratio is now exponential!

And if you read that and don't quite understand how it would affect you if you are in an individual sport...think again. When I competed in the sport of luge it was common to go back over a run and be overwhelmed by all of the opportunities for improvement, but it was critical because the smallest improvement can have the biggest net effect at the end of the run. By being honest with yourself and thinking of all of the possible opportunities you had to change the outcome is the first step to incredible levels of improvement in your performance and your results.

How British Cycling Beat The World

If ever there were a story I could share with you about how taking 100% responsibility and how making small improvements over a large number of areas can lead to massive results, it's the British Cycling team.

Before you say, "Yawn." let me help you for a moment. You see, I've met athletes who say they want to be amazing at their sport yet they forget to pack their socks in their gym bag. They can't find their mouthpiece or they left some other piece of vital equipment at home. They brush it off like it's no big deal, but it is a very big deal. (See "Life Skills" in Chapter 9)

In 2004 the British Cycling team was mediocre at best. I'm not talking about the guys who ride bikes outside, I'm talking about the guys who race indoors on massive Velodromes. If you have never seen track cycling in a velodrome you need to have a look. The sheer power that these guys and girls can create is incredible, not to mention the size of their quads! It's impressive.

But back in 2004 the Brit's weren't all that great, but they were close. Sir Chris Hoy (who at the time wasn't a "Sir" in British lore) looked at his one lap time which was roughly 17.4 to 17.5 seconds per lap. The world record was 17.3 seconds. He set his goal to ride one lap at 17.0.

That may seem like a lot of time to some, but when he did the math he realized that it was only a 2.78% improvement. To an average athlete they might look at that and think, "Well, if I could just peddle 2.78% faster then I would be the World Champion." That's the wrong approach.

What Chris Hoy realized was that if he could make a 2.78% improvement over a number of areas in his athletic life then he would easily reach his goal. He decided to improve his squat 2.78%. He wanted to lose 2.78% body fat. He looked for 2.78% improvements in things like aerodynamics, the weight of his bike, his nutrition, his sleep. The list of places he could find a 2.78% improvement was exhausting but exciting because the idea of improving 2.78% became very easy. Sir Chris Hoy went on to set the World Record.

So I ask you, where can you make small improvements in your life to help make your athletic goals come true? If you make small improvements over many areas you will improve faster than you ever thought possible. It's easy math, but it all starts by taking 100% responsibility and looking at all of the areas you can improve and then acting on those areas.

The Butterfly Effect

Edward Lorenz was a mathematician and a meteorologist who coined the term "butterfly effect" when he was looking to recreate the weather pattern of a hurricane. He noticed that as the hurricane grew, the tiniest change in input early on in the system could have a drastic change on the outcome of the final hurricane. Something as small as a butterfly flapping it's wings in California could change the wind so much that the final hurricane could end up in Texas or off the coast of California. The idea that a seemingly insignificant input can have a drastic affect on the outcome of something as large as a hurricane seems absurd. But it's mathematically true. And the same thing can happen to you if you take 100% responsibility for all that you do. The smallest improvement when you take ownership can drastically affect the outcome of your efforts whether you are in an individual sport, or in a team environment.

Goals. Strategies. Tactics

This book is all about helping you create a strategy for making your athletic dreams come true. The dreams you have are the Goals that you are looking to set. The Strategy you set is how you are going to get there. The difference between tactics and strategy is that a tactic is an individual action you might take like joining a new team, buying a piece of equipment, eating better foods or attending a skills camp... those are all tactics. How they fit into the overall strategy of what you are trying to accomplish is what makes the difference. Many athletes jump from tactic to tactic without having any sort of strategy other than "more will make you better". There is a huge difference. After reading this book you will know what tactics you need to adopt, which one's you shouldn't bother with, and how they all fit into an overall strategy or your athletic success.

When you take 100% responsibility for all of your actions your goals, strategies, and tactics immediately become more targeted. Instead of being vague about what you are doing you now have a laser focus on what you want and how you want to get there.

Be Curious

You are reading this book because you are curious. You want to learn more because you want better results. You want to win. I want you to win too.

In this book I cover a lot of topics. There aren't any pictures (it's not that kind of a book). People told me I should pare some things down but I thought to myself, if I was sitting with you face to face would I want to hold that information back? No. So that's why I've included what I've included.

When we are curious we ask better questions. We don't think, "Why did that happen to me?" we ask, "How did that happen?" When we are curious we ask, "How can I make that better?" instead of thinking, "I have no idea how that happened?" One question leads to great answers, the other leads to dead ends. This book is all about helping you get great answers, and how to ask even better questions to get even better answers.

I read an article about Steph Curry, a professional basketball player that you may have heard of. While the article was all about these techno gadgets he likes to use with his trainer (tactics) there was a comment that really summed up one of the greatest athletes of our time. He's curious. And within curiousity comes a greater level of intelligence. I thought that definition was great. But my question for you now is this:

How do coaches define you as an athlete? Would they say

you are curious? Or a hard worker? Are you tenacious? A dim yet talented lightbulb? What else do coaches say about you?

More importantly, how would you like people to describe you as an athlete?

Conclusion

By taking 100% responsibility for everything that happens in your life, you immediately feel a sense of control, and even relief. When you look back and say, "THAT is what I could do to change that outcome." you feel empowered and ready to learn. No matter how large or small, if you are extremely honest with yourself and your coaches, you will accelerate your learning and your results.

The British Cycling Team is a great example of not just one athlete, but a team of athletes, coaches and support staff who embraced the idea of taking 100% responsibility led by Sir Chris Hoy. It not only led to improvements but to Olympic Gold and created one of the most dominant teams in Cycling history. That same success can be yours when you apply this principle. Even small changes can make a huge difference, just like the flapping of a butterfly's wings can have an impact on a hurricane.

Decide today to take action. Increase your curiosity so you can find new strategies and tactics to reach your goals and be prepared to do this even though others around you may be quick to blame others for their bad results.

Watch This Video:

**www.AthleteSpecific.com/
100%-responsibility**

Take Action With These Steps:

- Think of a time when you were quick to blame someone or something else for your bad result. Write it down. Now write down what you could have done to change the course of that result.

- Being honest with yourself is a critical step in shifting from a responsibility giver to someone who accepts responsibility and therefore can change his/her results. Has there been a time when you weren't honest with yourself and your responsibility? Write that down and decide to take action.

- Sir Chris Hoy looked at his results and decided to make small improvements across a number of areas in his training and his equipment and won Olympic Gold. In what areas can you make small improvements?

- After you decide what areas you can improve (and there should be a bunch) take action immediately. If there are areas where you may need outside help, take action now and reach out to those who you may need help from. Don't delay. Take action...now.

- Increase your curiosity. It's almost become cool not to act curious. Don't fall into that trap. Identify one aspect of your sport, or your performance that interests you and take action on that curiosity. Maybe it's getting online and doing some research, or pulling out a book at the library on that topic. It doesn't matter what it is, just take action to feed your curiosity.

Chapter 5
Flying From Runway to FL50,000

> *"We can keep digging and digging; but if we don't take time, consistently, to look up and look where we are truly going, we will dig ourselves a trench that we can never get out of and that is going in the wrong direction."*

Jonathan Edwards
Olympian, Speaker, Author www.AthleteSpecific.com

I was flying from Boston to San Diego when it hit me. This journey of being an athlete is very much like being on a plane and you are the pilot. The entire journey is made up of, not just time on the runway, but time spent at all of the altitudes to make that trip come true. You will spend lots of time on the runway but you will also spend time at all of the different flight levels, each one giving you a unique perspective of your path below.

When you are in a plane and you are cruising at 36,000 feet, you have a very different perspective than when you are down on the runway. It is from these different perspectives that you can really start to think strategically about how things are going and what you need to do to reach your destination.

Flight Level: The Runway

When It Happens: Practices. Training. Game Day.

How You Will Feel: Fatigued. Tired. Potentially in pain. Emotions are raw at this level.

When you are on the runway you have your head down training and competing. You are on the ground level working on your skills and your abilities. This is where you are doing your work and this is usually where all of the pain and suffering takes place. It's where you're doing your push ups and your planks. It's where you will be doing your weight room work and your skill work on the field play. This is where a soccer player is doing footwork with the ball and where a skier is working the gates. It's where a hockey player is doing skating drills and where you are competing in a game situation. It's where the grit and the hustle are applied and it's where you feel the most fatigue.

Flight Level: 10,000 Feet

When It Happens: In between sets. Timeouts in games. In between periods, quarters or halftime.

How You Will Feel: Still fatigued. Breathless. You are looking to recover between sets. Between shifts. Between runs. Emotions are softened just a little but you know you're going to be right back in it in a few moments.

This is where you step back from a drill and you get with your coach for immediate feedback. It's where a team takes a timeout and says, "Ok, you did this great. But that thing we just did there, yeah, we need to do it differently." It can also be when you take a break in between sets in the weightroom. "Ok, just did a set of twelve. How did that feel?" This is a *mini-perspective* jump where you step back just slightly to get a quick view of how things are feeling and make immediate adjustments based on your immediate results.

Flight Level: 20,000 Feet

When It Happens: Day after events or training sessions. Could be Sundays but could really be any day of the week depending on your schedule.

How You Will Feel: Residual soreness and fatigue from training and competition but more relaxed because you are not at Runway level. Stress and anxiety may still be high because of your focus on a competition coming up, or the thoughts of a past, poor performance still in your head.

At this level you may be in a locker room taking off your gear. You may be home watching television, or you may be in a restaurant just thinking about how things went in your last competition or how you are going to manage a future competition coming up. It is in these moments where you get out of the immediate stress of competition and training to take a look at how the last phase of your training has gone. A recent competition gives you perspective on how things are going based on the intensity of that last competition.

Flight Level: 30,000 Feet

When It Will Happen: The end of a long season or offseason.

How You Will Feel: Tired but rewarded for all the work you've put in. You've probably come a very long way from where you started. The sheer volume of work you have completed regardless of your competition results is worth a big old pat-on-the-back.

It's at the end of an offseason or competitive season where you can look back and see how things went and how you improved. You will be able to review with your coach just what you need to work on for the upcoming phase of your training. This is a time of excitement as you look forward and a bit of regret as you look back. You will always feel that there was something more you could have done to prepare yourself, but don't focus too much on that. Look forward to the next phase and how it will fit into your overall goals.

Flight Level: 40,000 Feet

When It Will Happen: The end of a year which includes the main competitive season, and the off-season.

How You Will Feel: Relaxed. From this perspective you will be able to look at how your past training and competitions fit into your overall goals.

Without the stress of everyday training and competition you will be able to get a larger perspective for what it is you are doing. You'll ask yourself, "How is this all going?" From here you will take a further step back to look at how your development so far will help you reach your goals. From this perspective you can work proactively towards your future and not be mired in the immediate, reactive emotions of training and competition.

Flight Level: 50,000 Feet

When It Will Happen: Can be typically every four years culminating in an event like the Olympics or at the end of high-school or college.

How You Will Feel: More relaxed but with a larger swing in emotions. At times like this, larger decisions are made usually revolving around staying in your sport or retiring.

At this flight level raw emotions tend to be gone. You've had enough time and distance from your competitive and training environments to get further perspective and a feeling of how all of this fits into your larger life plan.

Commit To Every Phase

It is very easy to let emotions get the best of you. The best athletes eliminate that temptation by not making rash decisions at the wrong time. It's not a matter of resisting temptation but to remove temptation from the conversation completely.

When you commit to next season, commit to next season. When you commit to a four year plan, commit to the four year plan. Don't think about quitting in the middle of a practice, just practice. Don't think about walking off the field during a game either. Conversely, don't think that just because you've made one great play you're going to get a scholarship to college or compete in the Olympic games. (I talk more about this in **The Highs' Aren't So High And The Lows Aren't So Low** in Chapter 24)

When you commit to each phase of your training you will naturally want to set goals around each phase that you will measure your success by. By understanding that it's not going to be a very smooth path getting to those goals you won't be affected when you have a bad practice or a bad game. Committing to every phase takes the roller coaster ride of emotions out of it. When you're in, be in. There will be a time when you will know it's time to be out.

Are You Boiling A Frog?

I doubt you have ever tried to boil a frog but bear with me for this all-important analogy.

If you take a frog and toss it into a pot of boiling water it will hop out of the pot immediately. It doesn't take long for the frog to realize that the boiling hot water is not good for it so it jumps out as fast as it can.

On the flip side, if you take that same frog and put it into the same pot but this time the water is cool, the frog will stay in the water swimming around enjoying the little froggy pool. But if you slowly turn up the heat, guess what happens? The frog won't notice that the temperature is rising and he slowly cooks himself to death. (I know, I know, it's not a pretty story.)

The truth is, this is exactly how many athletes operate. They put themselves in an environment that seems ok on the outside. They train and they compete, never really taking a step back to assess how the environment really is affecting them. Testing the pot for hot water so-to-speak. Ultimately, they boil themselves.

You must step away from the hot pot every so often to know just what is going on. How do you really feel? Is your body recovering? Are you rested? Are you in the right training environment? Are you headed in the right direction? These are just some of the questions you can ask yourself.

Take a Rest

In my work as an Athletic Development specialist, sometimes the best advice I give athletes is to rest. While others coaches will provide more work in an effort to outwork their opponents **an already hard working athlete needs permission to take it easy. (Just a side note: There is usually an inverse relationship between how motivated an athlete and how much rest and recovery time they need. The more motivated, the more rest.)**

If you are a hard working athlete putting in tons of training time in addition to thinking about your sport all the time, you probably could use some time off. If you are dealing with nagging injuries that don't have time to recover, you probably need some rest. If you are working and working and working and aren't getting the results you want, you could use a rest.

An actual rest gives your body time to heal, but it also allows your mind time to rest and refocus. When you are in it every day and doing, doing, doing, you will get mentally stuck. Your brain will play the same mental thoughts over and over again. That's ok if you're having great results, but if you are stale, then you really need that break to get mentally refreshed as well as physically refreshed. As a gauge, I like to tell athletes that if they **don't** have a little, "How do I do this again?" feeling when they get back, they probably haven't rested long enough.

You Have To Have Valleys To Have Peaks.

The human body is not like a car engine. You can't just ask it to run high RPM's all the time and not take time to change the oil or gas it up. You are the same way. I have worked with a number of athletes who are on, year round. There is never a chance to rest or recover. There is no opportunity for the body to super-compensate. In the quest for "more" the body and the mind is never able to take a break and then recover to a level higher than it was before.

I recommend that every athlete should take a solid week off, preferably two, at the end of every season. That's roughly four breaks a year for a total time off of one to two months. What does "off" mean? No technical practices. No weight room work. Just "active rest" that's made up of very light physical activity that is significantly different than what the athlete might normally do. For example: A hockey player might play a light game of soccer or basketball every day to get the blood flowing and stimulate the body in a very different way. Outside of that he or she should do nothing but sleep and eat and hydrate. A break from any sort of academic work is also advised although I understand that's not always possible.

Another example might be a soccer player who takes a holiday and goes half day skiing every other day. On opposite days she can play in the pool and then sleep and eat and hydrate. Not only does this provide a physical "cleanse" it also provides a mental one as well.

You have to plan the valleys in your schedule. I worked with an athlete once whose family could just not get their head around taking time off. All they could see was that he had this tournament and that tournament. He had winter hockey and spring hockey and summer hockey. I said, "Listen, when can we get a solid week off between those sessions?" A quick look at the calendar and we were able to pencil in four separate weeks that were roughly three months apart. I took a pen and made the dates stand out even more and said, "We're going to start there. See those weeks? You're going to do absolutely nothing."

"Nothing?" they asked absolutely dumbfounded that I would suggest such a thing. "Yes, nothing." At the end of that year, this athlete had his best performance of all time. He scored the most points he had ever scored and had the least amount of penalties as well staying injury free. Four weeks off was the beginning of establishing a plan that made that all happen.

Gratitude

An emotion that very few coaches ever talk to their athletes about is a feeling of Gratitude. We get so wrapped up in wins and losses, games and practices, training and no training that we really miss the larger perspective on things. I would say that this Flight Level is a level 100,000 when you put it all into perspective.

You are on an amazing journey where you can not lose. Sure, you may lose a game or an event, but in the grand scheme of things a bad day doing your sport still beats a great day at work. None of this is a waste of time and all of it will help shape you as a person for the rest of your life. I can't tell you enough how much every coach, teammate, and fan affected who I am today and how I look back on even the smallest game and have good thoughts. You will have an incredible experience winning and losing, learning and unlearning. There are a lot of people who would love to be in your shoes and it is truly something to be thankful for.

A great way to start every morning is to just look up from your pillow and say "Thank you." Who do you say it to? Everyone. Your parents for giving you the resources to learn how to play. Your coaches for taking their time to watch you and pass on their wisdom to you that helps you improve. Your teammates for being by your side on this journey. Your competition, sometimes called "co-opetition", for challenging you and helping you get better. Your equipment. Your mouthpiece. Your lucky underwear. And to the big ball of magic in the sky that guides us on this journey. Whether you call it God, spirit, stardust, Unicorn farts, it doesn't really matter. (Yes, I said Unicorn farts.) Just know that it is all amazing and you should be thankful for it no matter what the result says on the scoreboard.

Conclusion:

As an athlete it's important that you will have moments when you are in it, and doing it, and loving it, and hating it. You will feel all of the emotions that sport can give us along with joy and elation, and pain and frustration. That is why you need to step back, often, to get another perspective on all that you are doing. Just like you get a different perspective when you are sitting in a plane, the view looks very different from 50,000 than it does when you're sitting on the runway.

By taking frequent opportunities to rest and recover, you can assess just how things are going. Are you on track? Are you healing and recovering? Are you happy? These valleys in your training and competition schedule will provide you the opportunity to have higher peaks than you've ever had before.

And while you may have times when it all seems too hard, and you're too tired, take some time to be grateful for it all. What and who should you be grateful for? All of it. If you're waking up in the morning with an alarm and thinking, "ugh" you don't have enough rest. Seek to wake up every morning rested and recovered and say, "Thank you." To who? Everyone and everything. It's going to be a great day when you start your mornings like that.

Watch This Video:
www.AthleteSpecific.com/flight-levels

Take Action With These Steps:

- Read through the Flight Level sections in this chapter and take a moment to think about when you can have changes in perspective and the value that will give you.

- When was the last time you had a really good rest?

- You have to have valleys to have peaks in your performance. Look back on when your last valley was and identify the peak that came after it. Do you see a trend?

- There is so much to be thankful for as you pursue high performance sport. Who and what do you have to be thankful for? Make a list and start your day by saying "thank you" to it all.

Section 2

Preparing For Game Day

"Champions do not become champions when they win the event, but in the hours, weeks, months and years they spend preparing for it. The victorious performance itself is merely the demonstration of their championship character."

Alan Armstrong
is an American Writer best known for his Newbery
Medal Honor Book "Whittington".

What is Game Day? Well, it's any day that you need to compete at your best.

"Wouldn't that be every day?" No, not at all. Or should I say, "I hope not!" Although in some competitive environments it may feel like every day is a day you need to compete at your best. I'm talking about days when you play a game against another team or a day where you have a competition that you need to be "up" for. It could also be a tryout in front of a prospective coach or team official. College football players compete in the Combine every March in Indianapolis, but they will also have a "Pro Day" that happens on their college campus where Pro Coaches come to see them play. In addition to the fourteen games they will play in a season, those are all days when an athlete needs to compete at their highest level. You may have a similar situation.

In this section we are going to discuss thoughts and techniques that will help you prepare for your best Game Day. Much like looking at a set of architectural drawings before a building goes up, this section is designed to introduce principles to help you set the foundation to be prepared for a successful Game Day. We will go into more detail on how to have your best Game Day in Part 3, but don't jump ahead. Without understanding the principles I cover in this chapter you can't have a solid Game Day.

Chapter 6
It's All About Peak State

---

*"A clear vision, backed by definite plans, gives you a
tremendous feeling of confidence and personal power."*

Brian Tracy
Canadian-born American motivational public
speaker and self-development author.

It's nine in the morning and I can't feel my fingers.

I'd been training in the sport of luge for nine years at this point. I'd
been a World Cup medalist and had finished fourth at the Olympics. I'd
done this before. A thousand times. But today, when it really mattered,
my heart rate was through the roof and I couldn't feel my fingers. It
wasn't that my hands were numb from the cold, it was a beautiful sunny
day and my warm up was awesome. Those were bad nerves I was
feeling and I didn't need them today. Not this much.

It was National Championships and I'd been waiting for this day for
over a year and was more than prepared to have a great performance.
After my normal warm up I was jacked up and the numbness I felt in
my fingers was a sign that I had blown waaaaay past my Peak State. I
went on to have one of the worst races of my life and was confused as
to why that just happened.

Before that day I hadn't ever really thought about Peak State.
Surprising since I had already gotten to the Olympic level without giving
it much thought and consideration. I mean I had always "warmed up"
and gotten ready to compete but obviously that wasn't' working right
now. I had over-cooked myself and my body and my mind weren't in
harmony.

What Is Peak State?

Peak state is **a zone of optimal physical, mental and emotional readiness** that allows you to compete at your best. I like to call it a "zone" because it gives me a visual representation that I can get to that state of readiness from a number of different approaches.

Prior to that day when I had that really bad race when I was so nervous and couldn't feel my fingers, I always felt that getting ready to compete was like climbing a ladder that got narrower and narrower the higher up I climbed. Like I was trying to climb to this perfect little point way up at the top.

Through this whole experience I learned that Peak State was not a little tiny target I was trying to hit, it was more like an area I was trying to get close to. Kind of like a golfer hitting a "lag" putt. He's not trying to get it in the hole from really far away, he's just trying to get it close to the hole. Peak State wasn't at the top of a mountain either, as I had thought about it in the past, it was like getting on an elevator and trying to get to a couple of floors somewhere up the building but not totally through the top of it.

This was a complete revelation to me. I had always done the same warm up, over and over and over again and never had to adjust it. It was my bread and butter routine that got me ready to compete and I had used it for years. But now, under the conditions I was in, I didn't need as much of a warm up to be ready. In fact, my warm up had gotten me way past ready to the point that I wasn't going to be able to have my best performance. I was no longer at my Peak State but was somewhere beyond it in a place of fatigue and stress and nervousness.

But why?

Peak State is a moving target that can be hard to hit some days. Some days it will take more effort to get there and other days it won't take much at all. What this means is that if you are a pretty stable individual and, day to day, your demeanor and your overall approach to your sport is the same, then getting into Peak State will be pretty routine. You'll be able to do your same warm up, eat your same breakfast and get on with your training and competing the same every day. You don't change much so neither does the target.

But if your demeanor changes from day to day, ebbing and flowing along with the demands of life, then that Peak State target starts to move a little bit too. One day you may need to get your heart rate up for longer to get the body warm, other days you may wake up out of bed and be ready to go. That's what was happening to me.

The scenario I was competing in was US National Championships. I was a year removed from the US National Team and was trying to get back on as a singles competitor and was obviously feeling the pressure. I had won the overall World Cup on the B World Cup Circuit the year before and had even beaten some of my US teammates who were on the national team already. I had been training very well and had already posted some very fast times that would put me on the podium come race day. I had been thinking about this day for a really long time and probably could have rolled out of bed and been ready to race I was so ready. But because I didn't consider that I was already ready and my mind and body was already really close to my Peak State, I blew right past it by treating that day the same as every other day.

As it was, my race was horrible. I lost by a small margin but overall I just didn't feel right. When I sat in the handles at the start, besides my hands being numb, I felt uncomfortable in my suit and my heartbeat was pounding in my ears. Not good. I was way past my peak state.

Why Peak State Is So Important

Peak State is a combination of mental, emotional, and physical preparation that allows you to compete at YOUR highest level and leaves you open to performances that you haven't quite been able to pull off yet. I say "yet" because every athlete can share moments when they did something amazing in practice or competition that surprised even themselves. I remember making saves as a goalie where I thought to myself, "Holy cow! How did I just do THAT!"

When you see an Olympic event, or a World Championships final in any sport, you are seeing the "cream of the crop" competing at their Peak State. For those athletes they are firing on all cylinders and are as amped up and ready to compete as they need to be to perform at their best. It's like Goldilocks and the Three Bears accept we aren't talking about porridge. We are talking about being mentally, emotionally and physically ready to compete at our highest level. We're not too hot, or too cold, we are juuuuuust right.

You have your own Peak State right now, although you probably haven't really maximized yours yet. As you become more experienced in your sport, reaching your Peak State changes. Mistakenly, many athletes think that the better you get the less of a warm up you actually need and this simply isn't true. For those athletes who compete in the 100 meter dash at the Olympics, an event that takes less than ten seconds to complete, they may have warmed up for hours to get to their Peak State.

How Do You Hit Your Peak State

Depending on your sport, you have been probably doing some sort of "warm up" to get your body ready. If you are in a team sport you may have been doing some sort of "dynamic" team warm up that may or may not be appropriate for you. Or if you're in an individual sport you've probably been throwing your earbuds in and cranking up the tunes getting yourself ready to train and compete doing any number of warm up activities. Whatever it is you do, you are ramping up your body both physically, mentally and emotionally.

However you've been handling it, you need to understand that getting yourself ready is a very personal experience. Every athlete is different and what works for one athlete may or may not work for another. I've seen athletes do everything from dance and scream to taking a nap. That's why you don't want to follow a warm up routine of another athlete blindly while not listening to your own body and your own needs. It is critical that you listen to your body during your warm up, then assess that warm up against your performance for that day. When your performance (training or competition) is over, you want to think back to all the things you did to try and get to Peak State to see if what you did actually helped you reach your Peak State. Did you feel good? Were you nervous or tired? Jittery or sleepy?

Just as an example, I found that if I did my warm up back in my hotel room that I didn't need to do as much once I got to the track. At the track I may be trying to run in snow or trying to get physically warm outside in the cold which obviously made it more difficult. My routine went something like this:

- 7:00 AM Wake Up
- 7:00-7:15 Meditate and Visualize what I needed to do that day. (Race, Practice, etc)
- 7:15-7:35 Shower, Brush teeth, drink water.

- 7:40-8:10 Whole body stretch.
- 8:10-8:30 Breakfast
- 8:30-9:00 Drive to track and prepare for session.

Once I got to the track I would prepare for my training and/or the race and would end up completing a smaller warm up again that was modified based on how good I felt. If I was cold and needed more I did more. If I was already warm and felt nervous or excited I might do less or change the music I was listening to in order to tone me down a bit.

So the question is...what do you do to reach your Peak State? What have you done in the past? Do you have a consistent routine or do you just wing it? If you are part of a team and do some sort of team warm up, does it help you? Is it just right or too much? Or not enough? What else do you need to do make it work? What do you need to eliminate?

Take a moment and put the answers to these questions in the box below. Do it now:

How Do You Know If You've Reached Your Peak State?

By assessing your performance and linking the effect your warm up had on it you can decide the following:

1. You were below your Peak State.
2. You were in your Peak State.
3. You had overcooked yourself and were past your Peak State.

This is something only you can truly assess, but working with a coach can help you understand just where you are. When I worked with Dr. Jerry Lynch, he was able to help me make changes to my warm up like changing the music I was listening to and toning things down to keep my heartrate from blowing up. My normal practice and training warm up consisted of something very heavy and hard like Jane's Addiction or Nine Inch Nails (Google it). But he recommended toning it down on game day because my body was already ready. By amping it up with hard music I was throwing more fuel on an already burning fire. I didn't need that.

Peak State is Not The Point Of The Needle

As I mentioned earlier, getting to my Peak State was no longer like trying to reach the fine point on the end of the needle. Or trying to sink a long birdie putt on a golf course trying to hit everything perfectly so it ends up in that very tiny hole. Just thinking like that can make you feel tight and pressure filled. Now it was more like a lag putt where a golfer does everything well enough so that the ball sits close enough to the hole that on the next putt he's sure to get the ball in the hole. He's trying to get the ball "close enough" to be in a position to sink the putt and not trying to thread the needle which can put a lot more stress on the mind of the athlete.

When I was young I thought that everything had to be absolutely perfect, from what music I listened to, to the sequence of my stretches, to what sock I put on first. If anything in that sequence was off then I would be off. This created a lot of stress for me and tends to create a lot of stress in others too. (See Chapter 22: Visualize Doing Imperfect...

Perfectly)

When I changed my approach and realized that I wasn't trying to reach some "perfect" Peak State I could relax and have a much better chance of competing powerfully. You can too.

Conclusion:

To have your best performance you must be in a Peak State to do it. What is Peak State? It is a mental, emotional and physical state where all systems are optimized for your best performance. The key words here are that it is "a" state that is specific to you. There are many ways to reach your Peak State. While you may have some sort of routine to reach it, you may need to utilize different techniques to reach it depending on how you feel each day. By keeping track of your results in practice and competitions against your warm ups and movement prep activities you will be able to narrow down what works and what doesn't for you.

Keep in mind that Peak State is not an exact "point" you are trying to reach. You are not aiming for perfect here. By listening to your body you will adjust accordingly based on how you feel and will be able to reach your Peak State no matter what is going on in your day to day life.

Watch This Video:

www.AthleteSpecific.com/peak-state

Take Action With These Steps:

- Grab your journal and write down what it is you do to get yourself ready for practice and competition. Don't over think. Just write down what it is you do.

- If what you do differs between your practice and competitions, ask yourself "why?". Is it because of the environment or are you just being lazy? How does that affect your performance?

- If you understand that you play like you practice and practice like you play, what can you do to make your preparation for practice similar to that of your competition?

- Take some time to get online and research the habits of elite athletes and how they prepare for competition and practice. What habits can you adopt to help you become an elite athlete?

Chapter 7
Understanding The Four Ages Of Every Athlete

"Nothing in life is to be feared, it is only to be understood. Now is the time to understand more, so that we may fear less."

Marie Curie
Polish and naturalized-French physicist and chemist who conducted pioneering research on radioactivity.

Have you ever competed against someone and said any of the following statements? (Or their variations.)
- She is NOT (enter age here)!
- He is a beast!
- There is NO WAY she just started playing!
- They have to have forged her birth certificate.
- That kid plays like he's been playing forever!
- That kid is so talented but he acts like a baby.
- And others...

You Can't Compare Yourself To An Outlier

Sidney Crosby grew up in Halifax, Nova Scotia, Canada and quickly became one of the top hockey players in all of Canada. As a junior player he was a man amongst boys and quickly rose to prominence in Canada's national sport.

His rise in the sport was meteoric and he had success at every level, including the professional ranks, where he became the youngest captain of a Stanley Cup winning team in history. And did I mention that he also scored the gold medal winning goal at the Olympics in Canada? It's a storybook career that still continues.

Culture can have a huge factor on athletic expectation and Canada is one of those places where the culture of hockey is...how you say...crazy? The competition is huge and the environment is such that if you're kid isn't playing "A" level hockey at fourteen years of age well, they should just quit, and they often do.

On the other side of the spectrum you have an athlete like Johnny Gaudreau from New Jersey. At 5'8" (maybe) and 165 lbs (soaking wet), he currently plays in the NHL after four years at Boston College and finishing his career there as the Hobey Baker winner and the best player in college hockey. The Calgary Flames ended up drafting "Johnny Hockey" 104th in the draft and he is currently lighting up the NHL.

Now Sidney and Johnny are different ages and came from different backgrounds but let's just say they were playing in the same year and comparisons were able to be made between the two. Sydney, man amongst boys, versus "little" Johnny hockey. You probably wouldn't have mentioned them in the same breath they were so different. Sydney is what you would call an "outlier." He was so advanced that it is unfair, and unwise, for any athlete to compare to him.

Looking Long Term

Josh is a pretty good hockey player for his age. He skates well but is pretty small compared to his peers. When body checking begins next year he is surely going to get run out of the game. His stick skills are solid and his skating is above average. Overall you would say Josh is "young" compared to his buddies but he's pretty quick and can skate well.

The chances "now" look a little bleak for Josh. But the long-term looks pretty solid if he can stick it out.

Tanner was 225lbs as a fifteen year old. He would run people over and no one could get around him he was so big. He lacked "foot speed" but had a cannon for a shot and was drafted into the WHL as a fifteen year old. Eventually, the game of hockey advanced around him and he was no longer able to keep up with smaller, faster skaters. The size advantage he had as a fifteen year old, that made him a game changer, had now become a disadvantage as skaters flew by him getting the loose pucks he was normally able to corral.

At fifteen Tanner was the next big thing, literally. Josh is skating by people but is really small. Sydney was winning games and was playing with kids much older than him. People were worried that Johnny wasn't going to have the size to compete ultimately, but he did.

All of these athletes have withstood the challenges of the game, but how? How have some managed to continue while others drop around them?

The Four "Ages" Of Every Athlete

At any point in time during an athlete's career they have what is considered to be four "ages" and they are:

- Chronological Age
- Biological Age
- Psychological Age
- Training Age

Understanding the four ages of every athlete can really help you identify where you are right now and what sort of development you might expect over the next few years. Really understanding these ages will enable you to look down the road a little bit while other athletes, parents, and coaches around you are fixated on the "now" in addition to thinking of the doom and gloom that will fall upon their athlete if they aren't winning right now. While most athletes are waiting for an excuse to quit I'm going to give you more years to stick it out. (Sorry. Not sorry.)

The Chronological Age

This is pretty easy to understand as it is your actual "age". Jimmy is ten and two months. Sally is nine and six months. Jimmy was born in January. Sally was born in October. You get it.

When an athlete is born can be extremely important as it can drastically affect an athlete especially during years of puberty. A difference in age of six months can have a huge difference especially during the years of Peak Height Velocity where kids are growing like weeds. Height and weight differences can really make a difference for young athletes. A pitcher who towers over her team can often rifle a softball way faster than a shorter competitor. In contact sports like hockey and football, those bigger kids can just dominate a game, and therefore help a team win. Therefore, most coaches are drawn to pick those kids as they have a greater impact sometimes than a smaller, more skilled, athlete at those ages.

Depending on how some sports are organized, age can have a huge effect. If you are born in December and you are competing against kids who are born in January of the same year, well that's a full year of growth. While it might not be a big deal when kids are 8,9,10 years old, it makes a huge difference when growth spurts start to kick in. If you are an athlete who is older in Chronological Age but you haven't "filled out" you are probably pretty frustrated. Conversely, if you are young chronologically but you are big like Tanner was, you may be winning just on your size alone.

Biological Age

Sometimes you can have athletes who just "fill out" early. Or they "grow like a weed". We all know those kids and marvel at their development. We say things like, "What have you been eating?!" Or, "Who did this come from, the Milk Man?!" Referring to an athlete whose height doesn't mimic Mom or Dad's height.

These kids can either be slightly larger or grossly larger than their teammates; but either way, the way their body has developed is faster than their peers and it gives them a distinct advantage.

Sidney Crosby was arguably that type of kid as he got to Junior level hockey. And probably even Midget level hockey. He was a man amongst boys and that was confirmed when he went to the NHL and still dominated amongst men who were ten years older than he. Even though he was still a boy his body was physically mature. So you could say that while his Chronological Age said "eighteen years old" his Biological Age said "twenty-five".

Another great example is Auston Matthews of the Toronto Maple Leafs. In his first year in the NHL at nineteen years of age he is one of the leaders in scoring - In the entire league! He is playing against athletes significantly older than him with tons more training and playing experience. Why is he doing so well? His biological age is so advanced. He's bigger, faster, and stronger and because of that he's able to do more things than most kids his age. He is a man amongst boys at only nineteen years old.

Psychological Age

We all know these kids. "Oh, he's an Old Soul". Or she's, "Wise beyond her years." Conversely we have also heard things like, "I wish he would just grow up!" lol.

These are the kids who, while their birth certificate says they are twelve, act like they are six. Or sixteen. It can go both ways. Kids who are advanced Psychologically are usually more aware of situations than their peers. They can think through plays and performances better than others. I go over this more in the Three Key Abilities section but want to lay this out for you now just so you get a basic understanding of how it fits in. By having an advanced Psychological Age an athlete can also go through the four competency phases in Chapter 17 more efficiently as well.

Athletes with advanced Psychological Age can usually "outsmart" their competitors. As coaches, we can share with you advanced topics and techniques and you are usually able to apply them in competitive situations (which is really fun especially in a team setting). As a Coach we wish all of our athletes, no matter what their age, were more advanced Psychologically.

On the flip side, athletes who have young Psychological Ages are usually "a step behind". They are the kids who you "just wish they would grow up!". You don't want things to "pass them by." And they frustrate you when you just wish they would "smarten up" a little bit.

Since you are reading this I'm going to put you in the more advanced Psychological Age category. That's not to make you feel superior over your teammates or competitors (or maybe it does), but by understanding this Psychological Age thing, you're going to have a better understanding of your teammates and your competitors and how you can help/beat them.

Training Age

Your training age describes how long you've been practicing your particular sport, which sounds simple enough but time spent in all sports can add up.

Let's say you've been a gymnast for a bunch of years and then you picked up ice hockey. While you've only been playing hockey for five years, that gymnastic "base" has given you a platform to build your ice hockey specific skills. But you can see a difference in athletes who have been playing one particular sport for a very long time. There can be advantages obviously, but an athlete who is "athletic" has a foundation that you can then layer Technical Ability on.

Putting It All Together

I meet a lot of parents who have athletes with a combination of these ages. They may be Psychologically "old" but may be young Biologically. Or they are advanced Chronologically but are young Psychologically. And while all parents wish they had a Sidney Crosby in their house just to make it easy, I bet if we interviewed Sidney's' mom, she might tell us that Psychologically he showed the same signs of immaturity that you might be experiencing in your house.

When dealing with the three ages of an athlete you really want to understand where you sit on each of those scales. You can map it out. On a scale of one to ten would you say you are Biologically and Psychologically "old" for your Chronological Age? Using Tanner as an example above, he was a twenty-year old in a fifteen year-old's body. He was biologically VERY advanced. Yet Psychologically he was pretty young and was unable to grasp that he really needed to work on his conditioning and agility to make it to the next level.

You can go down the list of every athlete either on your team or who are your closest competitors and graph them out. Where do they sit Chronologically, Biologically, Psychologically? How long have they been competing in the sport? What kind of advantages does that give them? How can you keep up? And most importantly, can you tough it out while you wait for your abilities to catch up? In the next chapter I talk more about how your abilities will help you withstand the storm.

Conclusion:

Every athlete has four "Ages" to describe them. They have a Chronological Age, a Biological Age, a Psychological Age, and a Training Age. When you understand the four ages you can understand why certain athletes may be winning at certain ages and why other athletes lose. While winning and losing is important to assess an athlete's development it doesn't provide the entire picture. An athlete may lose today because they are outmatched Biologically. Or perhaps their Training Age is young and they don't have the experience but in time, they will succeed. When you put it all together you get a solid understanding of what the currently affecting wins and losses, and how the four ages will affect outcomes long term.

Watch This Video:

**www.AthleteSpecific.com/
the-four-ages-of-every-athlete**

Take Action With These Steps:

- In your journal write each of the four "ages" on the top of four separate pages. Chronological. Biological. Psychological. Training.

- Now under each age, write down how you think you stack up against your current competitors. How do they stack up? Are they older or younger in each of the "ages"? How does that make you feel? What can you do about it? Is there anywhere you can apply some patience?

- What steps can you take to improve your Biological Age, your Psychological age, and your Training age?

- I don't need to remind you that you can't do anything about your Chronological Age. Right? (Other than doctoring a birth certificate but I'm not condoning that!)

Chapter 8
Understanding The
Three Key Abilities

---

*"Believe in yourself! Have faith in your abilities! Without a
humble but reasonable confidence in your own powers you
cannot be successful or happy."*

Norman Vincent Peale
an American minister and author of
The Power of Positive Thinking

To have success as an athlete in ANY sport you must possess
three key abilities. They are:
Physical Ability, Technical Ability, Tactical Ability

Your
Three Key Abilities

Technical
The "Doing" of Your Sport

Tactical
When To "Do" What You
Need To Do When You
Need To Do It

Your Ability
To Perform
Competitively

Physical
Your Ability to "Do" Your Sport

**A young athlete may be able to get by with two out of the three
abilities, but ultimately, to have the highest levels of success, they
will need all three. Or at least a high percentage of all three.**

Physical Ability

Physical Ability is fairly straightforward. It is the ability to do what it is you do when you need to do it. When we talk about strength and conditioning, agility, balance, speed, etc. those are all physical abilities. Without physical abilities we can't do what we want to do. We can't apply our Technical and Tactical abilities that I will talk about in a moment.

When we combine our understanding of the Three Ages from the previous chapter along with our understanding of Physical Ability we can see why our athlete is behind, or why they are slow, or not competing as well as they should. We can also uncover some flaws in the foundation that may look like small cracks now, but when we build that three story house on top, things might just go sideways.

In the example of Tanner that I shared a few pages back (the hockey player who was really large for his age) you can see how his Physical Ability dominated when he was young. But that asset turned into a liability because no one was able to see the two other Abilities and really hammer home what he needed to work on. His Physical Ability was advanced because his Biological age was also advanced. This is typical for kids who grow up fast, and are able to out muscle their opponents.

I was talking to a parent the other day who has a son who plays fairly competitive ice hockey. While his son is small and quite quick, he was left off of a travel team in exchange for a much larger, less skilled, player. The father was a bit upset because the coach told him something to the effect, "He's big, and he can help us win."

Does this mean the smaller player can't help the team win? No. But the common thinking is that the larger player will help the team win NOW. This dad then went on to tell me that it would probably be his son's last year playing because at the rate kids were growing, his kid would probably not make it next year.

What a short-sighted attitude. I explained to this dad that both he and his wife were both five feet ten inches tall, at least. His son would most likely grow to that height or potentially taller which was a fantastic size to build muscle on. As a strength and conditioning coach the first place I look to see an athlete's potential is Mom and Dad. If they are short, then maybe I might think that this athlete won't be a big guy. He may be a "late bloomer." In that case great things are possible if we can just be patient.

Physical Ability Is The Easiest Ability To Improve

Physical Ability is the easiest ability to improve. We can take an athlete and get them in the gym, or with any gravity challenging apparatus, and kick Mother Nature in the butt. We can accelerate strength and conditioning with a well planned strength program (more on that later). But no matter how you do it, it needs to be specific to this athlete.

Physical Ability is the foundation of all of the other abilities. Without it, you can't apply the Technical and the Tactical abilities. But it's important to understand where an athlete is in their development in order to accurately decide just what needs to be worked on. If an athlete has a set of parents that looks like the athlete will be the right size for their sport and they might be blooming late, we can just hang on while that growth spurt comes that we've been waiting for.

I mentored a father whose son was a very good lacrosse goalie but who was quite small. The father understood fully that his son was probably going to get the same growth spurt that he got his junior year of high school into college. Unfortunately, this was probably going to mean his son was going to get passed over for other goalies right now who were larger and more athletic. But the father understood that his challenge was keeping his son from quitting now and not sticking with it which would mean he would miss the benefits of that size and strength later. This was a very wise dad and ultimately we were able to help his son stick with it while his Biological Age caught up to his Chronological age and his Physical Ability improved. Too many parents would have not thought this through and their son would be pumping gas.

Technical Ability

This is the "what" you do for your sport and here are some examples to get you thinking in the right direction:

Football Quarterback - Throwing technique.
Figure Skater - Skating ability.
Hockey Player - Shooting, Passing, Puck Handling.
Lacrosse Player - Shooting, Passing, Stick skills.
Basketball - Shooting, Passing, Dribbling. Ball skills.

Swimmer - Stroke technique, all disciplines.
Boxing - Striking Technique

Hopefully that is enough for you to understand just how Technical Ability works and what you would be working on. It's the "what" you do, not necessarily "when" you do it.

Technical ability comes from an application of Physical Ability to your sport and a lack of Physical Ability can limit technical application. A coach may describe someone with a lack of Technical Ability as "Slow, inaccurate, sluggish, etc"

I worked with a hockey player who had gone through this amazing growth spurt of about three inches in a month and a half. Because of his size advantage and his ability to lean on offensive players he was a dominant force on defense.

But he was weak.

His Physical Ability was quite low because his muscles hadn't quite caught up to his height yet. He was tight and stiff because his musculature was stretched tight like a rubber band. This lack of physical strength really showed when he got the puck in the defensive end and was trying to make a pass out of the zone. He could see who he needed to pass to but from recognizing what needed to happen to actually making it happen would take way too long resulting in a picked off pass, or a pass that was too slow to get to his teammate on time.

It was kind of fascinating to watch as I sat with his dad. Here was a really good kid, (good person, good athlete) who loved the game but who was struggling technically because his Physical Ability was lacking. His ability to do what he needed to do wasn't there so the Technical Ability wasn't there, yet.

Parents invest thousands of dollars on technical camps every year hoping that their son or daughter will gain the skills necessary to be great at their sport. Sports like Gymnastics and Figure Skating require thousands of hours of technical training at a very young age in order for an athlete to be ready for those critical years where Technical Ability and Physical Ability meet. But for many athletes the Physical foundation doesn't allow them to apply their Technical Ability effectively. If that's you,, investing in your Physical Ability might get a better return on that investment. After the increase in strength, your ability to apply your strength along with your Technical Ability will improve.

Tactical Ability

Your Tactical Ability is your ability to do what you do, when you need to do it. So this is where you must apply your Technical Ability using your Physical Ability at the right time and at the right place on the field of play.

This is where you take the X's and O's that you learned in practice and now apply it in competition, and this is where a lot of athletes break down.

You've heard of athletes who are great in practice but not in games? Is that you? Well, this is where it all comes together. Where an athlete takes all of that training that increased their Physical Ability and their Tactical Ability and actually shows it in performance.

Breakdowns in Tactical Ability are usually psychological and come from an increase in stress and the need to perform in front of coach, teammates, mom and dad, family, friends, etc. It's where the rubber meets the road and all of the hard work comes together.

Depending on the sport, Tactical Ability may involve teammates like in hockey or soccer. It may involve competitors like hockey and soccer, or perhaps judo or wrestling. Or it may not involve competitors directly such as in sports like swimming, gymnastics, skiing, bobsled or archery.

Sometimes 'tactics" may involve, what costume to wear or what music to pick like in Figure Skating. Tactics can also (unfortunately) involve which coach to please and what time to bring the orange slices for half-time.

When my friend Ruben Gonzalez decided to become the World's first-ever four-decade winter Olympian, not only did he need to brush up on his tactics on how to get down the track safely, he needed to negotiate the International Luge Federation and their bureaucracy. His dream almost didn't happen because they were concerned he was going to be an embarrassment to the Federation because some athletes in the past had tried to do what he was trying to do and failed miserably. He needed to show them what his plan was and how he was going to execute it. He needed to negotiate, not just the course, but the people in charge.

Unfortunately, I've seen a number of athletes lose their opportunities because they were unable to negotiate the tactics of their team or their organization. It's sad to say that this is even something to be considered, but I find that usually an athlete's inability to negotiate with team or organization has more to do with their lack of ability in one of their Three Key Abilities. And this leads me to the crux of this whole book...

How I Look At Athletes In Competitions

Years ago I was coaching a youth lacrosse game in a new program in Canada. In this particular game it was U14 so we had a bunch of thirteen year old kids, a couple fourteen year old kids and a couple of twelve year old kids.

We were getting clobbered.

Helping me out on the bench was a great guy named Clint who was the director of the program. We were playing the team from the major city next to our town and Clint was pretty wound up and wanted to beat them pretty badly. Every play that we did well on Clint was a model of positivity encouraging the kids for their effort, but every play our guys lost Clint was getting increasingly agitated.

Clint was standing next to me on the sideline and the rest of our team was further back on the bench out of earshot. Clint leaned over to me and said, "What the heck is going on?" At one point Clint was getting pretty rattled and I said, "Listen, you can break every one of these plays down to the Three Ages Of Every Athlete and their Three Key Abilities.

He said, "The three what?"

For the next half a quarter I explained to Clint just what you read here in this book. But now I was able to show him exactly how it played out on the field. Here are some examples:

Example 1:

The Scenario: A young defender on our team (Player A) sees an open teammate up the field about forty yards away. He turns to make the pass which seems to take forever to get to the intended target. A player on the opposing team (Player B) sprints in front of the pass and picks it off and then starts a fast break which results in a goal against us.

What really happened? Player A is a young player chronologically (He's 12). He actually made a pretty advanced play psychologically. He picked his head up and saw the open teammate which was awesome and was a pretty advanced move Tactically as well. Nothing in this play was really wrong because if he held onto the ball he was going to get crushed by an opposing player. The only thing that was unfortunate was that his Physical Ability was a little weak and the play took too much time to occur. That is how Player B was able to pick off the pass.

What Everyone Saw: A player making a bad pass that got picked off and a goal was scored.

What The Player Felt: This player was pretty bummed about the play and hung his head. The energy around this play was pretty low. The parents in the stands were bummed and all of that negative energy gets focused on the athlete.

What I Saw: I was excited for Player A to make that play because it showed that he was doing the right thing Tactically and Psychologically. As a Coach, I want the player to focus on making the right play Tactically because as this player matures I know the Physical Ability to make the play happen will come. We just need some patience.

What You Need To Take Away: Anytime you make a play that is Psychologically advanced or Tactically advanced for your Biological or Physical Age you should be excited. If you can have patience while those around you are shortsighted you should have peace of mind. Many athletes who win NOW based on Physical Ability or Biological Age NEVER develop their Psychological Age or Tactical Ability. If you can grind it out and get through this phase of your development you will be ahead in the long run!

Example 2:

Player A is a fourteen year old who is quite tall for his age but very skinny. Player B is thirteen years old and really fast and strong for his age. There is a ground ball closer to Player A, but as he goes to pick it up he backs off as Player B sprints in to get the ball. Player B then goes in and scores on the goalie.

What happened? Player A saw the ground ball and started to go for it but then slowed up so he didn't get run over by Player B.

What Everyone Saw: Player A looked soft, like he didn't want to take a hit. Even though he is much taller than the other players on the field he now looks like a wimp.

What The Player Felt: Internally, Player A is a little confused. He feels bad for not getting the ball but he doesn't quite understand why he didn't go for the ball. He feels that everyone is expecting him to be a bigger force on the field but he's just not quite there yet.

What I Saw: First thing I look for is recognition. Player A saw the ball and made a move to go get it. Out of his peripheral vision he saw a much larger and faster player barreling down on him, and here's the key: He did just what you or I would do naturally if we were standing in a street and saw a car coming at us. We'd get out of the way! While everyone is looking at Player A and calling him really mean things under their breath, I saw the beginnings of the right actions currently covered by an undeveloped Physical Ability. I also saw Player B score and think he was awesome. I looked at Player B and was thinking he should really be playing up a level because his size and speed puts him in an older category.

What You Need To Take Away: This type of example can come at ANY age group. I've seen it happen at U8 and I've seen it happen at the college age in competitive sports. In this case if you are Player A you just need more time for your body to catch up to your mind. It takes a lot of confidence to feel like you're not going to get hurt in a situation like this. This player needs more time in practice to work on body contact and to really learn how to use his body as a tool.

If you are Player B you can't walk away too confident. Playing in situations like this too often can lower your guard and put you in a situation to get hurt in other games against better competition.

Progression Thoughts: Listen, I totally get it. In sports we are supposed to be all tough and put our body in harm's way in order to win the event. This isn't just a men versus women's thing either. In all sports there is some level of disrespect for your body. I see too many athletes drop out of a sport because they are forced into a situation where they aren't ready for the body contact and yet their Technical and Tactical abilities are coming along nicely. There is no need to rush, but there is need to progress an athlete through stages of contact so they can feel confident. That being said, if an athlete is small physically it makes no sense to put him or her up against athletes who are larger physically and have them be in a situation where they can get hurt.

Example 3:

Player A loves to run. This athlete has been gifted with an

advanced Biological Age since birth. People say things like he's been "growing like a weed" and "what do you feed that kid?". He is head and shoulders above the rest of the kids his same age. He's fast on his feet and quick to react and has great hand-eye coordination.

What Happened: In the last game he played...get this...the entire game. While his team lost 12-6 he scored five of his teams goals and took every face off. He played on both the power play and the penalty kill.

What Everyone Saw: One kid, on a huge team, dominating everything. His coach, in an effort to win, played him as much as he possibly could. Player A was absolutely gassed at the end of the game but you could already see signs of his fatigue and frustration in the second half when he started to not pass to open teammates who he thought wouldn't be able to catch the pass. He also made some bad plays but everyone gave him the benefit of the doubt because he was doing everything.

What the player felt: Player A was exhausted by early in the second half and gave it his best effort...at times. He is angry at his teammates for not being any better than they already are. He feels like he's "doing it all" and he is. He is continually frustrated and angry at losing all the time because he has no one around him who can help.

What I saw: I saw an athlete not being challenged. Sure he was being challenged physically, and any time an athlete is in a competitive environment they are either being challenged, or they are wasting their time. In the first half Player A scored four of his five goals while his team was losing ten to four. The other team played their second and third string players in the second half and Player A was so tired he could barely do anything against them. He continually missed making passes to open players and tried to run through two and three defenders at a time not recognizing his open teammate or even looking for them. While this game was a good conditioning session for him, he lacks the Technical Ability to protect the ball and Tactically he isn't learning any team concepts.

What You Need To Take Away From This Example: Player A

is a good kid as I believe all kids are. He's just not being challenged properly. His coaches aren't helping him because they are not teaching him how to develop the necessary Tactical Abilities to survive at the next level. I would rather he make the right pass to an open player who then misses the pass than for him to try and dodge through three players. That tactic might work at this level occasionally, but it certainly won't work as his competition gets more advanced. This player should also be playing up in order to be challenged appropriately.

Conclusion:

Every athlete has three key abilities on which all of their success and failures are based. You have a Physical Ability which is the base that all other abilities are layered on. It is the ability to do what it is you need to do and when you need to do it. You have a Technical Ability which is the "what" that you do. And you have your Tactical Ability which is the understanding of "when" to do, what it is that you do. A young athlete can get by on two out of the three, but to make it big, you need all three.

Watch This Video:

**www.AthleteSpecific.com/
three-key-abilities**

Take Action With These Steps:

- In your journal, write down all of the qualities you need to be successful at your sport. What does an elite athlete need? Strength? Speed? Quickness? Agility? Balance? List them all.

- Now make a list of the qualities you have and make a second list of qualities that you are not yet strong.

- Make a similar list for your Technical Abilities.

- Now decide which Abilities you want to improve first and make a commitment to improve them starting right now.

- Make an additional list of your Tactical Abilities and make a plan to improve those abilities where you are also weak.

Chapter 9
The Three Layers

"If I accept you as you are, I will make you worse; however, if I treat you as though you are what you are capable of becoming, I help you become that."

Johann Wolfgang Von Goethe
German writer and statesman.

I hope you enjoyed the last section on The Three Key Abilities. Usually, I will get emails from parents, athletes and coaches who say, "You know, I've never been able to say it the way that you just said it." So thanks.

When you look back to every single play in your career you can break down your success and your failures to those three abilities.

But in addition to those three abilities of physical, technical, and tactical there are three layers that I place on top of them. They are the glue that hold the abilities together and they are as follows:

1. Belief
2. Life skills
3. Resources

In this section I'm going to discuss these three layers and will probably help you uncover places where you're totally sabotaging your success so let's get started.

Belief In Your Abilities

Connie was an incredibly talented athlete who had all of the physical, technical and tactical abilities you could imagine. On paper, and on the field, Connie was a game changer.

But Connie had a crack in her foundation. A limiting belief in her Tactical Ability that held her back from making the big play. Connie was in her twenties, but her limiting belief was caused by a combination of events that happened when she was eight years old. Yes...I said eight years old.

Turns out that when Connie was eight years old she was given the chance to make the last shot to win a game, which she missed. While she was obviously bummed about missing the shot, it was a flip comment by her dad that did the damage. "Connie," he said "If you don't grow up you're never going to make that shot."

Did I mention she was eight?

Unfortunately for Connie this created a little loop in her brain that wondered when she was going to grow up. Even in her twenties she didn't feel grown up and therefore choked whenever she got an important chance in her game.

Now this is an unfortunate example but not too uncommon. Any number of experiences and inputs can put a crack in the foundation of an athlete's belief. Over the years I can't tell you how many athletes I have run into with stories of incredible physical, technical, and Tactical Ability only to have them derailed by a lack of belief in any one of those abilities.

Your belief in yourself is incredibly important and tends to get stronger over time. Small successes lead to bigger successes which lead to better performances. These steps increase confidence in your ability and your belief becomes stronger.

Life Skills

I've met a lot of talented athletes who sabotage themselves because they can't manage...life. It can be school, work, girlfriends, boyfriends, parents, jobs, you name it. An athlete's ability to manage all of the tasks of life is incredibly important.

I worked with a professional football player who would have lost his head had it not been attached to his neck. Another athlete I worked with got his girlfriend pregnant and became a dad at the ripe old age of... nineteen, which basically put an end to his athletic aspirations because he now needed to earn money to support his new, unexpected, family.

In an ideal situation an athlete is managing three things: training, competing, and recovery. It is these three things that allow an athlete to withstand challenges and take advantage of opportunity. But life is obviously more complicated than that for most athletes and that is where additional skills have to be acquired in order to manage it all.

Probably the most important skill that an athlete needs to posses yet is never taught formally is time management. Now that I have used that term "time management" I will tell you that you can't manage time at all. It's like trying to grab jello. You may think you're doing a great job trying to grab it but it just slips through your fingers and what is left just melts and drips out of your hand.

No. Time management is not really what we are looking for. Activity management is more like it.

In Chapter 3 we talked about Deciding What You Want. When you know what you really want then all of the potential activities that pop up in your life can be weighed against what it is you want. For example: Do you want to play professional sports? Well, your friend has asked you to go to a party friday night but you have a tryout Saturday morning. Do you go?

Here's another example: You're still in school and you have an exam on Friday morning at 8AM. You also have a big game on Friday night. You are planning on pulling an all-nighter to ace the exam. (bad idea BTW). What do you do after the exam. Do you go home and sleep? But wait, your mom wants you to go shopping with her and you haven't had a chance to hang out in a long time. What do you do?

Life is full of these small decisions. If you don't know what you want you will constantly be pulled in all directions. But when you have committed to a decision about what it is you truly want, these decisions are easy.

One of my favourite books on the topic of "time management" is **Getting Things Done** by David Allen. I can't recommend this book enough because when it comes to a life skill that will be with you forever, your ability to manage your time and the projects that you commit to within that time, is vital.

Resources To Develop Your Abilities

I was sitting in the stands of a hockey game watching a young hockey player with a ton of talent. I had been hired by the family to help them navigate the next steps for this athlete as he was starting to get noticed by some of the junior teams in Canada. It was a great game and it was obvious that this athlete had a ton of potential.

But I was worried.

During the game the parents kept commenting about the families of the athletes on the rest of the team, and specifically about the best players on the other team. They would make comments about the money that the other families had and that their family didn't have. These were good people working two jobs with their son and a daughter both in hockey, which is expensive. But their focus on the other families was almost maniacal. They were resentful of the wealth of the other families and felt that there was no way their son was going to make it with all of the resources that these other families had even though their son was proving that he was quite good. The truth is that in addition to the Three Key Abilities, and your belief in those abilities, you need to understand the Resources that you may or may not have to improve those abilities.

I was getting really tired hearing the parents moan and complain about how good all of the other athletes had it when their son was doing quite well. I told them flat out that if they kept talking like they were talking they were going to "complain" and "jealous" their son right out of the sport.

A family's attitude about the resources they have, or don't have, is really important. As an athlete you need to understand that, while it would be nice to have unlimited resources, it is rare that the athletes who have all of the resources succeed. I've seen many athletes from families with incredible access to resources do quite poorly overall because of an expectation of success that they weren't ultimately willing to work for. A number of years ago I coached a group of athletes at one of the top recruiting events in the country. Of all of the athletes who made the trip, one ultimately played in college. Can you imagine which athlete that was? The athlete who came from the poorest family.

While you can argue all day that a family with more resources would have more opportunity than an athlete who came from a family with less, I can argue that an athlete who comes from a family with less is potentially more hungry, more willing to work hard, and more driven than all of the other athletes combined. I have seen this over and over again.

Resource #1: Time

We all have the same amount of time given to us each and every day. The billionaires of the world have created more out of the same amount of time than the guy who works at McDonalds. What you do with your time is your choice, and all day long you make decisions about how you spend your time.

Over the years I have coached athletes from all walks of life. Many of the most successful athletes I have coached lived a full life outside of their sport. Many of them had great relationships. Participated in clubs and other extra curricular activities. Many played other sports in addition to the main sport their biggest dreams were wrapped up in. And they all went to school and even had jobs occasionally.

Time is a finite resource and one that, when it's gone, is gone. If you choose to watch the television and sit on the couch eating Doritos, you're choosing to spend your time in a way that takes you away from your goals. You will constantly be given choices on how to spend your time. I would argue that the more time you can spend working towards your goals the better.

But what about "Down" time?

I fully understand that an athlete who devotes every second to their sport can become a rather boring person, perhaps even a little crazy. It's good to have "balance", but again, most athletes will lean toward **not** doing something as opposed to working on something related to their sport. It's human nature. There will be times when you can just let loose and turn your mind away from your sport. This can be incredibly healthy for the mind and the body. I can attest to the fact that when an athlete takes a solid break from their sport at the end of the season, they not only come back refreshed physically but also mentally. Ironically, one of the biggest mental benefits I have seen is the athlete's ability to notice a difference in themselves physically due to the break. Let me explain:

I was a three sport athlete in addition to my Olympic aspirations in the sport of luge. Every fall when I returned to sliding after a spring and summer of lacrosse I always noticed how strong I had gotten and how much I had improved physically from the year before. Each spring, when I had returned to play lacrosse after a winter competing in hockey and luge I would notice how much stronger I had become when I picked up my lacrosse stick after a long break. That new experience I had with my body was extremely motivating. I felt stronger than I had before and with that newly understood strength I was excited to go out and use it.

In North America, we are so concerned with taking time off. With the proliferation of all of these travel teams and Junior programs, kids are playing the same sport all year long. I'm all for skill and strength improvements but what is missing is the ability for the athlete to take a mental and physical break from their sport. This break always gives an athlete increased perspective about their body and how they compete. **Any sort of "rust" that may accumulate on an athlete who has taken a break is quickly dusted off only to be replaced by the new shiny ability they have gained as well as a fresh perspective.**_

As athletes become more and more advanced in their sport the best advice is typically to encourage them to take a break. While it seems counter-intuitive, in my experience, the better an athlete becomes the more rest opportunities need to be prescribed. I had great success training a bobsledder who was injured with shin fractures. The National Team coach had this athlete doing so much sprint work that it ground the athlete down physically and eventually off the team with injuries. It wasn't that the athlete was burned out...he couldn't walk, let alone push a bobsled.

My first bit of advice was to scale his training so far back so that he could finally heal. Then, by applying some advanced strength and conditioning assessments we realized that this athlete could benefit by doing much less volume than any of the other members on the team. Instead of doing sets of five we would do sets of one. Sprint workouts were done with extremely low volume. What happened? This athlete tested as one of the top athletes in the offseason program and went on to make the Olympic team.

Filling your time by doing "more" is rarely the right plan of attack. (See: More Is Not a Plan in Chapter 11) But for most athletes there is plenty of time to do it all AND take the requisite breaks to recover and refresh.

Resource #2: Energy

In order to train effectively, and to compete effectively, we need to have the highest level of energy that we can create for every session. Think of it like having your gas tank topped off before heading out on a car ride.

But just like you would be taking that car ride and topping it up with gas, you're not trying to do it like your parents usually do. They probably drive their car until the warning light comes on that they need more gas and then they find a gas station. No, for you, the goal is to be able to drive either a little bit, or a lot, and then have your tanks topped off as quickly as possible before the next session.

It's All About Recovery

In Chapter 11 I talk about how More Is Not A Plan. More training isn't the answer if you are doing it in a fatigued state which is tired, hungry, sleepy, run down, etc. Being fatigued creates sloppy training and all that does is reinforce sloppy performance, and sloppy performance doesn't work so well on game day unless your competition is even more fatigued than you are.

You want to maximize your recovery between training and competition so that you can come back and be competing and training more frequently because the more frequently you can train and compete at a high level the better you will become, faster. Does that make sense? If it takes you less time to recover between sessions the more often you can train. And if you can train more often you have more opportunity to learn the technical and tactical skills you need to compete at the next level.

In this section we are going to talk about what you need to do to improve your energy levels so that you can recover more efficiently and get better faster, sooner.

Too many athletes think about artificial ways to up their energy levels when they haven't even really maximized the two that are the easiest to control. There's a reason that Red Bull and Monster Energy Drinks are multi-billion dollar brands. In a world where people aren't getting enough sleep or eating correctly, and people lack discipline to really take control of these two areas, it's no wonder people reach for these products.

Your energy is a limited resource. Your body has two main sources of fuel in the body, sugar and fat, and when you combine that with a body that has had enough sleep, good things can happen.

Sleep

It might surprise you that for ten years my wife and I owned a bedding store. Seriously. But not just any bedding store. We sold thousand dollar sheets and thirty-thousand dollar mattresses. Not to mention multi-thousand dollar duvets, pillows and featherbeds. We still run that company online at www.GreatCanadianDownCompany.com. I learned a ton about sleep by working in that industry so I come at you not just as an athlete and a coach but as someone who knows a lot about the rather murky industry of bedding.

First thing you need to understand is that your need for sleep is genetic. While your daily need for sleep fluctuates as you age, you have a daily numbers of hours that you need and if you are short of that number you start your day off in a fog.

Whatever your sport, the physical demands of training and competing, and recovering from competing are extremely high. When you rest, not only does your body repair itself but your brain repairs itself as well. Overnight your brain "rinses" itself and resets itself, taking all of the inputs for your day and wiping itself clean. An athlete who is in full-on training may take an average of ten hours a night to sleep, and take a nap, on average. Some are more. Some are less. If you are going to bed every night after ten o'clock and then getting up at 6AM to go to school for 8AM you're probably not getting enough sleep.

Without enough sleep, everything else you do is compromised. No matter how much effort you put into your physical training, or your technical training, your brain's ability to function will never be what it could be if you had enough sleep.

Here are some tips to make sure you are getting enough sleep:

- Dedicate a week to going to bed very early so that you wake up naturally with no alarm clock. While this will take a bit to adjust to, by the end of the seven days you will start to see just how much sleep you really need.

- While you probably have an alarm clock to wake up in the morning, be sure to set a reminder alarm so you can go to bed at night. When it goes off, turn off the phones and leave them in another room, put away the homework, no television in the room. Just go to bed. Learn to be bored so you fall asleep. (Be sure to read the Visualization section in Chapter 22 to take advantage of this time.)

- Turn off all screens roughly two hours before you are supposed to fall asleep. Staring at a blue screen triggers the brain to think it's daylight and disrupts your natural sleep cycle.

- Invest in a sleep sensor instead of an alarm clock. The Aura sleep sensor is my favourite. https://www.withings.com/ca/en/products/aura/sleep-sensor-accessory If you are disciplined and can put away your phone for the night, download the Sleep Time App: http://www.azumio.com/s/sleeptime/index.html

- Use a white noise machine to eliminate all ambient noise that could possibly disrupt your sleep.http://www.nosleeplessnights.com/best-white-noise-machine-reviews/. A fan or a humidifier running in your bedroom can also do the trick.

- Make sure your room is completely black when you sleep. Any small light in your room can stimulate your brain to want to wake up. If you wake up in the middle of the night to go pee, improve your aim and don't turn on the lights. I like to sleep with a soft t-shirt over my eyes. An eye mask can also be helpful. Try this over-ear version for best comfort: https://www.amazon.ca/Sleep-Master-smblu01-Mask/dp/B0015NZ6FK

- Use a humidifier to maintain moisture levels in the room and to help with dehydration: https://www.amazon.ca/b?ie=UTF8&node=2224061011

- Keep your room cool at night with a window slightly open for fresh air. Keeping the room around 65-68 degrees allows the body temperature to cool which stimulates recovery and improves sleep quality.

- Invest in a great duvet and pillow and travel with them at all times. A high quality duvet and pillow makes any mattress better. Check out: https://greatcanadiandowncompany.com/collections/duvets-and-comforters

These are just a handful of tips to ensure a great night's sleep and to make sure you are getting just the right amount of hours that you need to recover. Being chronically tired isn't helping your athletic performance or anything else for that matter. Become an expert in your sleep and watch your performance across all areas of your life improve.

Nutrition

Athletes are some of the worst eaters I know. Because they "burn so much off" they will eat pretty much anything. And don't think I'm being judgmental here. I did it too. In fact, it would shock you what I ate when I was competing. I just didn't really care too much about "what" I ate. It was really about "how much" I could eat.

For lots of athletes they are in a constant state of hunger because they are burning so many calories. They can eat and eat and eat and they usually do. But if you can up the quality of your food intake then the body responds in amazing ways. Read this quote below:

"Let food be thy medicine and medicine be thy food."

Hippocrates - 460-370 B.C.
Considered the Father of Western Medicine

When the body is well fed and watered it can burn energy more efficiently and it can heal and recover quickly. Think of a car burning clean fuel instead of fuel that has all sorts of gunk in it. When it's clean the engine runs better and the fuel flows through the fuel lines easier. When it's gunky, the fuel lines get gummed up and the engine has to work harder because it's trying to pump through all this extra sludge.

What you eat is very similar.

Taylor showed up to her strength and conditioning session with me and was her normal bubbly self, but her lifts were...meh. It was Thursday, so it was the end of the week, but Taylor was usually able to put up better numbers than these.

As was normal, her mom made sure she was the first car in the lineup so she could pick her up right after school. They drove quickly over to my gym so she could train with me before she headed back to school for some science club she was part of. This was par for the course three nights a week for Taylor and her mom.

What's up Taylor?" I asked.

"Oh, not much. Just tired I guess." she said. But her overall demeanor wasn't the same as she always was. Something was up. After some probing I learned that Taylor and her mom grabbed a gatorade and a burger on her way over to train. Some french fries too. She had polished off the last of the fries before she came in to train, and with all of her energy going to digesting that pile of food in her belly it was no wonder she was a little less than explosive.

This led to a long discussion about food and food timing, as well as what she was eating in general. We barely lifted the rest of the session and just talked about her diet. As is typically the case, Taylor was your standard North American high school kid plowing down a bowl of cereal on the way out the door followed by lunch at school and a dinner on the run between activities. Another meal in the car on the way home where she would shower and cram for the next day's classes. Pretty normal.

Taylor struggled with staying focused during class and despite her outwardly bubbly demeanor she felt really burned out inside. She loved sports. Was pretty decent in school. Had a boyfriend. But was a pretty hearty coffee drinker who didn't have time to party and was hoping to get a scholarship for hockey in Boston.

Now Taylor, by most accounts, was a pretty "normal" kid. Unfortunately, in today's world of youth sports she had been playing hockey and "forced" to specialize since she was a freshman. She told me, "With all the focus on school and hockey she had little time to focus on sleep and nutrition. Right?" I wasn't amused.

An athlete who only focuses on school and sports is like a car enthusiast who doesn't put oil in the engine and gas in the tank. The car can look real pretty, will run well for a few miles, but will eventually come grinding to a halt. Taylor was on that path. We spent a lot of time working with her and her mom to help her address her needs for better nutrition and more sleep and over the coming months her performance improved tremendously.

It's a little outside the scope of this book to get into nutritional details. There are a tremendous amount of resources for healthy eating and lifestyle choices easily found on the internet. (I list a bunch in the end of this book.) Let me leave you with these thoughts:

- Calories matter, but quality of calories is more important.
- Much of what your parents know about nutrition from the days of their youth has changed. The quality of the food that we eat is much different than it was twenty years ago.
- Clean food over processed food.

- Watch your sugar intake. (That includes fructose, glucose-fructose, and any other "ose's")

- There is a lot of research now about the benefits of fat and how it can transition an athlete from being a sugar burner to a fat burner for sustained energy.

- Be sure to read the "Everything Else" section in a couple pages.

Water

Of all of the performance enhancing products you could possibly put in your body, water, is still number one. If you are hydrated properly you will sleep better and everything else you eat will work better in your body. Your body is made up of around 60% water (it's not 98% as some people think). And that water is there to help with everything from your digestion to how thick your blood is. Water helps to create saliva in your mouth and it's the transport system for nutrients and their byproducts in and out of your cells. Water also helps keep you cool by sweating. If you can't sweat then you can't cool your body effectively and increased body temperature leads to fatigue and poor performance. (Which can be a little weird to wrap your head around if you compete in a winter sport.)

Many athletes develop a problem where they feel hungry but really it's a signal from the body that it's thirsty. As an athlete, if you are getting triggers that you're thirsty you are definitely not drinking enough and you'd be doing yourself a huge favour just carrying a water bottle around all day that you sip on. I have a water bottle on my desk that I constantly fill up throughout the day. Do I also get up to use the bathroom? Sure. But your body does become more efficient processing large amounts of water so don't worry, you won't be going to the bathroom every fifteen minutes for long.

Each one of your cells relies on water to transport energy into the cell, and to help get rid of the toxic byproducts of exercise. The lactic acid you feel when you are working really hard needs a place to go and if the fluid level in your cells is adequate then it will be able to flush it out properly. If you are dehydrated that whole process slows down and you're not operating as efficiently as you could. While there are all sorts of recommendations of how much water you should drink and when, just drink...more. When you wake up in the morning have a glass of water. You'd be surprised how much water weight you lose at night just from breathing and drooling into your pillow. Don't believe me? Weigh yourself before you go to bed and when you wake up in the morning. For me, it's about a pound and a half. So drink up.

You might want to stop drinking water close to bedtime so you don't get up in the middle of the night to pee. While you want to be hydrated you don't want to be interrupting sleep if possible. Drink enough during the day and you will be fine. I will stop drinking fluids around 6PM but will have a small glass of water just after I brush my teeth before I go to bed

While you can drink too much, it is extremely rare. Your kidneys will excrete excess water from your system so it's very hard to over do it. Just like it's hard for a highly trained athlete to get enough calories, it is equally as hard to get enough fluids. A constant sipping during the day is ideal.

I worked with one of the top nutritionists in the United States who also worked with the top professional football players in the NFL. He told me that of all of the nutritional recommendations he gave these multi-million dollar athletes, there was ONE nutritional recommendation that made the biggest impact. It was water. Remember, I'm not a doctor and any of this advice you should run by your own medical professionals. Well, let's just say I was peeing all the time. Eventually my body did get more efficient at utilizing the water I was taking in and I didn't pee as much, but to start you're going to want to be near a bathroom. After a month I felt fantastic though! My recovery improved and I had great sleeps. If you aren't drinking water during the day get started as soon as possible.

Without water an athlete is like a racehorse running in deep mud. You see the potential but it's just really slow.

How do you know if you're getting enough water? Your pee should be light in color and have no smell. (Unless you eat some asparagus or some Sugar Smacks the day before. Then it will stink.) Otherwise your pee should be odor free. If you aren't getting enough water your pee will be darker and it will be stinky. And to be honest, that's just the start. When you are drinking enough water you are sipping it all day long. We're not talking eight glasses a day, we're talking gallons of it.

Since we are getting really personal, I should mention that water also helps the poop move, too. When the body is dehydrated it looks to anywhere it can to pull water into the system. One of those places is in your large intestine where the poop goes after your food has been digested and is getting ready to let loose. If you are dehydrated that poop gets really hard and you won't want to go. When you do go it feels like your birthing a lacrosse ball. Enough water and that poop should be soft and slide right out. (TMI perhaps?)

While it's optimal to drink plain water I understand that tap water can stink where you live and you might not want to drink it. There are lots of options for water dispensers at home. You can always buy five gallon jugs of water and refill them at the grocery store. We have a dispenser in our house and for a couple bucks a jug we get it delivered right to our door. **Buy distilled water from a reputable source for the purest water you can buy.**

Another consideration is the quality of your local water. Our local waters are growing increasingly dirty with chemicals, pharmaceuticals and other pollutants. To see what the water is like in your area you can go to this website: https://www.ewg.org/tapwater/#.WbUuotOGN3l

Are things like Gatorade and other flavoured drinks ok? Yes, but to a point. While some people don't like the taste of water because it has no taste, drinking sugared drinks all the time can wreak havoc on your body, not to mention your teeth! I promise you that by spending time drinking plain water your taste buds will adjust. You won't always be searching for flavor in your fluids. Plain water is best and is most cost effective too. Not to mention there are less calories and your body isn't fighting the rush of sugar every time you drink a Gatorade or a soda. Stay away from those Super-mega-caramel-macchiato-double-sugar-calorie bombs.

Everything Else

So what goes in the "Everything Else" section? Well, things like supplements, caffeine, coffee, Red Bull and Monster Energy Drinks. Teas, vitamins, minerals, and anything else that falls into this category. (I could even throw some equipment in this section but I'll save that for the Equipment section in Chapter 25) There is a constant and never-ending stream of "aids" to help you shortcut your hard work. These products are marketed to you as ways to recover faster, jump higher, sleep better, lose fat, gain muscle, get a better car...you name it.

Here's the deal. Many people (not just athletes) look to these shortcuts for better performance. We are a society full of people looking to "hack" just about anything. But what's important to understand is that if your Sleep and your Nutrition are crap, no amount of the products you could possibly find in the "Everything Else" section will help you to the degree that they could.

I've worked with so many athletes who are such poor time managers that they get no sleep and then try to drink a Redbull to try and have a good workout. I once had an athlete pass out in my squat rack because they suffered from Adrenal Fatigue and had nothing left in the tank. They weren't sleeping. They weren't eating well. And they were trying to drink a ton of caffeine all the time trying to make up for it because they were "busy". It was ridiculous! Here's an athlete who thinks that they are going to somehow improve with no sleep and no nutrition over a long period of time. If that's you...cut it out. Dial in your sleep and your nutrition and THEN think about supplements to increase your performance. Remember this:

"You can't out-train poor sleep and bad nutrition.
And you can't out-supplement it either."
Jonathan Edwards - Olympian

Here are a couple quick thoughts on supplements that you may be able to apply to your training. Generally I can recommend these to 99% of all athletes. It's not a complete list but it's a place to start:

Creatine: Yes I still recommend Creatine. Found naturally in beef. Recommended for most athletes. Myths about protein affecting the kidneys are wrong and have been based on studies of people with already failing kidneys.

Protein Powders and Meal Replacement Shakes: Can be used if you find it's just too hard to ingest calories from real food. Just watch for any dairy intolerances. If you're farting a ton, it's probably a sign you've got an intolerance and probably not the best choice for you.

Multivitamin and Multimineral: Find a reputable Doctor of Naturopathic medicine in your area and purchase through them. Most over-the-counter multi's are useless.

Branched Chain Amino Acids: The building blocks of protein. Helps repair muscle damage after intense workouts or competition.

Caffeine: Ok in moderation. If you're looking for pick-me-ups all the time you really need to look at your sleep habits and your nutrition. Avoid getting your caffeine from sugary-drinks. Stick to coffee or capsules found over the counter at your local pharmacy.

Your Largest Stressor

You are going to have a lot of stressors in your athletic career. You can chalk up school, girlfriends and boyfriends, parents and siblings, homework, in addition to your practices and competitions; these are all stressors in your life. But one of the most stressful "stressors" in your life is the food you eat and anything else you put in your body in terms of nutrition and supplementation. It's all stress on the body.

When you're young, you can eat anything. Not that you really should eat "anything", it just happens. Grandparents take you for ice cream and then put brown sugar on your honey-nut cheerios for breakfast. Your parents get you pizza because you've been a good boy. It's easy to swing by some fast food place on the way to practice so you grab a burger. You're told that you should drink protein shakes to help you recover yet they taste horrible. It's all stress on the body..

But you feel fine! All of it. The chips, the candy, the slushies and the sugary coffees, you feel...fine. But I'm here to tell you that what feels "normal" to you now is not optimal. **Your parents, your friends, and even your athletic friends all feel "fine" because they no longer know what feeling good feels like.** And that's the same for you, you just don't realize it.

How To Cure Your Allergies

I suffered from incredible allergies to grass, mold, mites, trees, flowers and a whole host of other things when I was young all the way up into my twenties. I also ate anything for calories so I would put on weight because I was trying to keep my weight above 175 pounds. At the height of my Olympic training it wasn't uncommon for us to hit a McDonald's in Europe...every day. The order? Twenty-piece chicken McNugget, large coke, large fry, two cheeseburgers and an apple pie. I felt great, or so I thought. I would usually take one hell of a nap or go to sleep after that. While the sleep was partially induced by the crash from the sugar and carbs in that meal, I now understand that part of it was my body needing all the energy it could to digest that mess.

I know a very successful female hockey player who eliminated the protein shakes from her diet while she was out with a concussion only to find out that her stomach aches went away. It's obvious that if you're dealing with acute stomach pain you're probably not going to perform at your best, but most athletes never even realize how bad they feel because they can't feel anymore. It just becomes their new normal.

When I eliminated many of the foods from my diet that are known to be troublesome, my allergies cleared up. I had better sleeps and I even recovered faster.

Give Your Body A Rest From The Inside

When you give your body a break physically from your sport from the outside, give our body a break on the inside too. I highly recommend looking at Elimination Diets (it's not as harsh as it sounds) as a way to fuel your body but to just eat foods that we know are not highly-allergic. You'd be surprised how many foods cause adverse reactions in the body but we recommend those same foods for athletes. Things like nuts and seeds are full of "healthy fats" yet a nut can cause a reaction in your gut. I'm not talking peanut allergies either, I'm just talking about nuts in general.

Here is a partial list of highly allergenic foods:

Cow's Milk	Eggs	Peanuts	Shellfish	Fish
Tree nuts (Cashews and Walnuts)	Wheat (Bread, buns, pasta, beer, cake, etc)	Soy	Berries	Chocolate
Cinnamon	Citrus Fruits (Oranges, Lemons, Limes)	Corn (Corn on the cob, chips, etc)	Sugar	Mustard

	Coconut	Cinnamon	Pork	Other dairy products.Milk, Cheese, Butter, Yogurt, Sour Cream, Ice Cream :(,Whey

Note: This is a partial list and doesn't try to be a complete list. The point is, many of the common foods that athletes eat every day can cause them significant distress without them knowing it.

Elimination Diets Can Help

Elimination Diets help you find out just what your body doesn't like to eat that you may not fully realize. Take for instance Pizza. I love pizza. I have eaten enough pizza to probably cover the field in a large stadium in my lifetime. But I know that when I eat it I get a stomach ache and I want to take a big nap.

Pizza is a really big "social" food. You've probably had pizza with your family or with your team on multiple occasions. The funny thing is that if you polled all of those pizza eaters how they felt after they ate all the pizza they would probably say things like: sleepy, bloated, my stomach hurt, gassy, etc.

I'm sharing the following story in hopes that it will make you aware of what is possible when you listen to the signals your body is sending you.

All through Junior High and High School I suffered from really bad allergies. My nose was constantly stuffed. I was a mouth breather and my eyes constantly itched. I was so excited for winter when all of the trees and grass died so that my allergies took a break. But I was also allergic to mold and dust mites. And some foods.

I would go to the allergist every week for shots. I hated those shots and to be honest, they never really did much. I ended up feeling like I would never get rid of my allergies. They made me tired and I slept a ton because of it.

When I was twenty-three years old I was coaching lacrosse and I could barely breathe on the sidelines. Not like I was going to go into shock or anything, it was just a real pain-in-the-butt to breathe. It was at this time I was introduced to a nutritionist who explained to me one of the most important concepts that i wish I had known much earlier on:

Your Immune System Is
Like a Gas Tank

So we just talked a lot in this book about how food is one of your body's biggest stressors. What is it stressing? Your immune system. Your immune system is your body's way of defending itself against all of the "bugs" that are in our world.

Whether it's the flu bug, bugs on your food, or in your everyday space, there are bugs everywhere and a happy, healthy body, fights off most of them.

But what I didn't understand is that your immune system can get run down. Kind of like a gas tank in a car it can be "topped off" but it can also be "running on empty". And when it's running on empty that's when our body becomes more susceptible to all of the bugs and allergens that are in our everyday world.

When I was coaching and I was working outside with grassy fields and freshly blooming flowers and trees, I was a wreck. What this nutritionist taught me was that because of what I was eating, and the lack of sleep I was getting, my immune system was run down and I was defenseless against all of the allergy causing things that were in the air.

What was I eating? Well, I was eating what I had always been eating. A lot! I'd have cereal and milk for breakfast. I'd have a large roast beef sub for lunch and a can of coke. I'd have a snack at McDonalds in the afternoon and then go and hit the gym. For dinner it was always something great because my Mom is a really good cook and I was still living at home back then. I'd have a can of coke with lunch, dinner, and usually at night before bed. (Seriously.) And during my workout I'd have a huge protein shake that usually made me fart all day. (Seriously!)

But I was in the best shape of my life! I just look back on that time and wish I knew then what I know now about nutrition. All of what I was eating was wreaking havoc on my gut and wearing down my immune system which made me more vulnerable to the allergens that are out in the world.

Because I was training all the time, and coaching, my adrenal glands were pumping adrenaline through my system constantly. Because of that my immune system was already compromised. My tank was half empty and because of that my allergies were horrible.

Note: Just a word of warning before I write this section. I'm not a doctor, but I do follow recommendations by some doctors. In the end, we ultimately have to make decisions based on inputs from a number of sources and I want you to do the same thing. I was never exposed to the solution I'm about to explain to you by my Doctor. He had never heard of the solution my nutritionist recommended to me but when I explained it to him he was like, "Oh yes! That's a great idea. I hadn't really thought of that as an option but it sounds perfect."

The bottom line is that it is your responsibility to seek solutions. You can go to Doctor A and get a solution while Doctor B may have no idea what Doctor A is talking about. With the internet you have the ability to seek solutions that your Doctor may not be trained in. That's not to discredit them at all, it's just an opportunity to empower yourself and your own solutions. I saw a coffee mug that had written on the side, "Don't let your internet search interfere with my medical degree!" That's funny, but it's problematic. We have an incredible opportunity today to work with our medical professionals as a team. The amount of information, and potential solutions out there are incredible! And it's not possible for one person to know everything. Your solutions to create an incredible, high-performing body, are endless. And working with your doctors is a team effort. What I am about to describe to you is just that, a team solution. Had I relied on only one source for a solution I would have never found one. I encourage you to seek solutions and to be open to a team-approach to the solutions you need. Here's mine:

What this nutritionist recommended was that I go on a three day fast where I drank a mixture of water, honey, lemon juice and paprika. Sounds weird, I know, but the water was to keep me hydrated. The honey was to keep my blood sugar slightly elevated so I didn't get too grumpy. The lemon has a cleansing effect. And the paprika added a little spice to the whole thing which was also meant to cleanse the body. It was like a spicy lemonade and I just loved it, and while the recommendation was to go for three days, if I could go a little longer that was also recommended.

I ended up going for seven days! The hardest thing about it was having all sorts of free time where I would have been eating. They say that when a cigarette smoker tries to quit smoking that the hardest thing is not having something in their hand during the day. That was the same for me without food. I was looking to take a break to eat and because I didn't need to do that anymore it just felt weird. I would go to the fridge not because I was hungry but because my body was programmed to go to the fridge. It was weird I tell you! But a lesson I have never forgotten.

After the seven days of fasting I then went on what was called an elimination diet. I ate foods that are typically non-allergenic. For me that was chicken, rice and broccoli and I started to eat those over the next three days. After that I would add foods that I "normally" ate to see if my body reacted to them in any way. The first was milk and whoa did that feel weird. I immediately got phlegmy in my nose and throat and my stomach twisted up in a cramp. Milk was a food I had been drinking all the time! Protein shakes are based on milk protein. When I drank them after a workout I farted like an ozone-depleting cow but it was what an athlete was supposed to do, right? Wrong.

Milk was the first of many foods that were a staple in my athlete diet but my body was telling me that it wasn't happy and was fighting against it. The battle my body now had to wage fighting off the milk in my system was depleting my energy and my immune system was going with it. All of this was making me vulnerable to other allergens like other food, pollen, and everything else.

I spent the next month and a half adding other foods back into my diet that were commonly allergenic. Foods like eggs, fish, tree nuts (walnuts, almonds, hazelnuts, Brazil nuts), wheat, soy, shellfish, peanuts, etc. One by one, I added them back into my diet to see how they made me feel and one by one I eliminated the foods that made me feel bad. It was a long process but it was incredible to learn just what my body was dealing with. Foods that I had grown up on and eaten "forever" were some of the worst culprits, but if I hadn't taken the time to learn how they made me feel I would have never understood the toll they were taking on my body. I can guarantee that the same is happening to you.

Now you don't have to go through the same process I did. You probably know that there are certain foods that are making you feel sick or are wearing you down. So my question is, why are you still eating them? Take a minute and write down the foods you know aren't good for you but you're still eating them. Think hard because there are probably some on the list that have been recommended to you by well meaning coaches. Write them down in the box below and commit to eliminating them from your diet starting...now:

Resource #3: Money

When I retired from the sport of luge it wasn't because I wasn't any good anymore. In fact, the last race I competed in I missed making the National Team in a three-tier tie-breaker that came down to .01 of a second. Ouch. No, I didn't quit because I was bad. I just ran out of money and had spent about $30,000 over the previous two years to try and make the team. Had I been able to continue, I probably would have made the National Team the following season as others ahead of me retired or quit. But by that point I was pretty tired of a lot of things, and was ready to move on.

Money is an interesting topic for athletes and their families. The resource of money varies from family to family and no matter the level of wealth a family may have, there can always be more money. There is an endless array of opportunities to train and compete and they are only limited by time, energy and money.

It's important to understand that I have seen athletes from very wealthy families and very poor families make it to the upper levels of sport. I have also seen athletes from very poor families become world champion. I always enjoy hearing about athletes from "poor" countries who beat athletes from "wealthy" countries in international competition. In 2016, Leicester City won the Premier League in soccer with a salary base that was just a fraction of the other top teams in the league. The bottom line is that most people who have less wish they had more, and those that have lots wish they had more too.

I have also seen athletes from incredibly wealthy families completely blow it. The outsider views athletes with unlimited financial resources as somewhat gifted. But this focus can backfire. Your focus must be on what you can do with the resources you have and not on what you don't have. You must also believe that what you have is enough. You are not "less" because you have "less". You have the ability to come up with the resources for what you need.

The truth is, there are always opportunities to earn and raise money. The challenge is having the time to be able to earn/generate money all while training and recovering. This is where the entrepreneurial bug can start to kick in. If you only think of trading hours for dollars then there will be a time when you don't have enough time to do it all.

Fund Your Love Of Your Sport

But what if you had a business that could fund your ideal lifestyle. This is what Dale Begg-Smith of Canada did. A very talented freestyle skier Dale created an online advertising business that made him quite wealthy...by the age of 16. Here was a talented skier and a very successful business owner who was able to train and compete as much as he wanted due to the business he created to help fund his love of skiing.

The crazy twist in the story came when his Canadian coaches told him he was spending too much time on his entrepreneurial efforts and not training. Well, this didn't sit too well with Dale who decided he had had enough of the Canadian politics and decided to move to another winter-sports-crazed nation...Australia. (Wut!)

Along with his brother, Dale moved to the country that had a much smaller team but was supportive of his business aspirations and his Olympic dream. Over the next three years they lived and trained in Australia working on their company, all while pursuing their athletic and business goals. Three years later, after having fulfilled their obligations to the Australian residency requirements, they became Australian citizens and were now ready to compete for their adopted homeland. Sure enough, two years later, Dale Begg-Smith won Olympic gold for Australia.

Now that story has some crazy twists and turns in it. But what makes it fantastic is that Dale had a business that was mobile and supported his passion which was skiing. In fact, he and his brother set that as a goal, "to have a business that funds our lifestyle of skiing."

What if you had a business that funded your dream? There are countless stories around of people who started businesses to help fund their dream lifestyle. Or you could have a more traditional business that you operate in the off-season. Jeff Pain, a Canadian Skeleton athlete had a landscape company that he had started when he was a teenager. You can go on Kijiji or Craigslist right now and get a lawn mower and go door to door with this pitch, "Hey there, I'm so-and-so. I'm an aspiring athlete and to fund my dream I have started a company mowing lawns for $XX a cut. Would you be interested in supporting my dream?" With that pitch alone you could have enough work to pay for college. Not only that, you wouldn't need to be doing all the cuts yourself. You could hire it out and pay your mowers just a bit less than what you charge. Now you have leverage and that's what a true business is all about.

Sponsorship

Athletes underestimate the potential of sponsorship and the value they have as an athlete. Should you get a sponsor? What if you're just in a team sport? It doesn't matter what your sport or what level you compete at, there are always sponsorship dollars available, especially in today's world.

My friend Vickie Saunders of Australia has a company called: **The Sponsorship Consultants** and she consults with athletes around the world encouraging them to embrace the potential of sponsorship in their career. There is basically no athlete out there who couldn't benefit from pursuing sponsorship on any number of levels. I highly recommend you go to Vickie's website and download the free ebook and then get further involved with her education.

You = Athlete CEO

As the athlete, you are the center of your universe. You are really the CEO of your whole experience and act the same as a CEO would operate a business. Now if your family is made up of business owners, this concept will not seem foreign to you; but if your family is not made up of any business owners then this might be hard for you to comprehend.

As the CEO of the Company called "You", you are managing resources. That is what a CEO does. They manage the resources available to the company in order to create a desired product. In this case the product is you. You are the results of the company. A busy CEO has a lot on their plate just like you do. You may have school and family obligations. Your sport may be one of many sports that you are involved in, or you may be focusing on just this one. You may juggle relationships and time with friends. All of these obligations will be weighed against the goal of your company, You.

The CEO has to make many decisions about the resources in relationship to the company. Not enough time to train? Something must be cut elsewhere. That may be the chess club you are part of or the boyfriend you're into. (Don't laugh, I've seen it happen. She really liked chess AND playing soccer, but she had a boyfriend too) You may need more money so getting a job may be necessary, or you could look for a sponsor. Need more time to sleep and have more energy? Maybe missing your friends birthday next week to get a nap is in order. Whatever the choices they are all made in relation to the goal.

Conclusion:

In the previous chapter we talked about the three key abilities every athlete needs in order to have success on the field of play. But there are also three layers that we layer on top of those beliefs in order to have ultimate success. They are: Belief, Life Skills, and Resources to Develop Your Abilities which are Time, Energy and Money.

I have been around tremendously talented athletes who lacked belief in their abilities. I've also seen incredibly talented athletes who couldn't manage their time or their social responsibilities to the point that it completely derailed their talents. And when it comes to resources, well, I've seen athletes with incredible amounts of resources blow it all while other athletes with far less ultimately succeed. The bottom line is that no matter where you are and what you have, you have an incredible chance for success if you just stick with it and learn to manage your opportunities well.

Watch This Video:

**www.AthleteSpecific.com/
three-layers**

Take Action With These Steps:

- No matter the strength of your abilities, your belief in your abilities needs to be strong. An athlete with great abilities but no belief in their abilities is not a very good athlete. Identify areas where your belief in your ability is low and create a plan to improve them.

- As an athlete you have to train, recover from training, and compete in order to reach your goals. Everything outside of that is not essential to that goal. You must develop the skills to manage your time and the people around you to stay on track. What part(s) of your life are you currently letting distract you from your athletic goals?

- No matter how much time, energy, or money an athlete's has, they all wish they had more. How are you maximizing your time, your energy, and your money? What could you do to improve them?

- Brainstorm a list of all of the ways you can improve belief, your life skills, and your resources and commit to taking action on one item today.

Chapter 10
How To Create an Environment So You Can Learn To Win And Lose

"Losing is a learning experience. It teaches you humility. It teaches you to work harder. It's also a powerful motivator."

Yogi Berra
American professional baseball catcher, who later took on the roles of manager, and coach. He played 19 seasons in Major League Baseball, all but the last for the New York Yankees.

Every sport is designed to have a winner and a loser and the odds are you are going to lose more than you win. So you could say that learning how to lose is more important than learning how to win. That is why you need to create an environment of people and places around you where you can learn how to win, and how to lose, in order to constantly be improving.

Avoid "Light Switch" Mentality

Most people view winning and losing as either a good or a bad scenario. Kind of like the light is either on, or it's off. It's good, or it's bad. From, "OMG this is the best thing ever!" To, " This just sucks. I should just quit."

To become a great athlete you need to become more sophisticated in your understanding of how you win and lose. There is no good or bad when it comes to winning and losing. There is just...learning.

In this section we are going to talk about the people and places that you will build around you to do just that. From coaches, to friends and family, you are building a critical team around you that is going to help you.

Assembling Your Team

You won't reach your goals by yourself. It will take a team to make it all happen. But for many athletes much of your support team will be provided without you really thinking about it. You will most likely make a team and that team will have many of the supporting cast you need as already part of it. However, that doesn't mean you must rely on only that support staff. While many of those folks are great people, they aren't always the best people you might be able to have access to. I look back on my athletic career and in a trusting way I relied wholeheartedly on people who, I thought, were the best in the business. Turns out sometimes they are the only people who would take the job!

I can think back to bad advice from athletic trainers, strength and conditioning coaches, equipment managers, etc. I'm not saying that any of these folks were trying to do bad things to me, they were probably doing the best with what they knew at the time. However, I really wish that I had taken more responsibility on the advice that I was being given. A question I wished I had learned when I was much younger was, "Who else out there knows about this and what do they have to say about this?"

In no way do I want to put doubt into your head about your support staff. It's important to have an incredibly good working relationship with all of these people. You must be able to go to them and share your thoughts and concerns about being the best you can be. But you must remember that it is up to you to make sure the people around you have your best interest in mind.

Sometimes, a single person may occupy a couple of the support positions around you. This can be a good thing but more often than not it can be a problem. For example, after I retired from sport I immersed myself in the world of strength and conditioning. I enjoyed it. I was good at it. **And because I hadn't been naturally gifted with strength OR conditioning I found that I was really good at articulating it to athletes who hadn't really thought too much about the topic.**

When it came to coaching a sport like lacrosse, that I was

technically proficient at, I could apply my strength and conditioning knowledge to my athletes and could make them better fast. I'd like to think I did a pretty good job and had a unique understanding and an ability to articulate both skills to my athletes but at a higher level.

When Your Coach Can Be Trying To Do Too Much

There was a time when I ran a boutique strength and conditioning business working with a number of athletes from a variety of sports. Hockey, Lacrosse, Football, Bobsled, just to name a few. But my most intriguing athlete was a female figure skater who was fourteen years old. She was referred to me by her Physical Therapist who I knew and had developed a relationship with because I was known for being able to help injured athletes get back to competition.

I found this athlete to be really intriguing. Here was a very talented fourteen year old girl who had developed such bad tendonitis in her knees that she had an incredibly hard time doing any of her jumps. In fact, she had "lost" some of her jumps completely and wasn't able to do even the simplest of combinations. This was due, in part, because she was maturing physically and getting taller; but it was mostly because her knees hurt so much.

As I interviewed the athlete with her parents I learned that her Technical Coach also took it upon herself to have her athletes do the physical conditioning that she prescribed. I'll spare you all of the details but let's just put it this way, I asked the athlete how many times she jumped while on the ice and it worked out to be about 75-90 times per session on the ice. (Which is a LOT!) Immediately after their ice time the girls would do their "off-ice" conditioning that consisted of an additional 75-100 jump variations that took place on the hard concrete surface surrounding the rink. Is there any doubt why this girl had knees that hurt?

Training Should NOT Be Political

This is an example of how the Technical Coach was also trying to be the conditioning coach. In this case, there was a political wrinkle as well. The coach felt offended if her athletes were working with anyone other than her. Coaches can get very territorial and it turned out many of the girls were nursing injuries and didn't want to tell the coach because they didn't want to fall out of her favor and possibly miss out on ice time or other competitions.

This is a pretty nasty position for an athlete to be in. Unfortunately, there are some coaches who can't put their ego aside to do what's best for their athletes, which is ironic because most coaches really want their athletes to win. (Probably to soothe their own ego). With this athlete we had to set up a screen where she had "tutoring" for school that conflicted with her off-ice training. The tutoring idea was completely made up and was just an excuse so this athlete could rest and come train with me and not offend the coach. Over the coming months we slowly got her strong and flexible enough just to survive the on ice training and to be able to withstand the rigor of the technical training. In this case the coach was great as a Technical Coach, but as a conditioning coach, not so much.

You're Going To Need a Lot Of Help

Here is a list of some of the coaches and support staff you will need in your quest to be a great athlete:

1. **Technical Coaches:** These are the coaches who will teach you the "what" that you need to do in your sport.

2. **Tactical Coaches:** These are the coaches who teach you the "when" to do "what" it is you do.

3. **Physical Coaches:** Strength and Conditioning coaches or Performance Enhancement Coaches fall into this category.

4. **Physical Therapists:** For those times you get injured or are going through a growth spurt.

5. **Doctors:** While you will have traditional medical doctors I highly recommend getting opinions from Naturopaths as well. See below.

6. **Nutritionists:** While I'm not a fan of nutritionists who just follow the American Dietetic Association guidelines, finding someone who can help you tweak your diet for optimal performance is vital. There are a ton of resources available now so don't just listen to the status quo because it's rarely correct anymore.

7. **Sports Psychologists:** People like myself or others can help you with your mental game. Many athletes don't turn to people like this until they feel they have a problem. If you can seek them out early, you'll be bulletproof to the ups and downs of competition.

8. **Administrators:** While these people are rarely people who you can influence because they have many athletes to consider while making decisions, it NEVER hurts to be on their good side.

9. **Agents/Representatives:** If you are in a sport that has commercial viability, and you are above average in your performance and are nearing the top of your sport, you will have the need for an Agent or a group of Agents to help market you to contracts within your sport and possibly outside of it. Be wary. To these folks you aren't just an athlete. You are walking dollar signs that could make them wealthy if you reach your potential. Tread lightly.

Others: Naturopaths, Chiropractors, Massage Therapists, Energy Healers, Podiatrists, Dentists, Travel Agents, Mechanics, Web Designers, Social Media Managers, Agents, Promoters, in addition to Parents, Family and friends, and a ton more too long to list here.

The "Love" Of Parents. Family. Friends

Of all of the people in your life who can be part of your team, your parents, family and friends will be some of the most influential.

I use the word "influential" because they can influence you in a positive or negative way and even when they aren't trying!

The important thing to understand when dealing with parents, family and friends, when it comes to any sort of advice they may give you about your athletic goals, is that all of their recommendations come from love. Yes, love. They love you and here's the kicker to it all...they don't want you to be disappointed.

Now you've already heard me talk about "seeking disappointment" in CHAPTER XXX and that will help you as you work with parents, family and friends.

It's important to understand that with this category of people on your team, what they say to you carries more "weight" in your mind and seems more important. If some random stranger says, "Hey, when are you going to grow up and get a real job?" you can brush it off and not worry about it too much. But when your best friend says it, it's a whole 'nuther story. And when your Mom says it. Look out!

Remember, **what people say about you says more about them than it does about you.** We talk about that a couple of times in this book. And when you're dealing with people in this category they can have a real impact.

For many of the athletes I have ever been around, NONE of the people in their life have ever embarked on the journey they are trying to complete. Personally there was no one in my life who had been to the Olympics or who had played a sport in college. So much of the advice I got from my parents, friends or family was conceptual. They couldn't give me specifics but they could give me comparisons to other events in their life. My mom would often tell me how she dealt with certain experiences while being a professional opera singer and how they were similar to what I was trying to accomplish. While this sometimes drove me nuts it was valuable advice that I could apply to what I was doing.

With the internet it also makes it easier to figure out if the advice you are getting is legit. When your crazy Uncle Eddie tells you to drink a gallon of milk every day to gain muscle you can go online to see if he's pulling your leg. On the flip side of that, you can (and should) seek out credible guidance for ANYTHING you see online. Just saying. I saw a great coffee mug once on a doctor's desk that said, "Don't Let Your Google Search Interfere With My Medical Degree." While I get the joke, it can go both ways in today's world of easy information.

Your Friends

I'm not talking about Facebook friends or Instagram followers. I'm talking about your...friends. The people you hang out with. The people you've grown up with. The people who knew you "when" and the people who know you now.

Friends are an interesting category of people in your life because they love you as...you. They love the "you" they have gotten to know and you might be changing as you travel on your sports journey through life.

Let's be honest. Some of your friends, you are going to grow out of. Just like someone who goes on a diet and gets skinny. The habits that person follows now would be much different than the habits of their friends who are still overweight. This can cause some stress in a relationship and some of those past friends might feel uncomfortable around their "new" old friend and this can be a challenge.

A true friend is someone who believes in you and pushes you on even when they may not fully understand all of the specifics of what you're trying to accomplish. A true friend might say, "Listen, I would never do that thing you're doing but I love you and support you and want to see you succeed." They will also tell you when you're messing up and are veering off track. Either way, a friend is there to support you.

Friends need to know you support them, too. It's easy for some friends to start to think that their goals are far less important than yours. They might not even have any goals! It might seem that "little 'ol them" compared to "big 'ol you" doesn't need support, but they do. Part of being a friend is turning around and supporting them in their time of need and lifting them up and just being there. With today's technology it is so easy to stay in touch and be a part of people's lives even if you have to travel and compete at a distance. But no matter what your commitments are to your sport, you can always stay in touch.

Your Family

When I talk about family I'm not talking about your parents. I'm talking about your extended family. Brothers, sisters, cousins, step-brothers, etc. all have a special place on your team, or off it.

I've seen athletes with great families around them. Sometimes it's just a matter of you doing your thing and they are doing theirs. They can really get around your goal or other times they can be completely jealous of it. Either way, the challenge of the family dynamic is that sometimes those people are sleeping in the same house!

Family influence can sometimes be relentless. If it's positive, that's great. But if it's negative, it can be hard to get away from . Be sure to have time every day when you can be alone with your thoughts to gain clarity and to create some distance between you and negative family members. This can be hard to do especially with social media. I recommend, what I call, *The Social Media Upgrade*. Do what you can to mute or turn off the frequency of notifications of family members.

Or just follow so many great examples that the posts from your family members get somewhat drowned out by all the positive news and examples in your feed. Trust me, it's a great technique. If you have a negative family member direct messaging you...block 'em!

That being said, if your family members are really supportive, spend as much time with them as you can!

Parents

Parents take a special place in anything you try to do athletically. Let's face it, they've been funding your athletic dream longer than you can possibly imagine. It's not just the food they put on the table or the large amounts of money they have put towards registration fees. Just think of all of the equipment as well as countless hours in the car.

As I write this section I think of all of the parents I've ever been around. Some great. Some absolutely nuts. But all of them have one major thing in common...they all love their kids.

Love gets shown in a lot of ways by different people and what "love" looks like to one person can look a lot different to someone else. But no matter how your parents showed love to you, I can guarantee you that it's there. They want the best for you and this whole sports thing can be a bit strange depending on their upbringing.

Odds are that your parents never tried to pursue what it is you are trying to pursue. If your parents have a solid athletic background that's a bonus, but if they don't, that's ok too. You're going to be learning together.

The key to a successful parent relationship in sports is to keep the lines of communication open. Like it or not, you are a team. Your parents bring a lot of experience to the table and you have to respect that. Keeping them up to date about what it is you are doing and what it is you are trying to accomplish is key.

You have to understand that your athletic journey is as unique a challenge to them as it is to you. They don't want to see you disappointed, hurt, injured, or worse. They want it all to work out for you, but the challenge is that they will see your journey through their eyes and not yours. This is why having open communication and updates is important.

Adults tend to ask questions differently than younger athletes will ask them and this can cause a bit of conflict. While younger athletes will keep things inside as they try to figure it all out, parents are sitting there waiting for some bit of info that they can solve. (Especially the dads.) Moms too want to "make it right" and know everything going on in their kids head as soon as it's happening. (If you haven't seen the movie **Inside Out**, watch it with your parents.)

Just as you would talk to a coach or any other support person about how you'd like to be talked to, I highly recommend doing that with your parents. Many parents, in an effort to "help", end up losing touch with their kids because their delivery is off. If you need time to process things after a practice, tell them! If you're not talking to them they might take that as you don't care and that will frustrate them. The key is to have awareness to what it is you really need and to let them know.

The Car Ride Home

There is a lot of talk about "The car ride home." and how it can ruin an athlete's experience of sport. Depending on your age you may be going through this right now or have gone through it in the past. Either way, that time after practice or games can be an awesome time to bond with a parent or it can be a bit rough. Here's what I suggest to make it awesome:

In my experience, when most athletes get in the car after a game or practice, they need a few minutes to decompress. They've just gone from an incredible high of activity to the quiet car ride. Parents are excited to see their kids again and they are curious as to how things went and they will typically ask, "How'd-it-go?Did-you-score?How-was-coach?What-do-you-want-for-dinner?Did-you-ask-coach-why-you-didn't-play-more-last-game?Are-you-going-to-play-more-next-game? And on and on and on. (That was one run-on sentence for a reason. BTW)

If you are a talkative athlete and have a great relationship with your parents, great, but if not, then you need to help your parents help you by taking time to explain what it is you need. In my experience, parents are quick to respond positively when their young athlete comes to them with a plan and who says, "Mom, Dad, I love you and here's what we can do to make this awesome...."

The relationship with your parents is one of the most important relationships you can have in this whole sport experience. Keep them on the same page (or at least really close to the same page) by sharing with them what you know and how you feel and how they can help you be better. In the end they love you and don't want you to be disappointed.

The Chief Athletic Officer

As the athlete, you are the center of your universe. You are really the CEO of your whole experience and act the same as a CEO would operate a big corporation. Now if your family is made up of business owners, this concept will not seem foreign to you; but if your family is not made up of any business owners then this might be hard for you to comprehend.

As the CEO of the Company called "You", you are managing resources. That is what a CEO does. They manage the resources available to the company in order to create a desired product or service. In this case the product is you and you are the results of the company.

A busy CEO has a lot on their plate just like you do. You may have school and family obligations. Your sport may be one of many sports that you are involved in, or you may be focusing on just one. You may juggle relationships and time with friends. All of these obligations will be weighed against the goal of your company, which is you.

The CEO has to make many decisions about the resources in relation to the company. Not enough time to train and do it all? Something must be cut elsewhere. That may be the chess club or your boyfriend. (Don't laugh, I've seen it happen.) You may need more money so getting a job may be necessary, or you could look for a sponsor. Need more time to sleep and have more energy? Maybe missing that birthday party, or going to part of it so you can grab a nap before practice that night is in order. Whatever the choices you make they are all made in relationship to the goals you have set for yourself.

Conclusion:

In the world of sports we can put ourselves in incredibly pressure filled situations, but it's important that we don't make rash decisions. That is why we want to assemble a team of experts around us who can help us navigate this path effectively. We need people from doctors to agents to help us make wise decisions based on our long term progress and not short term wins or losses.

Just like the CEO of a large company you will assemble your team of experts around you. And some of those "experts" you won't have to assemble at all. They are your friends, family and parents and they just come along for the ride. But they can have a huge influence on you so it's important to manage them accordingly.

Watch This Video

**www.AthleteSpecific.com/
create-an-environment-so-you-
can-win-and-lose**

Take These Action Steps

- Take your journal and write down situations in your past where you might have overreacted to a bad result. How did you overcome that bad result? Can you apply what you did to future results?

- You need a team of people around you to help this make your dreams come true. Who do you have around you who is a positive influence on your team and who do you need to add?

- Who around you is more of a negative influence? Someone who may be dragging you down? What can you do to minimize their influence on you?

- Use social media to reach out to athletes in your sport who inspire you. Send them a well thought out note that compliments them and tell them how they inspire you. You may get a nice message back. They are people too so don't hesitate to give them support as well.

Section 3
Train. Recover. Compete. Recover. Repeat.

"Healing is a matter of time, but it is sometimes also a matter of opportunity."

Hippocrates
Also known as Hippocrates II, was a Greek physician of the Age of Pericles, and is considered one of the most outstanding figures in the history of medicine.

Chapter 11
The Primal Triad: Sleep. Eat. Move. Repeat

"Think in the morning. Act in the noon. Eat in the evening. Sleep in the night."

William Blake
William Blake was an English poet, painter, and printmaker. Largely
unrecognised during his lifetime, Blake is now considered a seminal figure in
the history of the poetry and visual arts of the Romantic Age.

When you look at the life of an athlete you really need to understand, what I call, "The Primal Triad".

Primal refers to a way of life that our cavemen ancestors really perfected. Now, while their life revolved primarily around survival, yours revolves around high-performance. While your caveman ancestor might be looking to outrun a bear or a lion, you are putting yourself on a starting line to see who gets the best time or some other performance.

The three main aspects of the life of an athlete achieving high-performance is this:

1. You must sleep.
2. You must eat.
3. You must move.
4. Then you repeat the whole thing.

Everything you do is designed to maximize your ability to move effectively for your sport. Another word for "move" might be "perform" and what you do outside of that either helps you perform better or it doesn't.

So when you think of it this way, everything you do outside of your training is designed to help you train more effectively, and more often.

Sleep: It All Starts With Sleep?

It is rare that I meet an athlete who is truly getting enough sleep day in and day out. People are often surprised that as an Olympic athlete training at the Olympic training center that I didn't get enough sleep. Looking back on the late nights working on sleds or partying at the Laughing Loon Cafe on Tankard Tuesdays. The truth is that social life happens and that is a large part of the lifestyle of being an elite athlete. That being said, I look back on that time with some regret. Knowing what I know now (and what I'm trying to impart to you) I would have done a lot of things differently.

But when it comes to getting enough sleep, it's really not just about getting "more", it's about getting the right amount for you, and this is something that wasn't truly taught to me until much later in my life. I know today that the perfect amount of sleep I need, per night, is seven and a half hours. If I sleep in, I take another hour and a half and sleep for nine hours. Any more and I feel like I slept four hours.

As a young athlete however it wasn't uncommon for me to sleep for ten to twelve hours on a Saturday. Eight or more during the week if I went to bed early enough. Many athletes I know today are lucky to get eight hours but are more prone to getting six or seven. Maybe.

I don't know what your perfect amount of sleep is going to be but I can tell you that it is different for all of us. Your parents might tell you that the average is eight hours, but that's simply not true. Depending on how old you are you may need anywhere between five and twelve hours per night. The key is to find just the right amount that you need and one of the best ways to figure that out is by using a sleep app on your phone to see just what your sleep cycles look like. I use an app called Sleep Tracker that shows me just how well I slept during the night by tracking my movement. It will also wake me when I'm at the peak of one of my sleep cycles so I'm closer to being awake than in a deep sleep. Have you ever woken up and felt terrible? But another night you may wake up early and feel great? This is most likely caused because you woke up in the middle of a deep sleep cycle and it makes it really difficult to get up. This is why sometimes you can sleep in and feel worse than if you had gotten up a half hour earlier. It's not about setting the alarm to get up at 6:30AM no matter when you went to bed. You may actually benefit from getting up at six, or five thirty, depending on how much sleep you need or when you went to bed.

When we are sleeping, we are recovering. For the athlete who wants to improve his or her performance, improving sleep quantity and quality can make a huge difference. We tend to overlook the sleeping quality of young athletes. Parents tend to think, incorrectly, that if they just get more sleep they will be better off. The truth is that quantity is just one aspect of sleep. Quality is almost equally as important. Here are some quick tips to improving the quality of your sleep:

- Make sure your room is as dark as possible. You're not a baby and need the light on anymore. No, you don't sleep better with the light on. When the world goes dark your brain signals the body to sleep and any light in your room can affect that circadian rhythm. A small green light on an electronic device or the awkward glow of an alarm clock can drastically change how well you sleep. Make sure you have blackout drapes on your windows or sleep with something over your eyes all night. Avoid any sort of electronics in your room especially tv's and computers.

- Keep your room slightly cool but with no major drafts blowing over you all night. Having a window slightly open so there is ample fresh air in your room and the temperature around 65 degrees fahrenheit or 18 degrees celsius is pretty much perfect.

- White noise blocks out unnecessary noises. You can buy a simple fan that creates a constant whir that drowns out other noises. Earbuds playing static can also work. I have the White Noise App on my iPhone that helps drown out unruly roommates or rowdy neighbors. Noise cancelling headphones are also nice, but if I use them too frequently they make me feel a little....off.

- Have a mattress that supports your body according to your bodyweight. Mattresses can dramatically affect your sleep quality so be sure you're not sleeping on a mattress that is too hard or too soft for your height and weight.

- High quality sheets and duvets can keep you dry and at the proper sleep temperature so that you aren't too hot or too cold. If you find your blankets make you hot and cause you to toss and turn you need to consider higher quality bedding and travel with it if you are headed to compete at other locations where you're not sleeping at home. Check out www. GreatCanadianDownCompany.com for great options.

- No caffeine after noon. Caffeine is found in everything from coke, Red Bull, coffee and even chocolate. Avoid any of those after lunchtime to avoid the lingering effects of caffeine that will keep you awake.

- Have a sleep routine. Put away your technology. Have a nice shower or bath with some Epsom salts, and wind down for the nights rest. Triggering your body that sleep time is coming can have a profound effect on how and when you fall asleep. Read a book that isn't homework or work-work and that will help wind you down. Do your affirmations and visualize for the next day without getting wound up or stressed out.

All of these tips will help you sleep better, and for a longer amount of time than you are currently which will allow your body to heal and recover from competition and training. The faster the body can recover the sooner you can train and compete again and the quicker you can make that cycle spin round the better you will be, faster.

Eat To Train, Train To Eat

Food is fuel.

To the athlete this makes sense but to the general public who aren't training to become a better athlete, food is eaten because of things like habit, social pressures, and emotional comfort. But for you, food is fuel.

There are two ways to look at the food you eat. First, it helps give your muscles energy to burn for when you are in training and competition mode. Secondly, food provides the nutrients to not only help refuel depleted energy stores, but also to provide the building blocks to help the body repair and recover from the physical damage training and competing does to the body.

For the scope of this book I'm not going to get into all of the details of a proper diet for you as an athlete, but just understand this: The quality of the foods you eat either help, or hurt your recovery process. The food you eat is either helping you get closer to your goals or taking you away from them. To give you some great perspective on food and and fueling your body for high performance check out the following resources:

Websites:

www.MarksDailyApple.com: Former world class triathlete, and now shredded 60 something year old, Mark Sisson writes a daily blog. It is an incredible resource of nutrition for high performance living.

www.RobbWolf.com: A "Paleo" website, many athletes swear by this lifestyle of living and eating. Incredibly detailed, his books are also amazing.

www.DanielAmenMD.com - Remarkably, the same eating habits that help your brain will help your body.

www.Bulletproof.com - run by Dave Asprey who was an out of shape tech executive in Silicon Valley, this is an incredible resource for people ready to take their body, and their brain to the next level. Listen to his podcast at www.BulletProofRadio.com."

www.TheHighPerformanceYou.com - created by the author of this very book, Jonathan Edwards. Check out my tips on how to hack your life and make it 1000x better. Not just for athletes either.

Documentaries On iTunes/Netflix or Youtube

Fat, Sick & Nearly Dead 1 and 2: Joe Cross was a successful investor who realized his belly looked like he had swallowed a sheep. He documented a cross country trip across the United States where he passed on the Standard American Diet of burgers and fries and just juiced. It's an eye-opening trip and worth the watch. While I don't recommend just juicing for high performance athletes, it does have its benefits and you would be wise to check it out.

Vitality: A documentary by Doctor Pedram Shojai, it's a look into the current medical system and while it is failing because it focuses on the treatment of disease instead of on prevention of them. One makes money and the other doesn't. A great watch to learn more about this rather broken system.

Food Inc.: IMDb calls is "An unflattering look inside America's corporate controlled food industry." You may have trouble eating food from the grocery store ever again. Food is very different than when our parents ate it. Watch this documentary for incredible insight into the food industry and how even the healthiest foods might not be so healthy.

Forks Over Knives: This documentary explores an incredible theory that most if not all, degenerative diseases can be controlled or even cured by eliminating the consumption of meat from our diets. While it does take some points from a debunked study the concept behind this movie is sound.

There are many more that I could list for you but start with those for now and start to learn about how what you are putting into your body is impacting your health and your ability to perform at a high level. I highly recommend getting your family involved when you are watching those videos as they can benefit everyone you love and not just athletes.

Move

Whether you are a gymnast performing a floor routine, a hockey player skating down the ice, or a heavyweight Olympic weightlifter, every sport has it's required movements to be competitive, and no matter what the sport, there is a strength and flexibility requirement to be world class. Your goal is to find out what that is and maximize yourself to be able to perform at the highest level.

How much you sleep, and how well you eat, is going to affect just how well you are going to be able to move, how often you are going to be able to train and recover from those movement skills, and how quickly you can heal in case you have an injury. So in reality, two-thirds of the Primal Triad that I have laid out for you here is responsible for the one-third that you get to perform with. The truth is, if you are not properly fueled and rested your performance will suffer.

It is beyond the scope of this book to get into specific training principles for every sport out there; but the overall concept I want you to take away from this chapter is that your sport has specific fueling needs depending on the demands of that sport. Your rest and your fueling will help make that movement possible.

Repeat

The concept of "repeat" is rarely discussed in sports but it is the cornerstone to all of your development. The idea is to train for competition and to be able to recover as quickly as possible so you can train and compete again.

The faster you can recover, the more frequently you can train and compete. The more frequently you can train and compete the more often you can be exposed to challenges and opportunities with which to learn. Everything you do from here is meant to maximize those opportunities.

Oh, and one last thing…

More Is Not A Plan

Improving your abilities takes tremendous focus and an environment called "Deliberate Practice." The answer is not "more training is better" it's that perfect training is better. This is not going to be a book with a full dissertation on Deliberate Practice as that could be an entire book on it's own. What I do want you to understand is that more is not always better. It's an idea (that comes from the athlete) that extremely focused attention to perfect technique in practice is going to reap higher benefits than sloppy training with poor technique. We are wiring the athlete just like we are wiring a computer, and if the wiring is sloppy then the application will also be sloppy.

When an athlete has great technique their margin for error goes down, however, Physical Ability will start to show through in poor technique as an athlete gets fatigued. This is where we might pull a pitcher from a baseball game when his pitches get sloppy. We may sub out a tired forward in soccer for a fresh one off the bench. We might see a golfer coming down the eighteenth fairway on a very hot day spray his approach shot wide because of fatigue.

Whatever the environmental condition, an athlete's physical ability will start to affect his ability to do what he does effectively. Your goal is to maximize your performance across all conditions.

Conclusion:

Your body operates, still, very much like our caveman ancestors operated ages ago. The slept. They ate. They moved. And then they repeated the whole process. Now you might not have to run away from a saber toothed tiger tomorrow, but you will have a practice or an event that you're preparing for. And to be ready for that event, your sleep needs to be on point. Your food needs to fuel you so that you are ready for the event and fully recovered from competition. And then your training needs to have prepared you to move effectively during that competition. It's a simple cycle that you repeat over and over.

But all of this work is strategic. You must be deliberate with your plan. The answer is not "more" as many people think it is. More training. More games. More. More. More. No, it is a simple cycle that is repeated deliberately. You need a plan.

Watch This Video

www.AthleteSpecific.com/
the-primal-triad

Take Action With These Steps

- Take out your journal and answer this question: On a scale of 1 to 10, how rested do you feel? Why did you give yourself that number?

- What can you do to improve your sleep environment according to the outline I laid out in this chapter?

- Do you eat for fuel or do you eat for pleasure? What foods/drinks or other edibles could you eliminate that would make you feel better? What would you replace it with?

- Do you move well for you sport? What would you improve if your answer is no? Who can you seek out to get better input on that issue?

Chapter 12
Creating Your Toolbox

"Losers assemble in small groups and complain. Winners assemble as a team and find a way to win."

Bill Parcells
Known as "The Big Tuna," he is an American Football Coach who coachd for 19 seasons and won two Super Bowls.

When it comes to improving our athletic abilities, and the qualities we need to withstand challenges and take advantage of opportunities, we are looking for coaches and other experts who can help us identify those qualities we need to improve and to make those qualities better. But here's a twist: sometimes they aren't the same coach!

It's true. Just like the coach I described in Chapter 10 who tried to do too much across multiple abilities, your coach may be able to identify what it is you are lacking and point you in the direction of someone else who can help you. You aren't looking for one coach who does everything, you're looking for multiple coaches who can help you get better across all of your abilities and add insight into areas you might be overlooking.

Start Bringing Up Your Weak Abilities

This is where the real "work" begins. This is where you look to create the well-rounded athlete you need to become in order to be able to withstand the most challenges and take advantage of the most opportunities. This is where you stop doing what is easy and start working on the Qualities you need to improve to the next level, and most importantly, to the level beyond that.

Imagine a stool that you would sit on and each one of the legs represents the abilities you currently have. If all of the legs are the same length but short, meaning they are equal but poorly developed, you can probably sit on that stool but it will be really low and you wouldn't be able to see too much. Let's say one of the abilities is really well developed and therefore long, but compared to the other legs that are short, you might be able to sit on the stool and balance on that one developed leg but it's going to be wobbly and you're probably going to fall off eventually.

If all three legs are well developed and evenly developed you're going to be able to sit on that stool, you could probably even stand on it because it's nice and solid.

It's All About Qualities

The best athletes have the appropriate qualities to succeed long term. What is a "quality"? Speed. Flexibility. Strength. Power. Coordination. Agility. Power. Explosiveness. These are all qualities that fall under the Physical Abilities that we spoke about in Chapter 8.

You have probably gotten by to this point relying on certain qualities and completely ignored others. Or maybe you were aware of the other qualities you need to address but just haven't taken the time to do so.

Take for example a soccer player kicking with the same foot all the time. Growing up, this soccer player got a better result kicking with his right foot than his left. Even in games, if he had a wide open shot at the net with his left foot, he would try and cut the ball back to his right foot in hopes of getting the same opportunity at the cage. It rarely came.

Now, this athlete has a few thousand kicks with his right foot and has all of the consequences that gives him. Strong left quad and weak right quad. Tight hamstrings and tight hip issues. Poor coordination with his right hip and a tight ankle. Along with a host of other issues.

Now it doesn't matter if you're a soccer player or not. Every athlete in every sport has a similar story of focusing on their strengths until their weakness becomes an issue that they might not be able to overcome.

This is only an example of a Physical Ability, but what other qualities within your Abilities are holding you back? Do you keep making the same errors in judgement tactically or technically? Maybe you're like a pitcher relying on his fastball when he really needs a curveball.

Take a moment to write down what qualities you know you need to improve but have avoided until now:

```



```

Motivation Comes From Within

At the time that I write this I have two young kids. Quinn, my son, is twelve and my daughter, Makena, just turned nine. You'd think having a dad who was an Olympian and an All-american would mean that they are little sports ninja's.

Um...not really.

As an athlete, I understand that motivation has to come from within. It's true whether you're seven years old or eighteen years old. And it's only something I think you realize when you really get older.

The experience of having my own kids, and having been a coach now for twenty-years, has taught me that there are some major underlying principles that need to be taught to have success no matter what age you really start at and that's what this book is all about.

As I mentioned in the introduction, I'm an only child of two musicians and wasn't born with some genetic gift of athleticism. I'm not a gifted athlete. Now you may have been birthed by some freakishly athletically gifted parents, or are part of a family where lots of the members are involved in sports. This book is going to help you just as much as those who were more like me. It's the fact that I was not a gifted athlete that makes me an understanding Coach who can help you.

Over the years I was increasingly disappointed by coaches who had been elite athletes prior to becoming coaches. While they reached huge athletic heights there was a component of their success that they couldn't truly grasp let alone teach it to others. I'm reminded of an Olympic athlete I once knew who told a bunch of young female athletes who were going to a sports psychologist that they would have better success going to a "spa" and get their nails done than to go for that frou-frou stuff. He never used a sports psychologist in his career (although he probably could have used one) and his lack of understanding of the needs of young athlete was insensitive. These girls were really hurt by what this coach had said to them and ultimately many of them quit the sport.

Elite athletes aren't always great coaches. They are inspiring to young athletes because all a young athlete can really understand is that so-and-so was an Olympian, or so-and-so played in college. While those are great accolades to have, and they attract interest, the true art in coaching is understanding all of the tools that a young athlete needs to succeed. **I call it creating the Toolbox.**

When You're a Hammer, Everything Looks Like a Nail

I worked with a well-known strength and conditioning coach who had a saying , "When you're a hammer, everything looks like a nail." What he meant by that was, if you're a strength coach you tend to think the solution to most athletic problems is more strength. If you are a physical therapist the solution to most problems is more physical therapy. A Chiropractor, more chiropractic adjustments. You see where I'm going with that?

As an athlete, think of it like you are building a house. When you build a house you need a toolbox to build different parts of the house. There will be times you need a hammer, but there will also be times when you need a screwdriver, or a set of pliers. You'll need glue, and staples and maybe some paint brushes.

The point is that as you build your athlete "house" you're going to need different tools in your toolbox to make all this happen.

You have a foundation that needs excavating and concrete. You need wood and nails for framing the walls. You'll need carpet and flooring, cabinets and electrical work, and shingles to keep the rain out.

But everyone's house is different, and for most athletes who become great athletes they know they have a house, they just don't understand how to build it. What they end up doing is thinking, incorrectly, that every athlete should have the same house.

The goal of this book is to help you understand the whole process. As a not-so-gifted athlete, and someone who has gone on to coach other athletes who have become collegiate and Olympic athletes, I want to teach you the Toolbox approach. I want to help you understand that by gathering the right tools in your toolbox you can build a better house. If all you have are nails and a pair of of pliers, you're going to get yourself in trouble. My goal is to help you fill that toolbox with ideas and people and resources to help you build your house. Do not build someone else's house. Just focus on building your own house.

I tell people today that my mind, and my body, are the result of all of the good and bad coaches, physical therapists, trainers, chiropractors, strength coaches, doctors and psychologists who I've worked with over the years. Some were better than others and In the chapter called "Take 100% Responsibility" I shared with you why that all matters.

Hiring Coaches and Trainers To Improve Your Key Abilities

Note: If you have come right to this chapter and have NOT read the Three Key Abilities Chapter 8 then you will want to go back and read that chapter before you read this section on how to find the right coach.

For many athletes, they play their sport, they get better, they make the team, they move up, they make the next team and on and on. But since the year 2000 we have seen an incredible increase in the amount of money spent on coaches and trainers and psychologists for young athletes. Unfortunately, many athletes go about this the wrong way and just think that more playing and more coaching should equal better performance, but this isn't always the case.

The way to get better as an athlete is to work on your weakness and to maximize your strengths. **While your competitors will just do**

this randomly you will be going about it strategically.

The key, now that you know your Three Key Abilities, is to look at your Abilities and see where you are weak. The best way to do this is by sitting down with your main coach (or two coaches if you have more than one) and strategically look at how you train and compete. Determine what your weaknesses are and which ones you can realistically improve by taking into consideration your physiological age, your biological age, your training age, as well as your chronological age. When you take all of those into consideration, you should then be able to pinpoint areas that you need to work on and then...and this is the critical step...seek out people who can help you make those improvements. THAT is how you hire the right coach.

Take Their Advice And Use It!

Once you have found a coach that can help you improve your abilities, it's time to go take that advice and apply it! Don't just pick the ideas you like and just use those. Take it all. If you are injured and are trying to get a second opinion I totally respect that. But if you are healthy and you have sought the advice of someone you respect, now is the time to go train and apply the advice.

Set Your Autopilot And Listen To The Feedback

When a pilot sets the autopilot on a jumbo jet he inputs the destination he wants to go to and then sits back and relaxes, right? Not exactly.

When the autopilot is set on an airplane the sensors on the plane are constantly making adjustments to keep the plane on course. To the outside observer looking at the plane on a radar screen it may look like the plane is flying along without any problem. The truth is that the plane is more OFF course than on course and the computer is making adjustments along the entire route. Left on it's own the plane would be only on course for a second before winds and weather would knock it off course.

You are the same way. As an athlete you have a dream that you are chasing. You can see it. Feel it. Sometimes you can even taste it.

So you set off today to practice, or maybe to a game. What happens during and after that game? You get feedback.

The Two Types Of Feedback (And The Kind In Between)

There are two types of feedback. There's the feedback you get from winning and then there's the feedback you get from not winning. We don't really like losing but it provides valuable feedback for us. Many people fear losing so much so that parents and organizations sometimes play without scoreboards so kids don't feel bad about losing. But losing tells us that what we've been doing up to this point isn't working. Let's say you were winning for three quarters and then ran out of gas in the last quarter. That's valuable feedback telling you that some of what you've been doing is good, but there might be some things you need to reevaluate. The feedback will tell you to keep going and do what you've been doing. It may tell you that what's you've been doing is "sort of" working. Or the feedback may tell you to scrap your current plans and start over. Whether it is good or bad or somewhere in between, you've got feedback and it is your job to listen to it and make changes.

The faster you can receive feedback the sooner you can act on it. With technology getting faster and faster, the ability for an athlete to receive feedback is quicker than ever before. Whether you are wearing a heart rate monitor or watching video of your performance you have the ability to get additional feedback even in the middle of a performance. The opportunities for feedback are endless and you should welcome them all.

How NOT To Respond To Feedback

I consulted with a female soccer player who had this terrible response of crying whenever she received negative feedback. Can you imagine how all of her coaches felt? Going back to our plane analogy, can you see how crazy it would be if the plane just stopped flying if the autopilot said that a gust of wind had just blown her off course?

Feedback is just information. As human beings we tend to wrap that information in a blanket of emotions and feelings that either make us feel bad or feel good. But what we need to do is look at that feedback just as a computer would. Simply inputs of "0"s and "1"s that affect our output somewhere down the line. When an electrician wires a switch in the house and it turns on the wrong light he doesn't break down and cry and walk away and quit. He removes the bad wiring and rewires it for the result he wants.

You can't ignore the feedback either. If you are headed for the edge of a cliff and I tell you to turn the wheel, what happens if you ignore that feedback? You're going to drive off the cliff! But ultimately you need to trust the person who is giving you the feedback enough to listen and then take action.

You also can't get mad at the person giving you the feedback. Imagine if the plane got angry at the autopilot telling it to adjust its course? Saying thing like, "You never believe in me!" Responding to feedback by getting angry at the person giving it to you just makes the person giving you the feedback stop, which ultimately reduces your options for feedback.

I see this last example happen a lot between young athletes and parents who are their coach. What starts out as solid feedback ends up spilling over to the dinner table. And the car ride to the game. It's endless and doesn't stop which can create a lot of tension between a parent and a young athlete. So that is why you'll want to...

Decide How You Want The Feedback Presented

I remember going to my first Olympic games and seeing how the increased television coverage could really help an athlete. Instead of having two coaches on the track with radios and one coach with a video camera we now had fifty cameras on the track. You could basically see every inch of every run. Talk about feedback!

But to some of the athletes this was way too much feedback and not what they were normally used to. It was overwhelming and ended up pointing out so many flaws that an athlete could feel horrible instead of inspiring them to improve. That is where I learned that sometimes too much feedback can hurt you. There's a difference in some feedback and I could break it down to this...

Macro and Micro Feedback

When we think of feedback there is Micro feedback: like talking about a missed shot, or a poor throw. This type of feedback usually revolves around a Technical Ability or a Tactical Ability.

But there is also Macro Feedback. Feedback that looks on a Macro level is rarely used and it can be incredible. Questions that uncover Macro Feedback are questions such as: How are you feeling today? Instead of looking with a microscope we're looking with a larger lens. Using the plane analogy Micro Feedback is like looking at things from runway level while Macro Feedback looks from the 30,000 foot level. As athletes we can get stuck looking at things from the runway level, but having feedback from the 30,000 foot level can really change your perspective and give you tremendous feedback to improve your performance.

Ask For Feedback

Early on in my Olympic career I shattered a bone in my foot. Pretty depressed over the whole thing, I flew back to Boston where I was scheduled to see a Dr. Thrasher (seriously, the surgeon's name was Thrasher) who was going to help make me better.

The great thing about Dr. Thrasher, and why he came so highly recommended, was that he wasn't just going to cut me open. He was a real mentor, and a fan of athletes. He was a great counselor in the process of what I was about to go through and he was able to give me multiple opinions about what the best course of action was to be.

Someone who is a great counselor looks at you and your situation as a whole. Dr. Thrasher asked me questions such as, "What are your plans this year? Do you have any major competitions you need to be ready for fast or can you take more time? How is this injury going to affect other areas of your life?" He would help me decide what was the best course of action for me and not just look at me as another body with a broken bone in his foot.

People who can give you counsel don't just look at the symptom There are lots of people out there who can give you feedback. From your coaches to your parents to your doctor and physical therapists, there are many people out there who can give you feedback. Many of them, however, will keep their mouths shut for fear of making you angry or speaking out of line and telling you something that they think you might already know. The point is that you need to go out of your way and ask for feedback. Dr. Thrasher showed me what it was like to receive fantastic feedback. It was an example I used later in my sports life when I asked Coaches to present feedback to me in a certain way. Every Coach is different, but great coaches will work with you to help you reach your goals, and the way that they present their feedback can be incredibly important.

Once you get that feedback you need to listen. You need to accept or reject the feedback and make adjustments and keep moving forward accordingly.

Seek Counsel And Not Opinion

When you are looking for feedback and advice on your path towards your athletic goals, it is very important that you seek "counsel" and not just the opinion of others.

There are plenty of people out there who will give you their opinion on anything, even though they have no earthly idea what they are talking about. Think about when people comment on politics, or the price of gas, or the war in the middle east. Lots of people will happily share with you their opinion on those things but many of those people have no solid basis other than their own biases and what they've heard on the news.

But someone who can give you counsel is a completely different story.

Someone who can counsel you on the decisions you need to make will help you take opinions and either help you choose between them, or help you find a solution that is a combination of some or all of those opinions.

For instance, if you break your leg and you go to one doctor and he tells you that you need to amputate, that's an opinion. So you go to a second doctor and he gives you a second opinion that maybe, with some specialized therapy, you can save the leg. Those are two drastically different opinions.

Hopefully, your coaches are great counselors, but this isn't always the case. Coaches can sometimes be more technically focused and not tactically focused. They need to have you be successful so they can be successful so sometimes their own bias comes into play. Think of the coach who wants you to play your sport year round and give up that other sport that you love. If they tell you you should quit playing hockey and only play lacrosse, that's an opinion. Someone who can give you counsel will ask you how much you love it and how playing other sports may be actually helping your other sports as well as a million other potential questions that help you find the right solution for you.

Only You Can Give Yourself True Counsel

Everyone will have their opinions and some are more justified than others. But it is you and only you who can truly take the opinions you get from everyone on your support team and decide what is right and what isn't. As an athlete we are bombarded with the opinions of others. Everyone from the Gatorade commercial on TV ("Fuel? Water?") to your parents. It's a never ending stream of advice and you have to filter out the good from the bad.

Sometimes you may not like the counsel of others but it may be the one thing you really need to hear and need to take action on. That's not a fun place to be but if you are not fixed in your ways, and that opinion can be presented to you in a way that makes sense, and you can see it improving your performance and helping you reach your goals, then you will be ok and will be able to move forward. But if you're set in your ways, no opinion will help you.

Over the years I've had athletes hire me for consulting only to completely not want to hear what I have to tell them. They are set in their ways and really just want someone to confirm their current false beliefs. Don't be that kind of athlete.

So as you navigate through your athletic life you will need to hear these opinions. Put them in your mental library and take what is useful and discard what is not. When you need it, seek outside counsel from someone who you can trust and move forward accordingly.

Hiring A Coach For Your Physical Abilities

When I was looking to make a comeback in the sport of luge I got online and started learning about strength and conditioning. I had been around strength and conditioning coaches my whole life at that point but made a very interesting discovery: I wasn't all that strong.

It might seem odd that with all the training I had done in my life that I wasn't strong physically, but that was in fact the case. All the years I spent involved with Olympic sport and I realized something very profound...that coaches can get into their own mental traps.

Whatever coach you are working with, I want you to understand this: **they will be teaching you the best of what they know. And you are doing the best with what you know.** What you know has gotten you this far, but to go further you must learn more. That is why you can find a coach who can take you so far, and then you will have to find a coach who can take you further. And while this may sound easy, some people want to work with the elite coach who has already trained Olympians, but depending on where you are in your training this may not be the right choice. That Olympic level coach might not be great for the young athlete. No matter what your age, the bottom line is you need to find a coach who can help you get the most out of your training for the quality you need the most **right now**.

So what qualities are there to work on?

Strength, Speed, Endurance, Mobility, Flexibility, Etc.

Every sport requires a component of each of the big three: Strength, Speed, and Endurance, but it's important to also consider your ability to move over a wide range of motion with strength and stability over that range of motion.

What you need will depend on your sport and who you talk to about your sport. If you are aware of the "hammer/nail" approach you will want to take many opinions into consideration. This is why having a coach or a mentor who can help you by being a good counselor to you will make the greatest effect.

It used to be that the overall consensus to training was that if you built a big base of endurance that you could then rise to a peak working to strength and power. But we know now that even in endurance sports an endurance athlete can drastically improve by getting stronger.

While it is out of the scope of this book to get into all of the training modalities that are available, the goal of this section is to help you find a coach who can help you with your physical ability. And when thinking about this topic it's very important that you give a program time. Consider this...

The Best Program Is The One You Are Not On

As you learn more and more about training your mind will start to wander to other plans, programs and athletes and what they are doing and who they are doing them with. Just remember this, you must give your training time to have an effect on you. You must have patience. Whether that's three months, six months, a year (it all depends on your goals) you need to allow your body time to adapt to the new training methodology and your body's adaptation to it.

Also, you must realize that your ability to recover will also have an affect on any training program you seek out. This is why I'm not a fan of training teams in a group because while they can be fun team building opportunities there are other ways to do that. Training is an individual project that is only limited by your physical, mental and economical resources.

Finding A Coach For Your Tactical Abilities

In my experience, I have found that most sport coaches fall into the tactical category. Many sport coaches you may have been exposed to when you were young are volunteers and have full-time jobs, families, and other obligations in addition to their responsibility as coaches. These requirements put a big drain on a coach's time and can limit his ability to learn more than what he currently knows. Even many paid coaches are what I would describe as Tactical Coaches. These are the coaches who focus primarily on the X's and O's of the game and really wish that all of their athletes could (depending on the sport) catch, throw, run, jump and otherwise be faster and stronger than they currently are.

A Tactical Coach will be able to tell you where to go and when to get there but won't be able to really tell you how to get there. Tactical coaches can be really good for athletes who have natural physical abilities and who are relatively new to a sport. These athletes already have the physical component down but need help with understanding the overall approach to the game. Athletes who transition from track and field, basketball, and rugby to the NFL often spend lots of time with tactically based coaches so that they can "catch up" to the rest of the team in hopes that once they catch up they will surpass those athletes because of their physical abilities that they developed in other sports.

Finding A Coach For Your Technical Abilities

Every sport has a heavy technical component at the highest levels. A quarterback in football needs to work on their overall release of the ball in order to be the most accurate passer. A golfer can spend all day analyzing his or her swing because the smallest technical improvement can make huge differences in ball flight and distance. There are even fishing coaches (Wut!!) to teach you the technical side of a sport that looks pretty straight forward. The truth is that all sports at the highest level get more and more complicated; and while the overall level of improvement might be small, the smallest improvement can make a huge difference.

You probably have heard commentators on TV say, "She's technically sound." or, "When he gets tired his technique breaks down." These are examples of how great technique can really affect a performance.

In my experience, great Technical Coaches have years of experience behind them unless they have developed some sort of revolutionary improvement. Technical Coaches have a great understanding of how the body allows an athlete to apply their expertise through an implement. Let me explain that: an athlete applies their physical ability THROUGH something. It might be a stick, a racquet, a pair of skis, or a ball.

Let's talk about a baseball pitcher as an example: a baseball pitcher uses his body to hurl a ball toward home plate. Ideally, that pitcher can do things with his body that allow him to throw the ball really fast, or make it curve, or make it wobble like a knuckle ball. A Technical Coach in this case would teach this athlete how to grip the ball and then how to use his body to create the proper technique to propel the ball to home plate with the proper movement on the ball.

A Technical Coach needs to have an understanding of body mechanics in order to do this. They might not know every muscle in the body or how they work, but in the case of the pitcher, the Technical Coach would need to be able to identify that an athlete's shoulder was tight or their hips were tight, or their back was weak, etc. That Technical Coach might then send that athlete to a Strength and Conditioning coach or a Physical Therapist who can help the athlete get their body into the position they need to in order to create the desired result.

A Technical Coach is the coach who helps you refine the "doing" of your sport. An athlete who is "technically sound" has the ability to perform at a high level while an athlete who is technically sloppy will ultimately make mistakes that keep them from performing at their best. Be sure to find Technical Coaches who can help you perform at your best.

Don't Fall In Love With Your Coach

While the Coach/Athlete relationship can be a very special one, it can also hold some athletes back. I have seen this again and again where athletes are loyal to a coach who they have worked with for a very long time. These aren't romantic relationships but they can have all of the parts and pieces and they act just like a couple in a romantic relationship would.

The challenge comes when the Coach is set in his or her ways. They may take a "this is the way I always do it" approach. It can ultimately hurt an athlete if the coach isn't doing everything he or she can to help that athlete get better.

There are many coaches out there with tremendous egos who get extremely possessive of their athletes. They are very territorial and get upset when other coaches come in to their area and have an effect on their athletes. It's not a good situation to be in if you are the athlete.

In every program I have ever been a part of, I tell my athletes to go out and seek additional information that can help them improve their abilities. Then, I tell them, to come back to me if and when they find any information they think will help them so we can discuss it. I first started doing this as a young lacrosse coach in a relatively new program in Bedford, Massachusetts. I would spend all spring coaching and then most of the kids wouldn't pick up a stick until the following spring. I wanted my athletes to go to lacrosse camps in the summer so they could a) keep playing, b) learn something new, and c) hear the same things I was saying during the season by college coaches to help reinforce my message and to invite buy-in to what I was teaching. There is a saying that a rope with three strands is unbreakable, but a rope with two strands can be broken. When the coach/athlete relationship is just two strands it can be broken, but when an athlete proactively seeks additional information (the third strand), and can then share and discuss that with his or her coach, a productive relationship gets even stronger.

Now I'm not saying you shouldn't trust your coach or develop a deep bond with your coach. That's not what I'm saying at all. What I'm encouraging you to do is to always view your relationship with your coach on a professional level and be confident that the relationship that you have is continuing to help your abilities to improve.

Just recently I worked with an athlete who loved his Technical Coach. Every month of the year this coach had some sort of program going on. It didn't matter if it was during the season or during the off-season, there was always a new program to join and as a loyal athlete he always signed up for what the coach had to offer.

After assessing this athlete and identifying what his needs were I recommended that he not sign up for the next program and let himself recover from a very long season and to heal up some nagging injuries. The father told me, "We can't do that. We always do Coach's programs." I said, "Yes, but are you just blindly signing up for his programs or are you looking at them strategically and understanding how they are helping or hurting your son?"

With that one question there was silence. They hadn't ever thought of it like that and I could sense that the family was torn between "disappointing" Coach or possibly being open to the fact that maybe his next program wasn't going to be in the best interest of their athlete.

These aren't always simple decisions. There are lots of dynamics going on but one dynamic that should never come into play is guilt. You should never feel guilty by not doing a coaches program, or be guilted into participating. It should serve a strategic purpose in developing your abilities and if it doesn't, you shouldn't do it.

You Will Probably Outgrow Your Coach

Every coach has their knowledge limitations and while many coaches want to have an impact on your performance as long as they can, the truth is there is usually a point where a coach needs to pass you on. Perhaps it's to another coach, another program, or even another sport! Seriously. As young athletes with long term athlete development understanding, you may find that your skills and abilities better suit you for a completely different sport. But that's the topic for another book altogether.

Your coach has abilities just as you do, and there may come a time when you need to move on. You may see a team with better equipment. You may catch a glimpse of an athlete doing one unique exercise that your coach never has you do, and because of that you think your current coach isn't good enough. That other coach over there must be better. That may or may not be true. Just remember that the grass tends to always be greener on the other side of the fence, until you jump the fence.

On more than one occasion I have encouraged athletes to try other coaches and programs. Why? Because I know that once they are over there they will realize that the work we were doing together was more appropriate for that athlete and that they will come back. Every time I have done that the athlete has come back, and when they do, they are more committed than ever.

I share these stories with you not to convince you to stay with your current coach, but to understand that there may be a time you do need to move on. Sometimes it just happens naturally. You move from high school to high school or high school to college. Or you move from your town to go train at a High Performance Center elsewhere. As part of the natural evolution of your development, there will come a time when it's right to move on from your coach.

What To Do When Your Coach Leaves (Your team, your club, you, etc)

Over time, an athlete can become pretty attached to a coach. And coaches can become pretty attached to their athletes, too. But occasionally, for whatever reasons, both personal and professional, a coach may have to move on, which can create a pretty big void for an athlete.

That being said, an athlete now must find a replacement coach to help them reach their athletic goals. While it can get very emotional with all of the five stages of grief coming into play (denial, anger, bargaining, depression and acceptance) an athlete still needs to look at their Three Key Abilities that I outlined in "Chapter 8" and find a new coach who can continue your development.

Today, more than ever, we can stay connected with a coach over incredible distances. Depending on what you are working on with that coach a simple Skype call once a week can work wonders. I work with clients all over the world via Skype and email and text with great results. If you'd like to work with me to help you improve your game just reach out. My contact info is in the Appendix at the end of this book.

When a coach leaves you it can actually be a blessing in disguise. As an athlete it is very easy to get very comfortable with a coach. Your coach may have become so comfortable in their position and with working with you that they no longer strive to make you better. They may not push you as hard because they know you too well. A new coach will look at you with fresh eyes and maybe some new tools in his or her toolbox. They will start fresh with a new assessment and new evaluations. They will infuse you with new energy and maybe even tick you off when they identify past mistakes your old coach was making with you.

Whatever it is for you, losing a coach isn't necessarily a bad thing. It can, in fact, be a good thing to your development so don't take it as only a bad thing if, and when, it happens.

Conclusion:

As the Athlete CEO your job is to create a toolbox of people who can help guide you and mentor you, providing feedback to help you improve the qualities you need to improve your game. Your role is to constantly be asking for feedback and then applying it to your game. Seeing how it helps you improve and how you can continue to improve. It is a never ending loop you will be a part of as long as you are a competitor.

When you receive feedback it's important to remove the emotion that can surround it. Don't take it personally. Just apply it, and see how it works for you. Feedback that works for you may not work for others, and the reverse is also true. What works for others, may not work for you.

If you compete long enough, Coaches will move on. They may

retire or move and you will have to adjust and find new coaches. Don't worry, this can be one of the best things to happen to you. The addition of fresh thinking to your training can be incredibly valuable so don't fear the move if and when it happens.

Watch This Video

www.AthleteSpecific.com/
creating-your-toolbox

Take Action With These Steps:

- Take out your journal and make a list of all of your weakest Abilities.

- Now make a list of coaches, other athletes, books, videos and other resources you can learn from to bring up those weakest abilities.

- Take action and make contact with one of those resources, now. And then make a plan to take action on additional resources that can help you.

Chapter 13
Don't Set Goals
Set Projects

"You can't accomplish a goal without accomplishing the small action steps necessary to complete it. Therefore focus on the small achievable projects that make your goals come true."

Jonathan Edwards
Olympian, Author, Speaker.

When it comes to the world of business and high performance the conversation usually heads toward the idea of setting goals. And while goals can be a pretty powerful thing, for eighty percent of the population people roll their eyes and think goals are the most boring thing on the planet.

As an athlete I set goals, but looking back on it I don't think it was the right focus. I set goals like, "I will make the US Olympic Team"

If I asked you to write down your goals you might set goals like:

"I will make the Varsity this spring"

Or.

"We will win the state championship"

But when you think of it, you really have no control over those goals at all. In fact, there are so many factors outside of your control that focusing on them can actually get you in trouble. Now, these aren't the same as affirmations that I will teach about in Chapter 17. Goals are a little different as I'm about to show you.

While people may disagree with me on the idea of not setting goals for athletes and not having that be their primary focus, what everyone will agree with is that in order to achieve a goal you need to become a different person than who you are now. That is a fact. If you aren't achieving your goals right now then you are not the person who is capable of achieving those goals. Yet.

So this is where I tell athletes...

Step One: Who Must You Become?

There is a great saying that revolves around the ideas of goals and dreams that says: **it isn't really the goal or the dream that is as important as who you must become in order to make those goals and dreams come true.** Let's say I want to try a sport like triathlon. Most people who hit their thirties and forties think that they need to do a triathlon to stay in shape and get fit so I'll use that as my example. The goal in this case is to complete a triathlon which isn't just one sport, it's three.

So the question then becomes: **Who must I become** in order to make that dream of competing in a triathlon come true. That is the base layer, the underlying question that needs to get answered. Now if I just wrote down the goal "I will compete in a triathlon next year in Hawaii" I'm probably not going to make it happen because I don't really understand what it takes to compete the goal. I need to understand the goal more fully. In fact, you could call it just a dream at this point because there is no real understanding of it at all.

Now if I went outside and went out for a run I would have done one thing correctly to make that dream come true which was to get out the door and take action by going for a run. But this is where people go really wrong on this and they don't break it down any further. By going for a run today, and going for a run tomorrow, and then going for a bike ride and a swim they are doing the things that a triathlete does but they aren't fully focusing on who they need to become to make that goal come true.

To understand who you must become you must first look at the athletes who compete at the level you wish to compete at and identify what you think you need to do in order to be successful. To use the triathlon example I would look at athletes competing at the level I want to compete at and think: "Well, they all have a body fat under eight percent. Most of them are quite tall (6'). They all own bikes that cost around $13,000. They all wear heart rate monitors. They train X amount of time per week. They go for massages once a week. They wear a certain brand of sneaker and a certain brand of bike shorts. When they run their VO2 is around XXX. They finish the swim portion in around 50 minutes. I would then look for training programs and coaches who could help me create a program for myself and my current abilities and then look to ramp up the daily habits to make it all happen. What I'm doing here is getting the bigger picture of what it takes to be a triathlete. The next step is to break this dream down further.

Step Two: Set Projects Around Your Abilities

So back in Chapter 8 we discussed the three Key Abilities and now is when they really come into play. As we look to identify who we must become we need to break that down into projects based around the three key abilities. We have our Physical Ability, our Technical Ability and our Tactical ability. Once we get an idea of who we must become in order to reach our dream of becoming that elite athlete we must break it down into smaller projects that we can then work on day to day.

The Physical Ability Project: This is where most athletes tend to focus last. They tend to think, "Well, If I was just bigger/faster/stronger/quicker (any of the "er's") they would make the team. Well, if that's true, then you need to set a project around the aspects of your Physical Ability that need to improve. You could have projects based on your flexibility or your maximal strength. Maybe your endurance needs work or your sprinting ability. Maybe your balance or your mobility needs work. Whatever it is you need to improve you need to write that project down and set it as something you will work on. "I will improve my VO2 max by 5% by losing ten pounds of bodyfat." Etc. What Physical Abilities do you need to improve? List those projects in the box below.

List your Physical Ability Projects here:

The Technical Ability Project: Let's say you're a golfer and your short game needs work. Or your putting. A project might be to improve your scoring average within 100 yards of the hole. Or let's say you're a hockey player and your stick skills need to improve. A project might be to improve your stick skills in tight situations. Or maybe it's something really small like working on your ability to relax unnecessary muscles while other muscles are working. What Technical Abilities do you need to improve? List those projects in the box below:

List your Technical Ability Projects here:

The Tactical Ability Project: Let's say you're a football quarterback and you need to improve your game when the pocket collapses and you need to scramble to your left, you would set that as your project to improve that aspect of your game so that you become a better quarterback in those situations.

Or you are a soccer player and you resist turning the ball up the outside of the field. Or maybe...maybe...when you get in front of the head coach you freeze and play poorly. What Technical Abilities do you need to improve? List those projects in the box below:

List your Tactical Ability Projects here:

Step Three: Set Projects Around Your Layers

It's easy to work on the Physical, Technical and Tactical Ability projects. It's fun. It's easy to understand and usually has very tangible results. Lift the weights and feel yourself get stronger. Change your grip and see the ball go in a different direction. Look the defender off and see the space on the field open up. Little changes can make very big results happen fast.

But where some of the biggest improvements can happen comes from working on your Layers. Improving on your Belief and your Life Skills and improving your Resources can make massive change. While the work on your Abilities can be a linear, step by step, progression; the work in your layers can be exponential.

The Belief Project: Remember the "glue" that holds it all together? Do you need to work on your Belief? Belief in yourself? Belief in your ability? Maybe a project you need to put into motion has to do with working on your mental game by working with someone like me. Or maybe you can find an older athlete mentor who can help you understand the nuances of your game better.

List your Belief Projects here:

The Life Skills Project: Are you hopelessly late for everything? Do you have work that never seems to get done? Is your equipment a mess and all over the place? Maybe you need to set a project to improve your time management and organizational skills.

List your Life Skills Projects here:

The Resources Project: Need a job? Or a sponsor? Looking to create a business to fund this whole thing? Maybe you need to submit an application for a grant for equipment. What can you do to increase your resources?

List your Resources Projects here:

It's All Possible

As you go through these projects you must believe that it is all possible. No matter what you have done before. No matter who has told you no. No matter who has told you that their drunk uncle Louie tried it once and didn't make it. None of it matters because you are ready for a new approach. A new paradigm. You have me as your coach and this book as your resource.

Shake off the past. Your results and the thinking that caused them are no longer relevant for you. You have a new way of thinking. Like taking off an old pair of ratty jeans and putting on a new pair. Sure, they may not feel as comfortable as that old pair you've been wearing but you know that once you give that new pair some time to break in they're going to feel awesome and look great too.

Conclusion:

It's easy to get into the false comfort of setting goals. Sure, goals are great. They help you set the vision for where you want to go but where the rubber meets the road is the place that projects are set. Those projects are the combination of ideas that will help you reach your goals.

Set projects for each of your Abilities. Improving your Physical Ability can be a project as well as for all of your other Abilities. Don't forget your Layers too. Improving your Belief can be a project. Heck, just overcoming challenges that you will face improving your other Abilities will increase your belief. By creating projects and then completing these projects one by one, you will reach your goals.

Watch This Video

**www.AthleteSpecific.com/
dont-set-goals-set-projects**

Take Action With These Steps:

- Take out your journal and write down three goals you'd like to reach for each of your three Abilities and each of your three Layers.

- Now break down each goal into a project. Do you want to run faster next summer? What Project do you need to put together to make that happen. Do you need to find a coach? Buy some running shoes? Buy a book? Break that project down into concrete steps you can complete.

- Now make a list of action steps you are going to take to complete those projects. Do you need get on the phone? Get a phone number? Call someone who can help you get that number? What is the first step you need to take?

- Now take those steps. Don't delay. Do something...now.

Chapter 14
Goal Getting 101

"Setting goals is the first step in turning the invisible into the visible."

Tony Robbins
American author, entrepreneur, philanthropist
and life coach.

Josh always talked about playing Junior "A" Hockey. Now if you're in the US, and you don't play hockey, you might not know that Junior hockey is, in fact, a big deal. In Canada, hockey is the number one sport in popularity and playing "Junior A" has become a big goal for a lot of people.

Josh would always tell me, "I just want to play Junior A. I just want to play Junior A."

Well guess what happened. He made the Junior A team. And in his first game something incredible happened...

In his first shift he was checked into the boards and blew out his knee and had a double compound fracture of his lower leg. He never played hockey again.

Harsh? Yes. Unfair? Maybe. Expected? Some might say, yes.

Let me explain...

Many parents are reluctant to help their young athletes set big goals for fear that they might be disappointed if they don't reach them. It's a modest approach and one that really bothers me as a coach. This is one of the worst forms of "love" I see as a coach. And if you are an athlete reading this ,and your parents haven't read this section, I don't want you to think badly of your parents. Not in the slightest. But I think it's important to understand that in some ways, trying to keep your athlete from being disappointed is one of the worst things a parent can do.

You see, sports is disappointing every...single...day. We constantly put ourselves in positions to be dissapointed so that we can work harder on our skills so that the next time we put ourselves in that situation we won't be disappointed.

So what happens as a byproduct of this type of thinking is that athletes set, what I call, **Ladder Goals**.

A ladder goal works like this: "Well my goal is to make (input next logical team/event/trip/tournament/etc). And when that happens then I'll set my next goal." (Which would be the next rung higher on the ladder.)

What an athlete is really saying is, "I don't want to **sound cocky**, and I don't want to **get my hopes up** only to have them come crashing down so I'm going to set this small 'stepping stone' goal, and then once I get there, I'll set the next goal.

While I believe that this type of thinking can work, occasionally, for the most part it really limits how an athlete can grow. It stifles potential in an effort not to disappoint. The ironic thing is that in an effort to avoid disappointment this approach usually leads to disappointment.

It also limits vision and it severely restricts the introduction and adherence to new habits that will lead to great success.

Set Big Goals and The Little Goals Will Take Care of Themselves

So that hockey athlete who blew out his knee and shattered his leg? Did he wish for that to happen? No. Did he reach his goal? Yes, yes he did.

But what if he set a goal like, "I want to have a long and successful career as a professional hockey player?" What do you think would have happened then?

Now this is a bit of a trick question. Right about now you're probably thinking, "Well yeah, he could have said that but still broken his leg." You are correct however when you set big goals you attract different people, ideas, environments and experiences to you that can help you reach your goal but also avoid bad experiences. With bigger goals you get exposed to better people and usually people with more experience. You're exposed to a better level of thinking and also a better level of intensity. This carries over into every aspect of your training and competing, and in Josh's case, would have kept him from getting injured.

In the example of this hockey player, he just barely made that Junior team. In fact, he made the last cut and because he was the low man on the totem pole the coach put him on a line that was to go up against the other team's "goon" line. (For lack of a better term). It was the other team's dirtiest players. These were the fighters and the players who were put out there just to wreak havoc on the other team.

Josh wasn't a player like that. He wasn't a goon. He was solid, and we had worked hard to make himself a solid athlete, but even the best coach can only prepare you so much against another player who plays dirty.

Josh's goal was to make that team and instead of thriving and being one of the top kids, his goal was a survival goal that ended up putting him into a bad situation and he payed the ultimate price.

I tried my best to get Chris to set higher goals. Those higher goals would have forced him to set better habits, and from better habits come better results.

Better Goals Force Better Habits

What are your current goals? Do you have any or are you just going with the flow and seeing how things turn out? For most athletes they have no goals. They show up to the next practice usually putting away their iPhone after having watched "fail" videos on the car ride there. They don't start to think about practice until they start putting on their equipment.

When you set goals you immediately put yourself into a different state. Let me help you with this so you can try these on for size:

Weak Goals	Strong Goals
"I'm just hoping to make the team"	"I will lead the team in scoring."
"I will be a starter this season."	"I will have a long, successful career as a professional in my sport."

"I will practice just as hard as my teammates."	"I will be the fittest athlete in every game I play in. No one will out work me."
"If I play my best I will be happy."	"I will perform the most difficult skills in my age category."

S.M.A.R.T. Goals Suck

When it comes to setting goals, many experts will tell you that you must set SMART goals. This stands for:

Specific
Measurable
Attainable
Realistic
Timely (or set against a timeline)
And while this is a nice idea in the world of business I find that for athletes SMART goals don't always resonate with them and here's why...

...they just don't FEEL good.

Many SMART goals in the world of sports are out of your control. Like saying, I'm going to finish in the Top Five in my next event. Or, I'm going to win the 100 meter dash next summer. While these sound like good goals you can't really control the outcome because there are other people involved. You have no idea what they are going to do on race day.

And while I have set SMART goals for myself in the past, I like to get my athletes to set SMART Habits to reach their goals.

S.M.A.R.T. Habits Rock

SMART Habits are habits that are Specific and Measurable and Attainable and Realistic and Timely. For example:

Let's use dieting for an example. Let's say that an athlete and his coaches have decided that if the athlete were to lose five pounds of body fat that it would help to increase his race performance. The next race is in three months. This gives the athlete plenty of time to shed those unwanted five pounds. While the goal here is to lose five pounds the REAL goal is to win the race. The goal to win the race is not a SMART goal but the goal to lose five pounds IS. Here's why...

While the goal to win the race might sound SMART, it fails in a couple of instances. Is it Specific? Sure it is. Is it Measurable? Yes, most definitely. You either win or you lose. Is it Attainable? Who knows? In this case it's a bit of a stretch to want to win this race, but attainable is not something that this athlete has done yet so let's say "no" it isn't attainable. Is it Realistic? Who cares! This is why I hate SMART goals. No one ever got anything accomplished who went for "realistic." (More on that in a minute).

Finally, is this goal Timely? Yes. It's an event, on a specific date. It's going to happen and then it's over. The athlete either hits the goal or they don't.

"Realistic" Goals Are Horrible

Realistic: Let's talk about realistic for a minute. In my opinion a Realistic goal is something that you know can happen. You've already done it before or it's so darned easy you know you're going to make it with your eyes closed. A goal like this involves no "stretch" at all. As an athlete we need to always be pushing our envelope. We need to be on the edge of our performance in order to exceed our earlier results. One of my favourite posters given to me by one of my earliest Olympic coaches said, "Only those who risk going too far can possibly find out how far they can go." I love that quote because it reminds us that as athletes we need to be pushing things just a bit. Now, that doesn't mean you ski off the edge of the cliff not knowing where you're going to land. Not being "realistic" doesn't mean being "stupid." That's not my point. I just don't feel that setting "realistic" goals means much.

Setting Realistic Habits.
The Key To Goal Attainment

Where SMART goals matter, and where being Realistic matters, is when you adopt the right habits to reach your goal. Take our five pound fat loss goal. Here are some of the habits that make that happen.

- Allow pizza and soda to one night per week.

- Complete four, sixty-minute sessions of Zone 2 Cardio per week.
- Two High Intensity Sprint sessions per week.
- No dairy. No gluten.
- Get seven and a half hours of sleep per night.
- Four technical sport sessions per week.
- Adhere to this program for twelve weeks.

Now these are just some of the habits an athlete might adopt to reach this goal. By no means are they all of the steps and athlete might take, nor do all of the steps need to be taken to have results. The specifics don't matter as much as the SMARTness of the new habits.

Are they Specific? Yes
Are they Measurable? Yes
Are they Attainable? Yes
Are they Realistic? Yes
Are they Timely? Completely

So let's talk about if these habits are Realistic? In this case, there's nothing unrealistic about adhering to these new habits. Many of these habits are just eliminations of what may have been bad habits. This athlete may be a soda drinking fiend who loves pizza. Restricting his or her soda intake to one night a week is just a change of what bottle you pull out of the fridge. No real strain of time, just a little discipline.

Some of the new habits may be unrealistic for this athlete but I sure would hope not. For a high-performance athlete there is nothing on this list that is out of the ordinary.

There Are No Unrealistic Goals. Just Unrealistic Habit Potential

Now let's say this athlete had a week to lose the same twenty-five pounds. Their new habits might look like this:

1. No wheat, no dairy, no soda, no grain.
2. Eat vegetables and boiled chicken only.

3. Four hours of Zone 2 cardio per day.

4. Two, two-hour weight room sessions per day.

5. No water.

6. Sleep twelve hours per day.

Is this habit list realistic? It's doable. It's really hard, but it could be done if an athlete had enough motivation, but it's pretty intense. Is the goal realistic then? It's possible, but it's probably not going to happen.

I exaggerated the above list to prove a point. I want your goals to be exciting. I want them to feel good to you. Do they need to be realistic? No. How you feel will tell you if they are attainable or not. Many athlete have goals that to the outside observer aren't attainable, but they are so inspiring to the athlete that they adopt new habits that were originally out of the ordinary for them. Because they were inspired by the "unrealistic" goal the new habits helped them stretch and reach new heights.

Let's Talk About Discipline

I know a lot of very high performing athletes who aren't disciplined. But you've probably heard a lot of people say that, "In order to be successful in your life you need to have a lot of discipline!" Well, it's simply not true.

The truth is you just need enough discipline to adopt the habits necessary to reach your goal. That's it.

To be successful in anything, you will need to acquire new habits you get there. Your habits up until now have gotten you this far, but to go further you will need to adopt some new habits. You just need the discipline to adopt the new habits and then you will reap the results of those habits. That's it.

Set Goals That Make You Feel Good

You may have heard professional athletes talk about how they, "Dreamt of this in the backyard/driveway/pond/etc since they were little." They were dreaming about being that elite athlete on the biggest stage. The bottom of the ninth. The fourth quarter. Overtime. You name it, those Pro and Olympic athletes were envisioning competing on that field of play and it made them feel good.

They weren't thinking of their high school gymnasium.

When you let your heart run wild and you dream about being the best athlete you can be, I don't want you to limit yourself. I remember watching the Olympics and seeing myself standing on the podium at the Olympic games with a medal around my neck. When I watched lacrosse I thought about what it would be like to play in the National Championships making saves and hearing the crowd roar.

I didn't visualize making the Varsity soccer team at my high school.

Why? Frankly, it wasn't as exciting to dream about. But that's just me. Whatever your goal, I want you to think about the highest goal that feels the best to you. The one that gets you excited. Play with some thoughts in your head and feel your body. What gets you a little jittery? That is the goal you need to focus on first and I'm about to tell you why...

Adopt The New Habits To Help You Get There

The reason I want you to focus on your most exciting goal, the one that gets you the most juiced up, is because when we look to set new habits we will only set new habits to the amount we are excited about our goals. If it isn't exciting then sacrificing for a new habit probably isn't going to happen. You may have heard of this thing called "willpower". it's a concept that within you is a level of energy that allows you to make a good decision or a bad decision. Let me show you how that works exactly: There's a brand new bag of chocolate chip cookies in the cupboard. Your goal is to not eat any sugar this week, but you're really hungry. What do you do? Well, if your goal is exciting to you and it's right at the top of your mind, and that goal of losing weight and looking great and feeling good is inspiring, then you may reach for something else. But if the goal isn't really that exciting to you, and you're hungry, then you'll probably just open up that bag of cookies and quite possibly eat the whole bag.

This is why I want you to focus on the goals that feel good to you because it is the goal that feels the best to you that is the one you will apply your new habits. If you're not that excited you just won't follow through.

Adopt Habits To Reach Your Biggest Goals

I wrote earlier about how certain goals become a byproduct of shooting for even bigger goals. There's a really bad saying, "If you shoot for the moon and miss you're still one of the stars!" (I threw up a little bit in my mouth when I said that, but it's true!) When I was playing lacrosse my biggest goal was to play lacrosse at a Division One school. By adopting the habits I thought were necessary to become that D1 lacrosse goalie, making my high school varsity my freshman year was no problem. It was a byproduct of the bigger goal. If I adopt the habits of being a Division 1 lacrosse player I'm certainly going to be able to play varsity lacrosse in high school.

I learned this skill from a Sports Psychologist I worked with by the name of **Dr. Jerry Lynch**. Jerry is an amazing man and his book ***Thinking Body Dancing Mind*** really set the tone for me in sport. His book helped me solidify something I was pretty good at already and that was "Acting As If" I was already the athlete I wanted to become.

Jerry put me through an exercise where he had me think of the best athlete in my sport. I knew just the guy to think of. Jerry then asked me what habits I thought this athlete would follow on a daily basis to become the champion he was. I created a list of about thirty habits that I thought this athlete would follow. Some were easy to see, others I had to speculate. The fun thing about speculating is that you typically skip all the fun stuff and your speculation goes a little higher than what might actually be true. For instance, you might think that athlete who you really respect doesn't drink beer and only eats organic sushi for every meal. It may turn out that he's actually a micro-brew fan who likes doughnuts instead. The bottom line? Have some fun with it and cut yourself some slack. But not too much.

What To Do Once You Have Your Habit List?

Once I had a list of all of those habits I knew were followed by my world class example, I looked to incorporate them into my daily routine. I knew that if I could Act As If I was already that world class athlete I too would eventually become a similar athlete.

The good news about all of those habits is I could adopt all of them. (Except the beer drinking of course because I was a bit young.) I could adopt them...now. And that's where most athletes go wrong.

Most athletes think, "Well once I'm a better athlete THEN I'll adopt that habit." This is the wrong approach. You adopt the habits and then you become the athlete you want to become. You don't become the athlete without adopting the habits. I'll get into why you won't do that in a future chapter, but for now understand that the sooner you adopt as many of those habits as you think you should to become that world class athlete then you too will become world class.

Eliminate Old Habits That Keep You From Reaching Your Goal

It's easy to look at that habit list and think...well that's a lot to do! Well, yes it might be. But it's a lot if you only think that you're adding to everything you are already doing. Many of the habits you want to adopt will actually replace bad habits that you might be currently following. **What habits do you currently want to eliminate?**

Maybe you stay up too late on your phone texting your friends when you should be sleeping. Maybe you eat too many carbohydrates. Maybe you don't take advantage of study halls at school and this leaves you with too much homework when you get home.

Or maybe you're way too serious about it all and need to unwind sometimes. Some athletes I know have to schedule in "down" time to blow off steam and relax. (Other athletes I know take Down Time to an extreme) You'll find your way, so don't stress.

What I want you to do is take an inventory of your current habits and see which ones you can eliminate. This list will be pretty interesting and it might be best if you have someone you trust have a look at your list. They will probably be able to help you add a few, or discard some that they may feel are important to keeping you sane. Just know that most young athletes will err on the side of keeping too many of their bad habits. I mean you need to have that daily two hours of XBox don't you? (Kidding.)

Create New Habits To Complete Your Projects

Human beings are creatures of habit and this we know as an absolute truth. From when we get up in the morning to when we go to bed at night (To when we get up in the middle of the night to go take a leak!) we operate by habits. Habits are a way for our brain to be able to relax and focus on other things. Think about it for a moment, if you needed 100% focus and concentration when you drove a car you wouldn't have a lot of people who liked to drive with you. But because of habits you can drive while you talk to your friend in the back seat, change the playlist on your iPhone and sip a drink from the drink holder, all because of habit. (Be sure to read "Why Your Momma Ain't A Race Car Driver" in Chapter 15)

Throughout the day there are hundreds of things we do out of habit and the truth is that your habits have created the life you currently live. Athletically it is no different. Your habits of how you prepare, perform, rest, recover and everything in between has gotten you to where you are now but in order to become an athlete who is going to compete at the next level you need new habits to take you there.

Identify Your Current Bad Habits

One of the best way to help create new habits is to first identify your bad habits and get rid of them. Bad habits are like small anchors you are dragging around with you that are slowing you down and holding you back. If you can release those bad habits then you should start to see improvements right away just because you're cutting out the bad habits from your daily life. For most athletes they are constantly thinking about what they can add to reach their goals. More running, more time in the gym, and more calories are just some of the things athletes look to add when they might be better off thinking to lose the habits of bad food, not enough sleep, and too much training. You may have bad habits that fall under each of the Three Key Abilities. You will have physical habits, technical habits, and tactical habits and some of those habits will be bad.

Eliminate The Bad Habits And Replace Them With New Habits

The trick to getting rid of old, bad habits that don't serve you is to not just eliminate them but to replace them with new habits. As you set projects around your Three Key Abilities, and your Layers, you're going to want to identify old habits that limit you and replace them with bright shiny new habits that better serve your new goals.

Consider these examples: If your bad habit is to not get enough sleep at night, your new habit would be to turn off all electronics at a time when you can then go through your new routine of getting ready for bed so that your body slows down and gets ready for sleep earlier.

If you reach for a sugary energy drink your new habit would be to always carry a bottle of water with you so that it's easy to grab for the water and not the energy drink. Save the energy drink for the games, but even then, you may not need it if you are getting enough sleep.

If your bad habit is to be late for practice then your new habit might be to get ready for practice twenty-minutes earlier than you normally do so you're not always late. A new habit might also be to say that, "You are always early to practice." instead of saying "I'm always late to practice."

The One Sentence That Can Change Your Life

When you find yourself falling back into old habits here's a little trick you can tell yourself that will get you back to your new habits. Tell yourself, **"That's odd, I don't normally do that (insert bad habit)."**

Years ago I had a friend who had the really bad habit of smoking when she got stressed. One day I started saying to her, "That's odd, I didn't see you as a smoker." I would say this over and over again any time I saw her smoking or could smell the smoke on her clothing. Over time, she started to tell herself that same thing, "That's odd, I don't see myself as a smoker. I see myself as someone who takes care of my body." Eventually she quit completely because she could no longer see herself as a smoker because she truly believed now that she wasn't.

Adjust Your Habits For Better Project Results

As athletes we tend to work in three month chunks or micro-cycles and you really need to give your new habits that much time to take effect and make a change. In fact, studies by The Cancer Research UK Health Behaviour Center say that, on average, it takes 66 days to install a new habit and make it automatic. But since we are also looking to make changes in the body, those changes can take even longer. If I need to improve my sprinting speed a new three month habit of working maximally in the weight room twice a week may start to show its effects right away, but the results in my Tactical Ability might take longer to show.

The point is, don't discard new habits and fall back to your old habits too quickly. Remember, 66 days. For you it could be longer. There are obvious bad habits that you know you should eliminate now like eating twinkies after practice or watching too much television when you should be sleeping. Habits like visualization and affirmation usage or better communication skills with your coaches or teammates may take a little longer to take effect; but just be confident and know that those new habits will make you better if you just stick with them.

The skill you develop of eliminating old bad habits and adopting new ones will be a skill you take with you the rest of your life. You will also be able to help others who are stuck in old ways of doing and thinking by helping them identify bad habits that are holding them back and by replacing them with new habits that can change their life. And you can always use that sentence I told you about on them, "Hey, you don't look like someone who would do that?" Powerful stuff right there.

Make The Good Decision Once

Commit to a new set of habits and set a time to revisit them. Don't negotiate with yourself daily. If it's going to be three months, or a year, whatever, stick to it for that entire set of time and then decide again at the end of that time frame if you should stick with it or not.

Lots' of athletes will think of a new habit they should adopt and then make a snap decision on it. Like you heard that Lebron James takes extra shots before practice so you decide you should take extra shots before practice. It's a snap decision. "Sounds good to me!" you say. So you do it for a day and then you forget about it. It wasn't a good decision. It didn't really fit into any of your Projects and therefore it didn't stick.

But if you hear about a good habit and then think about it for a while, marinate in it overnight. Let it soak in. Write it down in your journal and then see if it still resonates with you in a day or two. If it does then NOW you can add it to your habits and it has a better chance of sticking with you. You're not going to be thinking about it every day saying, "Is this a good idea?"

Your Competition (And Your Teammates) Won't Be Doing This

But Jonathan, I don't know anyone else around me who is doing anything like this. My friends like to party and Skype all night. I don't want to miss out on that social time. I mean, they are my friends and I don't want to lose them."

Here is one of the hardest lessons I can possibly teach you. **Your true friends will show up when you commit to your dreams**. They will be the ones who support you. They might not understand what you are doing, fully, but they will support you. Remember, this dream is in YOU for a reason and not them. They can't see what you see or feel what you feel. Because of that, what you do will confuse them and may even push them away a bit. But your true friends will come back to you and understand, "Hey, this is your dream and not mine."

Your competitors probably won't do this either. It can be confusing when your competitors beat you and yet you don't see them taking these extra steps as I've asked you to do today. Trust in the process and know that they are on their own path doing their own things. They have been gifted with certain athletic talents and you have been blessed with your own. But these extra steps are reserved for the athletes who want to be world-class. Who want to take it to the next level. You should be happy knowing that the majority of your competitors aren't taking these steps and **it will only be a matter of time before your habits outpace their habits and your results start to beat their results.**

Conclusion

It's nice to set goals. Goals are important. But what makes goals happen are the habits you eliminate, and the habits you add to your daily life that make them happen.

Goals can seem unrealistic to some, but your goals will excite you for reasons only you can explain. And even then, explaining your goals to anyone other than yourself isn't recommended. Why? Because your goals are yours and yours alone and don't have to be explained. They resonate with you and feel good to you. That is all you need.

When you have a goal that feels really good to you, whether it is "realistic" or not, identify the habits you need to make that goal come true. And don't forget to eliminate some of your current habits as well. It's easy to get overwhelmed thinking that you need to add more and more habits to your "to do" list. By eliminating the habits that won't help you reach your new goal you create some space for the new habits you'll need to help you reach your goals.

Watch This Video:

**www.AthleteSpecific.com/
set-smart-habits**

Take Action With These Steps

- Take out your journal and write down the goals that get you the most excited.

- Think of the top athletes in your sport and make a list of the habits you feel they would follow to continue to be the best in your sport.

- Make a list of your current habits that would keep you from reaching those goals. Commit to eliminating one of those habits starting today.

- Now make a list of the new habits you feel you need to adopt to reach your goals. (Hint: many of these habits will come from that list you created above.)

Chapter 15
Some Thoughts On Practice

---

*"Practice does not make perfect.
Only perfect practice makes perfect."*

Vince Lombardi
Is considered one of the greatest coaches of all times. The NFL
championship trophy is called
"The Vince Lombardi Trophy"

Now this is when the work starts. All of the thoughts, considerations and planning come together and the work begins. This is where champions are made, or should I say, this is where the possibility of becoming a champion is created.

You could say that practice happens all the time. It's not just reserved for the times when you are in the gym, the weight room, or on the field. It's when you are writing in your journal, when you're at the physical therapist, or walking through the mall.

When you have big goals, you're going to be thinking about them all the time. When you go to bed, when you wake up, and when you're in the bathroom too. You will be consumed by it.

In this section we're going to talk about how to implement a philosophy of training and how to get through the days when you really don't feel like training. Let's get started:

Playing Like You Practice and Practice Like You Play

Many athletes treat practice and Game Day very differently. Game Day is a serious day when results matter and it's time to get focused while practices are less serious and not as important. While it's true that there is an up and down feeling to the pressures of game day's and practice days, you can't have your best performance on game day if you haven't stressed your body and mind hard enough in practice.

For example: many of the goalies I work with will have a certain save percentage on game day that is really their "grade" for their game. A hockey goalie may have a save percentage as high as 95% on game day and yet their save percentage in practice may actually be higher because the shots they take in practice aren't as challenging as the shots they face in a game. When they face more challenging shots in a game they are often taken by surprise and are bummed that they weren't able to make a save that they never saw in practice.

There are three variables to every practice that you can manipulate and they are:

1. **Intensity** - Go hard or go heavy.

2. **Volume** - Do a lot of work or a little.

3. **Frequency** - Do it often.

When you consider these three variables in relationship to having your best Game Day ever, you can adjust the intensity, the volume, or the frequency so that Game Day feels easy.

Everything you do is to prepare you for a successful Game Day.

It All Starts With Practice

Numerous stories abound of athletes in every sport getting to practice early and staying late to improve their skills. For many athletes the idea of getting there early and staying late first comes from just having a great love of the game, but over time the act of getting there early and staying late confirms that they are working more than their peers. The extra repetitions add up, and over time, what is only fifteen extra minutes at a practice adds up to hours of extra practice time.

Jordan Prysko was a lacrosse player I coached a few years ago and I'll never forget one day after practice when Jordan took a bucket of lacrosse balls and tried to shoot them right handed (he's a lefty) through the hole in the time keepers box in the hockey rink where we were practicing. Ball after ball, Jordan shot at a hole that was just slightly larger than the ball itself. Each shot got closer and closer and some even bounced awkwardly off the edge of the small circle. Over and over and over again Jordan took shots from a distance of about fifteen feet away. After about fifteen minutes Jordan finally hit one and turned with his hands raised in victory while he walked straight off the floor. (He didn't even pick up the balls!) But he didn't need to. The effort Jordan put in that day was indicative of his work ethic overall and is it any wonder why he was recruited to play, and given a scholarship to, one of the top lacrosse schools in the country? With a work ethic like that any coach would crawl on his hands and knees to recruit a kid like that. What type of time and effort do you put into becoming the athlete you need to become to be great?

Balance Is For Ballerinas

As I got hot and heavy into training to become an Olympian one of the first decisions I had to make was to leave school for half the year in order to travel with the National Team. And for lacrosse in the summers I would travel for weeks at a time attending camps and clinics to improve my game. It wasn't too long after making those decisions that friends and family would start to wonder why I was doing what I was doing. They'd say things like, "You're missing out on all the fun this summer! Take a break. You're going to burn out!"

And while concepts like Burn Out can be very real, remember that what people say about you says more about them than it does about you. People who cry that you'll get too tired, or that you'll miss out are basically saying that they value those things more than you do right now, and that's fine. That's their choice. The idea that there is some magical balance in this world is a myth and it's changing every day for everyone. I know people who can't sit at a desk longer than thirty minutes before they have to get up and go out to smoke a cigarette. I also know businessmen who work for three months straight but when those three months are done they are somewhere for a solid month going fly fishing. You will find your right ratio of training/competing versus rest and recovery. And as athletes we know that within a single week we need to train and recover, and over an entire year we have seasons where we compete hard, and other seasons where our training and competition is lighter. Whatever you need is strictly up to you the individual and no one else can impose their idea of "balance" on you.

So don't let them.

The Myth of the 10,000 Hour Rule

You may have heard this idea that you need to spend 10,000 hours at your sport to become really, really good at it. The 10,000 hour rule is based on a very famous paper that was published back in 1990 by a gentleman named Dr. Anders Ericsson who proudly declared that it takes 10,000 hours to be world class at...well...anything. That's a lot of time!! It basically equates to 20 hours a week, 50 weeks a year...for TEN years! That's a lot of time. And not just the ten year part. Twenty hours a week? That works out to just under three hours per day dedicated to your sport.

How does that make you feel? For most athletes and parents I talk to it doesn't make them feel very good at all. They either have been spending a lot of time and aren't as good as they would like to be, OR they haven't reached that 10,000 hour total and they may then feel like they are running out of time to achieve it before their window of athletic opportunity closes. It's ok, I had those feelings, too. 10,000 hours? That's a lot. And the three hours a day? Not happening for most athletes unless they are in a full time training environment like the Olympic training center

It's All About Deliberate Practice

But here's what's wrong with the 10,000 hour rule, it takes into consideration (mildly) the idea of Deliberate Practice which I will explain in a moment. But most importantly, I find when people discuss the 10,000 hour rule it doesn't help athletes at all. It just makes you feel bad and that doesn't help anything.

I want you to understand that most athletes aren't chasing the 10,000 hour rule. Sure, you may have a couple hockey players who started playing when they were five and now they are eighteen years old and are tearing up the NHL. But the majority of the league is made up of players who started later and spent less time and they are still in the NHL and some of them are even All-Stars.

The point is that the 10,000 hour rule is a guideline. It's not a number that you're trying to hit like the high score on a video game, it's a generalization. If putting in 10,000 hours guaranteed you success then it would just be a game of starting early and then everyone would be a professional athlete which we know isn't true.

Why Momma Ain't a Race Car Driver

The example I like to give is called, "Why your mom isn't a race car driver." If the ten thousand hour rule was true, your Mom would have been a race car driver in her twenties. All that time behind the wheel would surely make her an expert race car driver, right?

Wrong.

The reason your mom isn't a race car driver is because of "deliberate practice." Sure, when she was young she was paying attention learning how to drive that car, but at a certain point, she just turned her brain off. She can shift gears and speed up and slow down all without really thinking now. She can use her turn signal and change the radio without taking her eyes off the road. In fact, she can probably drink a coffee with one hand all while texting with the other hand and driving with her knee. (I know, I know. Certainly NOT your Mom. I get it.)

The point is, your Mom got to a certain skill level driving a car and she didn't really need any more for what it was she was doing. She was going through the motions and her mind would drift to other things even while she was flying down the road in rush hour traffic.

The same happens when you learn the skills for your sport. If you're not careful your brain will shut off while you are playing. It's not like you're brain dead, you just aren't engaged. You are going through the motions and not pushing yourself accordingly. You are spending time doing your sport but that time is not really well spent. In that case, the time you are spending doesn't apply to the 10,000 hours.

Somedays You Punch The Clock

Even though you understand the concept of Deliberate Practice now, there will be days when you just don't feel like putting in that sort of effort. And that's okay! The truth is you can't have your A game every day, all day. Those are the days you still need to Punch The Clock. This refers to factory-line workers who come into work "just to put their time in" to get paid. Their work isn't exceptional but sometimes you don't need exceptional work to move things forward. Again, you're going to listen to your body to know whether you're going to be able to put in a great day, or if you're just going to have an average day. Either way, you'll have to punch the clock and get it done.

Get The Ball Rolling

The hardest part about putting in the time every day is getting yourself going and getting the ball rolling. Building momentum day by day, week by week, and year by year can constantly be a struggle. But if you revisit your goals, look how far you've already come, and by focusing on your progress you should be able to get yourself up to speed and then be able to keep the whole thing moving in a positive direction. Keep an optimistic view on the process and you will begin to see results.

For athletes, just like in business, much of the effort to become a success happens in the early stages without any real signs of reward. Those are the days where much work is done with very little reward and sometimes very few signs that things are going to turn out ok. I know in my own business where there are days you just want to pack it in and quit. Turn and try something new. But those are usually the days when the extra effort you put in despite the lack of results really starts to add up. **So don't be afraid to slog through the valleys to get to the next peak.**

Your Greatest Competitor Is Not Here

It's not uncommon that athletes move up through the ranks locally, even nationally, only to be disappointed with their results when they get to the national or international level. Let me explain:

I've been brought in to consult with a number of athletes who are really disappointed when I tell them that they are missing a critical piece of their development.. Or they haven't paid attention to their Key Abilities. I remember sitting down with one of the most talented lacrosse players in all of Canada. This kid was super talented and where he lived he was head and shoulders above his peers, literally. At 6'1 and 16 years old he had a long stride that allowed him to outrun his shorter opponents with little effort. His height gave him a visual advantage to see the field and therefore make great plays, and he worked hard on his stick skills so his technical abilities were also great. But he was skinny. His counterparts in the U.S. would be much stronger physically and had a mental confidence that he lacked due to his lack of size and strength. He was fine playing locally, and even nationally, but when put in a pool of athletes trying to get Division 1 scholarships, he wasn't all that remarkable.

I tell athletes all the time that they need to always be testing their skills and abilities to their max, frequently. Many coaches and parents fear doing this only to be disappointed when it's too late to do anything. I learned this as a young lacrosse goalie. I knew that I was the best on my team, and I got to the point where I was one of the best in my league; but to test myself I really needed to get out of my State and play against the top athletes in the country to know just how well I was really doing.

It's rare you are surrounded by the best athletes in your sport. Your goal is to get around the best competition as frequently as possible to see how your Three Key Abilities stack up. It is quite possible that your greatest competitor is not here right now. They are somewhere else in the country, or the World, depending on your sport.

You must be constantly evaluating yourself against the best in your sport. The good news is that with the Internet you can get online right now and pull up a video of the best in your sport. What do they look like? What is their body like? What do they do well? What don't they do well?

Conclusion

Great performances come from the repetitive deliberate practice of skills. There will be days when practice doesn't feel great at all and you will be "punching the clock" to put your time in. But day after day, and year after year, consistent, Deliberate Practice will lead to improved performance. You just need to put in the time.

Watch This Video

**www.AthleteSpecific.com/
deliberate-practice**

Take Action With These Steps

- In your journal, take a moment and write down what a perfect practice session would look like to you. What would you do? When would you arrive? How would you prepare? How would you cool down after the session? What would you do to prepare for the next session?

- Take time today to research the practice habits of some of the top athletes in the world. They don't need to be in your particular sport. The greatest innovations typically come from applying strategies outside your sport to your sport. How can you improve your practice sessions by applying the techniques of other athletes?

- What are some practice activities you do where you don't really think about them? What can you do to stay focused and attentive during those parts of practice in order to improve?

- What bad practice habits can you eliminate starting today? What new habits can you replace them with?

Chapter 16
Dealing With Fear and Negative Thoughts

"Fear is peeing your pants.
Courage is knowing what to do with wet pants."

Dan Sullivan
Is the creator of Strategic Coach and this quote is from his Drill Sergeant
when he was a young private in the US Army. www.StrategicCoach.com

---

"Jonathan, but I'm afraid."

I understand. This is uncharted territory for you. It always is. Do you remember that quote I shared with you earlier? "Only those who risk going too far will possibly find out how far they can go." There will be times when you are afraid of getting hurt and other times when you are just afraid of...well...performing. Whether that's a new situation in training or a big competition coming up.

I could tell you something very cliche like "Fear is just: False Evidence Appearing Real" But then I might want to throw up in my mouth a little bit.

How about, *fear is just a physical manifestation that comes from having a lack of understanding of something.* The first time I saw the sport of luge (the first TIME!) I saw a guy on a sled hit the woods in curve ten breaking his sled and almost breaking himself. (The woods is the top of the curve. It's a lip that keeps you from flying out of the track and landing in the trees.) This guy was coming from the Men's start at the top of the track and my first run was from curve ten which was much further down the track so the speed was about a third of what he was doing. I was still afraid. Or so I thought.

To me, that **fear was really a physical representation of**

my body trying to help me prepare for something I didn't fully understand. Let me explain that in another way.

What most athletes feel as fear is really the mind helping the body to perform at a level that it has never performed at before. It's a totally new experience for you. The sensation of "fear" that you feel is really adrenaline coursing through your veins to help you see better, run better, and be stronger than you ever have been before. It's called the Fight or Flight syndrome and it's a built-in response to help you move. We'd be much better calling it the "Perform Better Syndrome". It was really designed to help you run away from a house on fire or a robber trying to take your lunch money. But when you are thinking about your sport and not actually participating in it, **that sensation of fear you feel is really not fear at all. It's your body ready to perform better than it has before, but with no outlet it just feels like butterflies and fear.**

When an athlete is afraid, I ask them, What is it that you don't fully understand that gives you that feeling of fear. There could be any number of a thousand things that could be causing it, but once we break down that area that is causing them fear then the fear usually goes away enough so that the athlete can perform at a high level.

Fear Of Pain

I work with a lot of goalies in a couple of sports and for many of them the fear of getting injured can be a real fear. The beauty is that we can usually solve that problem by putting extra padding on the goalie and protecting the area that causes them fear. Our goal is to allow the athlete to relax enough so that they can focus on the task at hand (which is making the save) so that they aren't getting hurt by the ball or the puck.

But what if you have fear of something you can't really protect that easily. Some athletes are doing triple back flips on motorcycles where going from two to three flips causes a lot of fear. What if they get hurt?

The Answer To Fear Is Always "Progression"

When I first started to compete in the sport of luge I learned fast that you don't just start at the top of the track and go all out on your first run. No, you start lower down and control your speed so you don't freak yourself out and get yourself into trouble. Each time you go to a new track you start a little lower down and then you move up as your confidence and understanding of the course improves. You are constantly in this balance of confidence and fear. Ideally you are in a position where your confidence is higher than your fear, but sometimes working with your fear can help you break through some plateaus.

Think of it like lifting weights. You may be doing squats and you load up the bar and it pins you to the floor. This obviously isn't good and you can really hurt yourself. Ideally you come into the weight room the first time and start out light. As you get stronger you slowly add more weight and move yourself up and up. If you have a day when you can't lift the weight, you don't just automatically go into fear mode, you take some weight off and then try it again.

The same is true in EVERY sport. In luge, if we had some fear, we would move down the track and scrub some speed. For my goalies in any sport I move the shooters so that the goalie has more time to react and move to the ball. For that motorcycle rider trying to do that third flip we get them to a gymnastic center in a harness where they can practice that flip in safety.

The only way to eliminate fear is to FLOOD the athlete with information about the task they are trying to complete. We then scale down the task using progression so that the athlete can relax and perform at a level that they are currently ready for. There is no use working through the fear and getting injured.

Feel The Fear And Do It Anyway

I don't want to sound like I'm contradicting myself. I mean, really, didn't I just say that there was no use working through the fear and getting injured? Sometimes that fear can help you push through a plateau.

As I mentioned before, the feelings you feel when you are afraid is actually a chemical reaction in your body preparing you to perform at a level greater than you have before. Your body is releasing adrenaline as well as other hormones that help your eyes to see better, your muscles to contract quicker and harder, and your heart to pump faster than ever before. You can imagine how all of that might FEEL a little different than you're used to especially if you're just sitting there thinking about it.

When you think about a task that is a challenge greater than what you've done in the past your body starts going into that fear mode. Remember, **our mind doesn't know the difference between what's real and what's imagined with feeling**. And if you're a young athlete thinking about that thing you're trying to do to reach your dreams you can pretty much guarantee that it's going to have a lot of feeling with it!

But if you understand that your body is just helping you to get ready to perform at a level you haven't yet performed, that in and of itself is exciting. Elite athletes look forward to that feeling and when it's not there...it's a problem.

When I qualified for my first Olympic team I immediately became nervous. Seriously. The Olympics were in February and I was feeling this way... in December. That was two months of feeling butterflies in my stomach and having shaky hands. I was a bundle of nerves that entire time and when we rolled into Norway ten days before the event to move into the Olympic village I was even more nervous. The feelings going through my body were intense and those feelings were there every single day. Just as I was getting used to it the morning of our event hit and I felt...

...nothing.

I was completely flat. I had absolutely nothing coursing through my veins. All week in training I was jacked up on adrenaline as the feelings of fear and nervousness coursed through my veins. But the day of the race I had to manufacture some nerves in order to perform at my best.

Looking Forward To Feelings Of Fear

As you improve you will look forward to those feelings of fear. You will understand that it is just your body's way of getting ready to do something that you haven't done before. When you understand what is happening in your body you will understand that it might just be the best time to try that new trick or skill or personal best. (Always keeping safety in mind)

So just because you feel fear doesn't mean you should stop in your tracks and turn around. Just know that it might be the best thing that could be happening in your body to perform at your best.

Replay Past Successful Experiences

Another great way to reduce or eliminate the fear that you feel is to think about past successful experiences you have had doing what it is you're about to do. If you're a quarterback and it's five seconds to go and you're on the five yard line and you need to score a touchdown because you're down by four points, instead of focusing on the adrenaline rush that is coursing through your veins you'd be better off thinking of a time when you 1) Made the same play in a game or in a practice. Or 2) thinking about a time when you successfully made a similar pass in a game or practice. By focusing on those two types of situations you have a better chance of making the current play than by focusing on something bad that could happen.

Focus On What You Want.
Not On What You Don't Want

Here's a trick for you...

Don't think of a pink polar bear.

No really. Don't think of a pink polar bear.

What do you see in your head right now? Probably a pink polar bear.

The bottom line is that your brain can't process a negative. It just can't. So when you tell it NOT to do something it automatically puts a picture in your mind of you doing exactly the thing you're not wanting to do. If you're fearful of a bad result, or doing something that may hurt you, the key is to replace the negative thought with a positive one of you doing what it is you want to accomplish.

I was playing in a lacrosse game once where we were down by a goal with less than thirty seconds to go in the game. Coach called a timeout and we all huddled up for one last play. It was a favourite play of our team that we used to run at the end of every practice. It was a bit of a gimmick play, but one that if we pulled it off would be epic.

In every practice our main attackman Zach would get the ball coming off a pick and he would always get a really good shot off forcing me to make a heck of a save.

In today's game we hadn't really played well as a team and it was a surprise we were down by a goal at this point in the game, especially when the other team had a really weak goalie. We just didn't get the right shots off during the game but we were really confident that we were going to pull off the play like we did every day in practice. Zach would rifle the ball, top corner, like he always did in practice. It was a sure goal.

So our Coach goes over the play in the huddle. We all knew the play so our confidence was building as he reminded us of what we already knew. The Ref blew the whistle to signal the end of the time out and we all put our hands in for one last, "WIN!" before we took our position on the field.

As Zach jogged away from the huddle coach yelled, "Hey Zach!"

"Yeah, Coach?"

"Don't miss." Coach said sarcastically.

Well guess what happened? We brought the ball in bounds and ran the play to perfection. Zach came off the pick and had a clean shot at the cage just like he always got in practice. He wound up and rifled the ball to the top of the cage like he always did in practice and the ball went...

...wide.

The final whistle blew and the other team ran cheering to their goalie to celebrate their big win. Zach walked back to the bench with his head down, frustrated that he didn't pull off what he did in practice every day. It didn't make any sense to him. But it did to me.

You see, the Coach should have never said, "Don't miss." Why? Because now the prominent thought in Zach's head was "not to *miss*" instead of seeing the ball busting the net in the top corner where he liked to shoot it. What the Coach should have said as he finished drawing up the play was, "And Zach's going to stick the ball in the top corner just like he does in practice." That way, Zach would have left the huddle with this positive image in his head of him rifling the ball past the goalie and sticking the ball in the cage, top corner.

So why did the Coach say, "Don't miss."? He probably wasn't thinking at all. If you asked him he'd probably say he was joking or being sarcastic. He was trying to cut the pressure by having a little fun. But by putting that negative thought in Zach's head his brain was seeing him miss instead of seeing him put the ball in the net.

I catch young athletes all the time saying things that don't seem like much to them but are actually a very big deal. It's easy to be sarcastic and say things that don't seem right. Of course no one wants to crash, or miss, or fall, or shoot wide. But when you speak it, you give that thought power.

Dealing With Negative Thoughts

Negative thoughts are very natural. Our brains are wired to help keep us safe so it's normal to have negative thoughts pop in our heads. The key is to not speak them verbally unless you are talking with a Coach who is 100% there for you to support you. What you speak about, comes about.

I have a favourite Starbucks where I like to go and write occasionally. Over the years I've seen this same group of women who sit and chat, and chat, and chat. I call them the "Dr. Phil Sisters" because they are normally gossiping about some strange people they see on that show. Personally, I hate those types of shows as they always showcase the negative. Most people would say, "But I would NEVER do those types of things." Then why would you watch it? It's like watching The Worst Chef In America TV shows. Why would you want to watch the worst when you can watch a show and see great examples of great chefs? Again, your brain can't process a negative so watching negative cooking shows just makes you a really bad chef. But I digress...

Well this day at Starbucks my noise cancelling headphones were out of batteries and I'm hearing this woman rant and rant about how her six-year old son keeps spilling the milk. Everyday he spills the milk. And she's always mopping up the spilt milk that her son always spills. And guess what she says? "I tell him EVERY DAY, Quinton DON'T SPILL THE MILK!"

I was in a rather frisky mood this day so I turned around and said, "And that's EXACTLY why he spills the milk."

"Um...excuse me?" she said.

I said something along the lines of what I'm telling you here. I said, "The human brain can't process a negative. So when you tell your son to not spill the milk he gets a little High Def 4K picture of himself in his head spilling the milk. Why don't you help him by saying, "Q you always do such a great job getting every drop in the glass. You're awesome and always so clean when you pour the milk. It all goes right in the glass."

She said, "Yeah, whatever."

So I went about my business and ended up leaving a few hours later. I hadn't been back to that Starbucks for a month when, lo and behold, the Dr. Phil Sisters were gabbing away. This day, thankfully, my noise cancelling headphones had fresh batteries so I wasn't able to catch up on the latest gossip.   But I did get a tap on my shoulder.

It was the woman who had the son and the spilt milk. She sat down and said, "You know that day you told me that I shouldn't tell my son not to spill the milk? Well, we all thought you were a total jerk for chiming in like that."

I said, "Well, thank you."

But she went on, "I went home later that night and I thought about it. And I tried it. I said, 'Q you are one of the cleanest kids I know and whenever you grab the milk I just know it's always going to go in the glass. Every last drop."

"And what happened?" I asked.

"He hasn't spilled it since."

We got talking and I told her about the first time I heard this concept. It was a concept used in race car driving to help drivers get out of a drift that could turn into a possible spin. Once they felt the car starting to lose control their main focus needed to be on where they wanted the car to go and not on where they didn't want to the car to go. Instead of staring at the wall that they DIDN'T want to hit they needed to focus on the road where they wanted to go.

The reason they did this was that their brain could then send the proper signal to their hands to steer the car. By focusing on where they wanted the car to go, their hands would steer the wheel to compensate and get the car back under control. If they focused on the wall that they didn't want to hit they would hit it every time.

So by focusing on the result you want, and not on the result that you don't want you pretty much guarantee yourself a good result. But by focusing on what you don't want, you'll get that too.

Here are some examples:

Negative Outcome	Positive Outcome
"I always hit the wall coming out of curve four."	"I see myself coming right down the middle of the straightaway out of curve four."

"In situations like this I always kick the ball too hard and miss."	"When the pressure is on, my body gives me just the right amount of energy to place the ball where I want it."
"When it rains I always lose grip on the ball."	"No matter what the weather, my grip adjusts to make the perfect pass every time."
"I always play bad at away games."	"No matter where we go, the field is the field and I play the same."
"I don't want to miss"	"I'm going to stick this ball right in the top corner and knock the water bottle off too!"

How To Re-Instill Confidence In An Athlete Who Has Lost It

Confidence. It's the base of every great athlete. It is the foundation that great athletic "houses" are built on. With confidence an athlete is capable of overcoming the toughest of challenges. Without it, and sometimes the simplest tasks seem impossible.

But how do we build confidence in you?

Many coaches lack the awareness that confidence is the key to your athletes success. All of the work you do in the gym, on the court, on the field, or anywhere else is designed to give you the tools you need to succeed. That is why you are doing all of those things your coach is asking you to do. But to a lot of coaches they don't realize that building confidence is the ultimate goal. It's not about doing more pushups for push ups sake. It's to get stronger in the chest and core so that you can have the confidence to dominate your opponent. (And it's not just push ups either. It's anything your coach asks you to do. Sprints. Squats. Or even that weird drill he learned from his old Russian coach years ago.) Sure, we are building explosiveness, and strength, and endurance, and balance, and coordination, but on top of all of that, we are building confidence.

But what happens when your confidence goes away? Maybe not completely, but enough that it affects your performance. Then what?

Let's Talk About How The Body Works

Your body is a pretty amazing tool that has evolved over thousands and thousands of years. It has adapted incredibly to different environments, from the one you are sitting in right now, all the way back to cavemen fending off Saber Toothed Tigers. And it's important to understand that the brain and the body combined are designed to do one thing above all others, and that is to protect itself.

So?

Well, if the body is designed to protect itself then why on earth would it put itself in front of danger?

Let's say you're about to try a new skill in your sport. Here's what your brain is saying during that situation. It says something like this, "Geee...that seems like it's going to be pretty cool if we can do it, but if we mess it up it's really going to hurt. I might even break something. Maybe we should do it just a bit slower? Or not so high? Or perhaps we don't have to do it against this person? I really shouldn't be doing this. It seems a bit out of my skill level. I'm going to shut things down just so I don't hurt myself." And on and on.

If you understand that the body's natural tendency is to avoid getting in the way of danger, you can see why your confidence might dip a bit here and there when we ask it to do something it thinks is dangerous.

When you understand the debate your brain and your body are going through as you ask them to do more difficult tasks, you can quickly see that a dip in your confidence is easy to overcome, if you want to.

Step 1: Are you looking for an excuse to stop?

This can seem a bit strange to some, but I've seen athletes who are burned out, or who are still competing to make someone else happy, or who just need a nap, who say that they have lost their confidence. The solution is this: Identify what is really bothering you. Take a nap. Take a break. Get some peace and quiet and really find the underlying cause. Are you stressed about school? Family? Relationships? Step away so you can step back with a clear mind.

Step 2: Modify the task at hand.

I work with a lot of goalies and the first step is to have the shooter step away so the goalie has more time to react and make the save. If the shooter is too close the anxiety goes up and the fear creeps in. When the fear creeps in the confidence goes away. What can you do to modify the task at hand so you can lessen the anxiety around it?

Step 3: Add protection.

Goalies can put on extra pads. Freestyle skiers add more crash pads to the landing area or put on a harness and use a spotter. Tennis players can use softer balls. No matter what the sport there are countless ways you can protect yourself, or your environment, to make things safer and to reduce the anxiety around practicing and competing. What can you do to add protection and reduce your anxiety so you can get your confidence back?

(Note: Remember way back in Chapter 3 when I talked about "Why you won't do what I tell you?" Well, it comes back to haunt us here: Peer pressure. From the figure skater who wears padded shorts over her tights to protect her butt when she falls to the soccer goalie who wears a padded shirt in practice to keep the bruises away. It doesn't matter who you are, when you focus on elite performance you will do anything to help it come faster. When you focus on your friends and what they think of you, then you get all confused and stop taking the steps to improve, which in this case involve wearing protection. Keep your focus on your goal and not on impressing your friends. It doesn't matter what they are wearing it matters what you wear to perform at your best. When your confidence comes back you can shed the extra protective equipment. OR you may find out that you perform even better with it. And then all of your supposed friends will start to wear extra padding too. Nuf' said.)

Step 4: Everything is possible with progression.

You can overcome lack of confidence by not getting to the point where you lose it. This is possible with progression. Baby steps.

When you make improvements ever so slowly you keep fear at bay and your confidence always remains high. By not biting off more than you can chew, you always stay in a Peak State that allows you to perform at your best without the risk of getting hurt, or injured, or having an overly bad result. By taking small steps you'll always be in great mental state and will be able to continue to improve.

Step 5: Suck it up.

There are times when the best thing to do to get your confidence back is to suck it up and just go for it. This can be the right response if your confidence has been lacking for a while and what you feel may in fact not be what you need. Sure, many times the signal from your brain is telling you you need to be aware of something real, but other times, it's just stuck in a loop that you need to get out of.

Now I'm not telling you to be stupid, but if your coaches and your support staff are telling you you need to go for it then you probably need to tell your brain, "Brain, I hear ya. But I have faith that it's all going to be alright and that I have the talent and the skill to pull this off. Now have a nap and let's go DO this!"

When I was learning how to snowboard I was on the side of a French alp on a really bad snowboard. (I didn't know it was bad, I just thought they were all that way.) I'd stand up and try to turn right away and fall down. Stand up. Try to turn before things got too fast. Fall down.

That's when some really snobby French ski instructor came over to me and said, "You American pig. You must not be such a, how you say, wimp! You must let the board get some speed you coward and THEN you can turn!"

Say what you will about the French. (Just kidding guys. You know I love you.) What this over dressed ski instructor with the tight pants was saying was, I needed to turn off my brain for a bit because the fear I was feeling, and my lack of confidence, was incorrect. I needed to suck it up and let that board get some speed. And when I did, sure enough, I could turn. It was the beginning of a great relationship! (With the snowboard. Not the ski instructor.)

Losing your confidence can be one of the most frustrating times in any athlete's life. You're stuck, briefly, thinking: I just had it! I was fine! And now I don't know what's going on!" If you follow the steps I've laid out in this chapter you will be able to overcome this brief period that lacks the confidence you crave. It's not the end of the road. It's just a phase. And you can work through it.

Conclusion

Fear can be considered a negative feeling, but when you realize that it is just your body preparing you for a great performance, you can flip the switch on fear.

By focusing on what we want, and not on what we don't want, we can harness that energy and use it to create the outcome we want to create. Most people get derailed by feelings of fear, when in fact, it can help you raise your performance to another level.

Watch This Video

**www.AthleteSpecific.com/
Dealing-with-fear-and-
negative-thoughts**

Take Action With These Steps

- Get your journal and write down an experience you had where you felt fear but eventually pulled through and had a good performance.

- Looking back on it, what did you not understand prior to your performance that makes sense now and which eliminated your fear?

- If you have a fearful thought in your head, write down how you could scale things back to a point where you don't feel fear.

- Write down an experience where you felt fear, but now looking back, you realize that energy really could help you perform better.

- Write down a time when you had a sarcastic comment that may have caused you to perform poorly. How could you change your words to have a more positive mindset in the future?

Chapter 17
The Four Phases Of Competence

"One of the best uses of your time is to increase your competence in your key result areas."

Brian Tracy
is a Canadian-born American motivational public speaker and self-development author. He is the author of over seventy books that have been translated into dozens of languages.

So you like your sport. You obviously think you're good at it (or someone who loves you thinks you're good at it). And you want to be better. Maybe even play professionally or go to the Olympics. Whatever your dream is, you're going to go through some phases as you learn new skills along the way.

Here's a quick tip: **you're never going to be "done" with learning in your sport**. There is a great quote that says "school is never out for the pro." So my question is...are you a pro?

You will constantly be going through phases where you learn a skill, master it, then learn something new, struggle with that and then master something else. But there is an actual science behind it that I really want you to understand. I find that as I help athletes understand the phases, and identify what phase they are in, they can relax a bit. They know that improvement and mastery will come.

The four phases of competency are as follows:

1. Unconscious Incompetence
2. Conscious Incompetence

3. Conscious Competence

4. Unconscious Competence

Those are some big words so let me translate for you. As you read through this section you will start to identify certain things you do and what phases you are in while you are doing those things. You can be in different phases for different skills. Many athletes I know who are early bloomers may be masters in one skill (like skating in hockey) but might be unconsciously incompetent in another (like stick handling). A young goalie might be really big physically and be Unconsciously Competent stopping the ball because of their size, but technically they may be Unconsciously Incompetent which can hurt them later.

Phase 1: Unconsciously Incompetent. (Translation: You don't know just how bad you really are.)

For any athlete who is new to a sport you automatically drop into Phase 1. You like what it is you do but you're really not aware just how bad you really are or what you really should be working on. You go to practice and go through the motions but you're just not really focused. There is so much to learn you're overwhelmed by it all. You don't know how to do things yet and you're really unaware of just how much work it's going to take to achieve your goal. (Which is probably a good thing because if you did you might just quit at this stage.) **Your love of the overall experience of what you are doing overrides the work that needs to come.**

Phase 2: Consciously Incompetent: (Translation: You know you're bad, and you see the value in improving the skills you need to improve.)

This is where the fun starts to begin as a coach. This is where your coach can start to see that the advice they give you starts to sink in a little bit and you begin to improve. You start to recognize the gaps you need to fill in and you work to fill those gaps. In this phase you start to recognize your mistakes and register a value to those mistakes. You then work to eliminate those mistakes and your performance improves.

Phase 3: Consciously Competent: (Translation: You realize that you're pretty good at what you do but it takes some significant thinking)

In this phase you're pretty close to mastery, but your concentration level is through the roof. You're not "In the Zone" yet. In your head you're working hard to put all the pieces together and make it work and you're doing well. But it's not easy. Yet.

Phase 4: Unconsciously Competent: (Translation: You're in the zone.)

In this phase you've mastered a particular skill and you don't have to think about it. When I competed in the sport of luge I remember moving from Phase 3 to Phase 4. Our coach Wolfi would be standing on the side of the track and as I whizzed by at eighty miles per hour I could say to myself, "Wolfi was standing in the exit of curve 9. But I knew I had reached Phase 4 when I could smell his cigarette smoke in curve 10. In Phase 3 I could think about it and could process it with one of my senses, my sight. But in Phase 4 I could use a much more subtle sense, my smell, that was only activated once my brain could process everything else easily.

Most athletes get stuck in Phase 2 and 3. What phase are you stuck in and specifically, what part of your game do you think needs the most work? When an athlete can start to identify what phase he is in, and can then work through those Phases, performance begins to really improve and this is where it starts to get exciting.

When you start to combine the understanding of these Phases with your understanding of the Three Ages of every athlete in **Chapter 7** then you really start to take control of your development.

Conclusion

If you understand what the phases of learning are, you're more likely to keep going when you start to struggle. It doesn't matter what the sport, you will go through the four phases of competency over and over again until you win. Just when you feel you've got it all figured out, you will play against better competition and go through the four phases again. It's a never ending cycle, and one you need to prepare for in order to be successful. When you feel like you don't have it figured out, realize you are just going through a phase and will soon be out of it. If you stick with it.

Watch This Video

**www.AthleteSpecific.com/
four-phases-of-competence**

Take These Action Steps

- Take out your journal and write down the skills and abilities where you are Unconsciously Incompetent.
- Write down the skills where you are Consciously Incompetent?
- Now write down the skills you have where you are Consciously Competent?
- And finally, write down the skills you have where you are Unconsciously Competent.

Chapter 18
What Will Keep You From Reaching Your Goals

"Environment trumps willpower."

Jonathan Edwards
Olympian, Speaker, Author

In my Sophomore year of high school, everything changed. The summer before I had attended the oldest YMCA in North America, Camp Dudley in Westport, NY. It was here that I was exposed to the Winter Olympic sport of luge that would ultimately alter the direction of my life.

Yeah, I know...what the heck is luge?

Well, since we are in the age of the Internet I will encourage you to Google that. If you are somehow reading this somewhere and you don't have access to the Internet, I will tell you that it is the sport in the Winter Olympics where we fly down an icy track at speeds of up to ninety miles per hour, lying on our back and going feet first. That's luge.

So I learned how to luge at Camp Dudley which is an incredible place that exposes boys from ages 10-14 to a variety of experiences, some athletic, some spiritual. I'm going to put luge somewhere in the middle. Seriously.

Two of my camp leaders had been alternates to the previous Olympic team and I thought it would be pretty cool to try the sport for a second time. I had tried it four summers before but really on a dare. This time it was part of a national recruiting process. If I did well I might have the chance to try it on ice sometime in the winter. We practiced once a week down a short road on wheeled sleds ending in a pile of wood chips.

After the summer I headed back to school where I was a pretty normal kid. My dad was the music director and I played Varsity Soccer, JV Hockey, and Varsity Lacrosse. (I owe it to Camp Dudley for getting me in incredible shape to make the Varsity Soccer team as a freshman.) I was a goalie in all three sports although I was now physically able to play all positions after having been a little chubby when I was younger.

The fall semester went well and I transitioned into hockey season with ease and that's when I got a phone call. It was Dmitry Feld from the US Luge Association inviting me to come to Lake Placid, New York to try the sport of luge but this time on ice. I was going to take part in the US Junior National Development camp where I would stay in the Olympic Training Center for two weeks with other kids from around the country. This sounded like a pretty cool experience to say the least.

I told my JV Hockey Coach that I wanted to go to Lake Placid to go try this "luge" camp thing. He was pretty confused but optimistic for me at least. He was disappointed that he was losing one of his goalies for a couple weeks but two weeks was only three games so he wished me luck. The school itself was not as receptive. They piled on as much homework as they could and told me I'd be responsible for every test and quiz that I missed. Ugh. I was going to Lake Placid in February so I had lots of time to plan and get my homework done ahead of time. It didn't really matter to me because I was going to go to the Olympic Training Center and that was way more exciting than missing school.

My friends at school had no idea what I was doing. "Luge? What the heck is luge?" "You're going to miss hockey! You're going to miss school! Why would you do that?" Most of my friends were pretty positive about it but some kids who were on my friend "bubble" were less than supportive.

February couldn't come fast enough and when I got to Lake Placid I was quickly immersed in the culture of the Olympics and the culture of training for them. The real Olympics were actually happening on TV while I was in Lake Placid which was cool. We could see the Olympians on national television and hear stories of them training back in Lake Placid. There was the weight room, the cafeteria, the Olympic hockey rinks and the ski jumps. Lake Placid is an Olympic town so everybody there has some small connection to the Olympics. The Olympics is part of the culture up there, in fact, you could say it is THE culture up there. When you walked into a store and they asked what you were doing in town, when you said, "I'm in the luge camp and I'm staying at the Olympic Training Center." the response was, "Cool. Good luck." Kind of like saying, "No big deal to us. You go on with your big-bad-self."

There were two groups of athletes coming to Lake Placid for two separate camps. Each camp was two weeks long and I was there for the first session. There were kids from California, Michigan, New York, Connecticut, Florida. Kids from all over flew in and we immediately went to work. We had roommates, two to a room, and we were busy. The normal day's schedule went something like this:

> 7:30 AM Breakfast
> 8:30 AM Take van to track for first sliding session.
> 9:30-11:30 Slide Three Runs
> 12:00 PM Van back to OTC for lunch and video review.
> 12:30-1:15 Lunch
> 1:15-2:00 PM Free Time
> 2:00-3:00 Weight Room
> 3:15 - 4:30 Physical Activity (Soccer, Gym, etc)
> 4:30-6:00 Work on sleds
> 6:00 - 7:00 Dinner
> 7:00-8:00 Homework
> 8:00 - 9:00 Free Time/ Homework (Mostly free time :))
> 9:00 Lights Out

So this was nowhere near what a typical school day was like. But it was the new normal for those of us at the US Junior National Development Camp. This was the lifestyle we needed to live in order to be on that path to make the Olympic team. As a group we got up and did this routine for the next two weeks and no one ever doubted it. This was just what you did and how you did it. It was the environment associated with training for the Olympic games.

After the first two weeks we had a small race and I did pretty well. Well enough I guess, that they asked some of us if we wanted to stay for the second two weeks. I was hooked so I said yes. School wasn't really happy about it but I figured I'd figure out the homework situation when I got back. The hockey coach wasn't too excited but he was still enthusiastic for me being up there.

I ended up staying for five weeks total and at the end of it all I won the Empire State Games Gold medal as the fastest Junior. I even bought my own sled for the next season!

At the time, I wasn't thinking that I would be on the Olympic team some day. The whole thing was just a ton of fun and I liked it. I was pretty quick in the races so that helped, but when it was over I headed back to school to pursue my lacrosse dreams. But I ran into something really interesting when I got back to school. You see, when I was in Lake Placid I was in this environment of training for the Olympics. If you were training there you were in the right environment. People understood what it was you were trying to do and they were optimistic for you. People loved to help and be part of it. They believed in your dream because, odds are, they knew someone who had already competed in the Olympics. That person they knew might not have done luge but odds were they knew someone, in some sport, who had competed. When I got back home, it was a different story.

When I got back home, kids were like, "Where the heck have you been?" "You did what?" "You lifted weights? That will stunt your growth." You trained three times a day? When did you do homework? My parents would never let me do that. You're nuts! Why would someone want to do luge? You really think you are going to be in the Olympics? Pfft."

I wasn't really prepared for that at all. I had just been in this amazing environment where everybody "got it" only to be slammed by all of these people who didn't "get it." It was an odd situation to be in and I can't say I was really prepared for it. Somehow, once lacrosse started the questions died down and I could focus on school and sports. But I learned a really interesting thing back then that has always stuck with me:

"What people say about you, or what you do, says more about them than it does about you."

Jonathan Edwards
Olympian, Author, Speaker

I'm going to cover this more in the next section, but I wanted to cover it here, too. The people around me when I got back home didn't have the experience I just had. They had no idea. And the words they used to describe what was really their lack of understanding of my experience hurt. It also caused me to reconsider the great experience I just had. Maybe what I just did wasn't that cool? Maybe thinking about going to the Olympics was stupid? I was a little rattled.

The whole experience I did have however, going to Lake Placid and then returning back home and running into this resistance, was something I have always taken with me. I learned some very critical lessons in that whole experience and it was this:

1. *Your dreams are yours and yours alone.*

2. *Don't share your dreams with anyone, until you're really, really ready to.*

3. *Environment trumps willpower*

4. *There are four things that will kill your dreams:*

   a. *Friends (or people you think are your friends)*

   b. *Family*

   c. *Place*

   d. *Inputs*

   e. *You*

When you understand these five critical areas and how to navigate through each of them you will be better equipped to withstand the pressures (and sometimes lack of pressure) from different people-influences you will encounter.

Your Dreams Are Yours And Yours Alone

When I went to Lake Placid that first time, it was obvious that even though we were all selected for the same development camp, there was a wide variety of kids within the group. Some were motivated and others weren't. Some were giving their all even while others were flat out lazy.

Within this elite group of kids, the dreams of each kid were quite varied. Some kids talked about going to the Olympics while others asked about how they thought it was crazy.

When I returned back to school the dreams that I carried around in my head, and shared with my friends, were now even more out of place. Most of them couldn't relate at all to what I had just experienced. Kind of like talking about a movie that they hadn't seen yet. If you told them the ending they couldn't even possibly comprehend it.

When I came back from Lake Placid after that first trip, I can't say that I was thinking about going to the Olympics as a goal just yet but I could see the path it was going to take. I could envision myself travelling to some of the tracks in Canada and in Europe that I had heard about. I liked the lifestyle of travelling and training and it sure sounded better than school! That's for sure. The bottom line was that I could envision being on the path that would take me to the Olympics.

When you talk to your friends about your hopes and dreams they can only see the outcome of your dream. They don't see the path. For me, the end of the path was the Olympics and that's a pretty huge goal to some. I mean, this is the Olympics that's on television every four years, and the only people who are on TV are actors and actresses and athletes and murderers and the President! That's huge! But you're just that kid who we sit next to in math class, why do you think you can go to the Olympics now? I mean last week you were that goofy kid wearing those really bad sneakers and now you think you're going to go the Olympics?

This was a lesson. **I was learning that the environment I was now in couldn't comprehend my dream because they didn't have my interest. They didn't have my experience and they didn't have my results that made me think I could continue.** What I realized was that my dreams were mine. They had been given to me and me alone just like your dreams are yours and yours alone. It's kind of like a dandelion that blooms in the spring. Those little seeds get blown around in the wind with their little fluffy parachutes. Where they land depends on if they grow or not. Some land in the street and the rain washes them into the gutter. But some land on fertile soil where they have a chance to grow. That's you! Just like that dream to go the Olympics was mine to now nurture.

I shared a quote before that has been really helpful for me since then: **"What people say about you or what you do says more about them than it does about you."** You are going to run into people who have some pretty choice words for you if you tell them what it is you are dreaming about. Maybe you want to go to the Olympics. Or maybe you just want to make that travel team this summer. That dream is yours.

Here's what I heard from some of my "friends", how I felt, and what they said really meant.

What They Said	How It Made Me Feel	What They Really Were Saying
You really think you are going to make it to the Olympics?	"You loser. Why on earth would you think you could make it to the Olympics?"	"I could never see myself going to the Olympics in anything."
"You're going to miss a ton of school if you do that."	"You're going to end up stupid with no career if you try and do that."	"I've been raised with the understanding that if I don't get a degree I'm going to end up living in a van down by the river."
"You're crazy!"	"I'm crazy."	"I could never imagine myself doing something like that."
"I had a dead uncle who tried that once. He went broke trying that."	"I'm going to end up like their dead Uncle."	"I have one example of someone in my life who I respected who tried that and failed."

The Words You Want To Hear That Are Rarely Spoken

The examples I listed above can be quite disturbing to a young athlete especially if they come from people you like to hang around. You may have girlfriends and boyfriends who are your best friends (up until now, potentially) and they've just made this comment that has sucked the life out of the dream that you are really excited about.

What you really wish they would say at the end of their comment is, "Hey that's awesome. Go for that dream! How can I help you?"

You can add any variations to those comments. You want desperately for the people around you to say, **"You can do it. I believe in you. I've never seen you do anything like that before but I know**

that you know that you can do it and that's what's most important."
You need to prepare yourself for the words of doubt and of skepticism
that comes from your friends. Those words are not meant to define
you, they are just a backhanded description of their own fears and
reservations. Those same words they use to describe you keep them
from going for the same dream as yours. The dream that has landed in
you, and not them. It has landed in you for a reason and now you must
protect it.

Outgrowing Your Teammates

My Olympic dream experience was kind of unique because I went
away from all of my friends to go experience something completely new
in a completely new place. None of my friends at home had any idea
what I was talking about when I explained the sleds and the ice and the
coaches and Olympic Training Center. They couldn't picture it or relate
in any way to what I just did.

But for most athletes reading this book you may be in a sport
where you have friends and even family who participate or who have
participated in the same sport. This is a unique experience because it
is rare to have teammates of equal ability with similar dreams.

I was lucky to see two hockey players from my high school in the
same class go on to play in the NHL and to become All-Stars. They
both were Olympians and they both had long successful professional
careers. I always wonder why the other players on those high school
teams didn't reach their same level. Every day they saw two examples
in practice playing the same game as they did but they didn't make it.

Part of it has to do with Deliberate Practice as I explain in Chapter
15. What you see a player doing is not necessarily what is most
important. It is what is going on inside the head of that athlete that is
most important. A romantic concept is the image of the player staying
late after practice taking extra shots at an empty net. Or of the athlete
doing extra wind sprints on the track or extra reps in the weight room.
These are great, and often they are in fact what you need to be doing,
but what tends to happen in these situations is you make the effort to
do the extra work and your friends and teammates give you a hard
time. They will say things like, "Oh, what, you think you're going to get
recruited? Play in College? Go pro?" They will yell out things like, "Take

a rest!" Or God forbid you miss one of those extra shots you take. The ridicule can be endless.

There is a saying that goes like this, "**When you find you're staring in the opposite direction to those around you, you're probably staring in the right direction.**" This is a perfect example. There will be a point when you outgrow your teammates. Something will click in you that will make you start to think that you can make your dream happen. Sometimes it happens in an instant, like when a lacrosse player I had the chance to coach made an incredible move around an All-American defenseman. It was at that point when he started to believe that he too could make it big. For most athletes it happens over time. A little belief here and a little belief there. A good result and then perhaps another one. Or it happens when a Coach who you respect tells you that you can do it. However you get to that point, you will hit a tipping point when you will have a dream that your teammates don't want as much as you do and you will have to set yourself aside and do the work you feel is needed to achieve it.

Don't Share Your Dreams With Anyone... Until You're Really, Really Ready

There is a school of thought out there that you should share your dreams with those around you so that they will hold you accountable when you're thinking about quitting. This is really popular with adults who are trying to lose weight or quit any number of bad habits. The idea is that you will proclaim to the world your intentions and avoid the inevitable ridicule when you stray from your goals. This might work for adults, it just doesn't work with young athletes.

The dream that you have within you is like a small bird in your hands. You want to hold it firmly enough so it won't fly away but if you squeeze it too tight you just might crush it. Hold it loosely enough for people to pet it and it will get manhandled and it will die.

Another way to look at it is like building a house. You read some magazines or saw some TV shows, and you want to build this really cool house. But it's in a style that none of your friends have seen before. You could tell them what you're going to do, but they'd probably say things like, "That's a stupid idea. That type of house doesn't look good around here. You've never built a house before" Stuff like that.

So you sit back and take in all of those comments and do your best to shake them off. You go back and read the magazines and watch the TV shows and get excited again. You even get on the phone with people who have built similar houses to learn how they did it. You decide to go ahead with the build, but instead of submitting yourself to the sometimes ruthless comments from people who just don't "get it" you find a plot of land to build your house that is a little bit off the beaten path. When people ask you where you're going you come up with some excuse not to tell them that you're actually headed to your secret location to build your house.

So a few months go by and all you've got done is the hole for the foundation You've been spending every day thinking about your house. You've got the plans and you can see in your head what the finished house is going to look like But one day your best friend finds your location by accident and says, "Hey! You said you were just going to the woods to hang out. But I see what you're doing! That house is stupid. Why are you doing that?"

I recommend you hold on to your dream long enough that you start to see some positive progress towards it. What you are trying to do is solidify that dream a bit. Like building a wall around your house. When the wall is just getting built people can step right over it and create some serious damage to your home. Wait until the wall is high enough and whatever people say or do they can't really affect the house. The house is your dream and you want to protect the house and start building that wall of protection first so it can withstand the doubters when they come. And they will come.

Beware The Black Crab

In the book "**Rich Dad, Poor Dad**" by Robert Kiyosaki he shares the story of the Black Crab. The story goes like this:

In Hawaii, fishermen will go out to fish for black crab and they make sure they have a bucket with nice, tall sides. That way when they throw the first black crab into the bucket he can't crawl up the sides and get out. The interesting thing however is that if you catch two black crabs, you only need a bucket with small sides. Why? Because when one crab sees daylight and tries to escape, the other crab will pull him back down. Instead of one escaping, they both get cooked. The fisherman knows he can relax because the "peer pressure" of the other crab will just drag them all back down.

This Is So Much Like Life!

Like many of the ideas you have learned in this book, many of them apply to the rest of your life as well. The Black Crab syndrome applies to a lot of people. I've seen athletes apply and get accepted to travel teams, or universities. Almost instantaneously, people who they thought were their friends end up dragging them back down to their level. They will say things like, "Who do you think you are going for something like that? You'll never make it. You'll blow your reputation. Maybe in a couple of years but not now."

There are two main concepts you must understand when you run into a friend who is a Black Crab:

1. You are making them look lazy
2. Your action challenges their beliefs.

You will run into this rather quickly if those around you aren't aligned or supportive to your goals. If you stay after practice for extra work you'll probably hear comments like, "She's crazy!" or smaller, more sly comments like, "Take a break. Rest!"

The Number One Reason You Won't Do What I Suggest - Peer Pressure

peer pres - sure
noun
social pressure by members of one's peer group to take a certain action, adopt certain values, or otherwise conform in order to be accepted.

When it comes to becoming an elite athlete you will start to run into resistance almost immediately. Whether it's something as simple as stretching after practice to eating better at lunch, someone, somewhere, will start to dig and ask you "why are you doing that?" But it's not a "why" that's based in curiousity, it's more likely a "why" that's coated in a healthy dose of "So, you think you're better than me?"

When I graduated highschool I missed the best graduation party of the year because I had been selected to play in the East-West Prep School All-Star game. My peers thought I was nuts. "How could you miss that party!" they asked.

I was the MVP. I remember the MVP. No one remembers the party.

Define What You Want And Need

When it comes to reaching your dreams and goals and completing your own projects you will realize something pretty important: They are YOUR goals and dreams. They are YOUR projects. And because of that, they are no one else's. Rarely do you have a group of people around you whose goals are exactly the same. Even as an Olympian I can tell you that within that group of Olympians training for the same sport, in the same sessions, there is still a spectrum of motivation and effort. My teammate Chris Thorpe would go back to his apartment and do an Eight Minute Abs fitness video even after he had done all the training sessions with the team. He ended up with a great set of abs (and he got all the girls) and no surprise he competed in three Olympic games and got two Olympic medals.

When I stood at the top of the Olympic track about to put the sled down for our first run at the Olympic games I realized that all of the people who gave me a hard time for being away from school, or away from my friends...people who didn't understand my dreams and my goals...they weren't there. They weren't standing at the top of the Olympic track because it wasn't their goal...it was mine.

You need to decide just what you want and just what you need to make your dreams and goals come true. And when you decide you will then make all of your decisions based on your goals. No one else's.

Just know this...

Environment Trumps Willpower

While these comments may seem like no big deal at first, they start to add up. It's like small layers of silt that end up on the bottom of the river. At first they aren't that big of a deal, but after a while they build up so much they can drastically affect the direction of that river.

I first heard the term "environment trumps willpower" as it related to food. Kind of like, if it's in the house eventually I'm going to break down and I'll eat it, sort of thing. But if the food's not there you can't eat it.

The same goes for reaching your athletic goals. You may read this book and get all excited and empowered (which is my plan for you) and you'll go out and do extra repetitions. You'll start eating better and maybe you'll start to stretch a little more after practice. You'll visualize and watch extra video...but then...

You'll run into a Black Crab with something sly like, "Hey, Courtney's having a party at her parents' house tonight and that guy you like is going to be there..." or, "Hey, we're going for pizza after practice, wanna come?" There is a scale of these subversive little invitations and comments that will chip away at your foundation. But your willpower will hang on for a bit, however, willpower has it's limits.

Willpower takes a lot of mental energy. That is why you're usually good in the morning or early afternoon when you're rested. But when you're tired and hungry and it's the end of the day, that is when you're the most likely to cheat on your goals and dreams. You'll say things like, "Well, just this once." Or, "A little pizza won't hurt." And before you know it you're now further behind than you were when you started.

Bad Environment = Need For More Willpower

Understand that the environment you surround yourself with has a huge effect on how much willpower you need to exert on yourself. As you read this book you're going to get excited and motivated and it's going to be pretty easy for you to do an extra set of squats if you're by yourself and none of your friends and family are around to pull you away from what you need to do. But if you're best friend is bugging you to get going because he's got to meet his friends at the mall you'll be quick to skip that last set, "Just this once." And so it begins.

Your environment consists of not just where you are and what you're surrounded by, but also by whom you're surrounded. This is where peer pressure comes in and can really affect what you do, when you do it and how you do it. And while your friends and family usually mean well, there is one thing even they don't fully understand when they casually try to pull you away from your hopes and dreams...

It makes them look lazy.

This is the primary reason your friends and family don't want you to reach your goals "But Jonathan, my friends and family love me. They want me to succeed, right?" Well, not always and they don't always know it..

You have incredible strength and fortitude locked inside you. Actually, we all do but the cold hard truth is not everyone believes that. They don't believe that they to can reach their goals if they just get off the couch and go for them, too.

Many people get locked up, worried about failure or losing friends family and other things that currently make them comfortable. They don't really want to get off the couch, and to be honest, you and I don't really want to either. But when we do, that's when the magic happens.

But to your friends and family who have known you since you were young, they know you don't make your bed in the morning and that you leave the cap off the milk in fridge. To them, your new goals make them look lazy. Subconsciously they think, "How does he think he can go to the Olympics?"

What your success does for them, because they think they are just like you, is makes them think, "If he made that happen, what could I have done with my life?" And as I mentioned before, while they may not think of this consciously, it is in their subconscious.

I have seen this happen with friends, but I have also seen it with parents. It can be as simple as a father or a mother who never earned more than $30,000 a year holding back their child from a college degree in finance that would earn them $100,000 a year, to an athlete who is trying to make the high school basketball team when his dad was cut from that team when he was that age. It can be conscious: It can be subconscious. Either way, your success, and potential success can make your friends and family look lazy so just be aware.

All Inputs Matter

When you come right down to it, everything you do, everything you listen to, everything you eat, everything you read, all of it either takes you closer to your goal or away from it. There is no grey area. It's very black and white.

The reason there is no "neutral"...when it comes to...anything, is because you are in a competitive environment and everyone involved is trying to improve as well. From the kid just starting out to the current world record holder, everyone is getting better. It's like swimming in a pool that's barrelling down the highway. Sure you might be able to float for a minute but the stream is constantly moving.

This is why it's important to be vigilant about all of your inputs all the time because they are either going to empower you or drag you down.

I was working with a group of athletes a couple of years ago and I noticed that every night one of the boys was watching some really gross murder/detective TV show online. Every night it was another really gross/twisted/nasty/dark show. I got pretty perturbed and said, "Why on earth are you watching that?" He said something to the effect of, "I don't know. I like it. It doesn't bother me."

I found this really interesting. First, I was curious as to how someone could not be bothered by watching the equivalent of a horror movie every...single...night. But I asked the athlete, why would you watch that when there are thousands of better more uplifting options available to be entertained by.

Now as a side note, I also noticed that there were some other athletes in the same common area who were kind of stuck watching this show as well. While they were working in the common area this athlete happened to have his laptop up and running first and therefore he was in control of the content. But I noticed that there was a female athlete in the room who was doing her best to do her thing but she wasn't super-excited about this particular show. The conversation was not just for the athlete who had the show on his laptop, but for all the other athletes in the room as well.

Watching negative...anything...news, movies, TV shows, YouTube clips, you name it...they affect you. On one side of the scale they might affect you a little. On the other side of the scale they might affect you a lot. The bottom line is that they aren't bringing you closer to your goal, they are bringing you away. Yeah, I know, where's the fun right? Great results are fun.

That athlete in question changed what was playing on the laptop that night omit to an animated movie that all the athletes remembered watching from when they were younger. The mood in the room shifted immediately. The interesting thing was, the next day, they all had a great competition.

Did that little change in what they were watching affect their performance for the next day? You bet it did. Where in the world of performance does it say, "Watch scary negative television shows the night before your competition." Going to bed tense and possibly upset does nothing to promote healthful, restful sleep. Remember, all input matters, all the time.

Dealing With Distractions

Remember back in Chapter 16 when I talked about the "Dr. Phil Sisters"? I'm sitting in a Starbucks trying to write and these voices kept interrupting what I was trying to focus on. My first approach was to turn on my noise cancelling headphones to drown out the noise but I couldn't because my battery was dead. As I sat down to write this section I realized how perfect that situation was to explain just what dealing with distractions is all about.

Distractions are going to happen. It's a fact. They just are. But you can either be derailed by them, or understand that they are going to show up and you need to create some tactics to deal with them effectively.

In one of the greatest productivity books of all time, **Getting Things Done** by David Allen, he talks about "Work as it appears." And that is exactly what a distraction is. It's work as it appears. You weren't really planning for it, but now it is annoyingly there and you have to deal with it. So what do you do?

Well, also from **Getting Things Done**, you can do a couple of things with work. You can 1) Deal with it. 2) Delegate it. Or 3) Discard it. I will add one more to the beginning and that's 1) Avoid it.

Distractions are really things you need to deal with that you really didn't think you were going to have to deal with. They can be a flash bulb in the middle of a race, or they can be a sibling busting into your room while you're studying. Either way, you have to deal with it quickly and effectively.

The first step is to control your environment as much as you can so that distractions can't sneak in and interrupt your concentration. Just like trying to put on noise cancelling headphones, there are things you can do to make sure you aren't interrupted. Locking a door. Finding a secluded training spot. Turning off your phone. These are all ways to control your environment.

The second step is to realize that when you are interrupted with a distraction you need to treat it like work. And like work, you can either deal with it, give it to someone else to deal with, or discard it.

Many athletes get completely derailed in competition when a distraction pops up. They don't know how to deal with it effectively and I want to give you this technique to deal with distractions effectively.

1. Know that they are going to show up. Do your best to control your environment, but outside of that, just be aware they are going to pop up from time to time.

2. Deal with them quickly. When a distraction pops up decide how you're going to handle it right away. Do you need to handle it? Can you delegate it to someone else? Can you just discard it?

When you take this fast approach to distractions you can quickly move on from them and get back to the task at hand no matter if it's a competition or a practice.

Conclusion

There are a number of things that can keep you from reaching your goals and all of them are within your control. It doesn't matter if it's a friend or family member, a teammate, or even yourself. You can control all of it to create an environment that will help you succeed.

It's important to understand that there will be distractions that pop up that will distract you from reaching your goals. Learn how to deal with them and how to remain focused on your goals no matter how large or small they are.

Watch This Video

**www.AthleteSpecific.com/
reaching-your-goals**

Take Action With These Steps

• Take out your journal and write down the consistent distractions you face that affects your training or performance.

- What steps can you take to reduce or eliminate these distractions?

- Do you have a teammate or a family member in your life that is keeping you from your goals? What can you do to reduce or eliminate that distraction?

- How can you adjust your environment to reduce or eliminate any distractions.

- Understanding that all inputs matter, what inputs can you eliminate that aren't helping you. And what inputs can you add to help your performance?

Chapter 19
Understand The Law
Of Attraction

"The Law of Attraction states that whatever you focus on, think about, read about, or talk about intensely, the more of it you will attract into your life."

Jack Canfield
Author of The Success Principles: How to get from
where you are to where you want to be.

As athletes we tend to focus a lot on the three Key Abilities. We have this very linear approach to our training and our thinking. We think that the more we train, rest and recover the better we will be. We have an input- output mentality that can be really hard to break.

But there are other aspects of sport that are not completely under our control but they are not completely outside of our control either and those things are referred to like "luck" or "good fortune." You've seen it where announcers use terms such as "the ball just seems to find him". Or, "the ball's really dropping for him today". These refer to situations and events that seem just a little out of the ordinary but are definitely to the benefit of the athlete.

But we now know through quantum physics that things like luck and good fortune can be attracted to you. They aren't a random occurrence but are literally created by the athlete.

Consider this great quote:

"What you radiate outward in your thoughts, feelings, mental pictures, and words, you attract into your life." - Catherine Ponder author of The Dynamic Laws of Prosperity

I want to share with you a story of Chris who was a lacrosse player I coached a number of years ago. I've changed his name to protect the innocent here but the story is worth sharing for a number of reasons.

Chris was a hard worker and was quite young compared to the rest of his teammates. He tended to get picked on by the older kids because he was so small and this didn't always sit well with Chris. The good natured ribbing didn't hit Chris the right way and it really worked a number on his self-esteem.

Chris was adopted, and there were issues in his adopted parents' house that really took a toll on him. He felt victimized by some of his teachers and really wanted to quit playing lacrosse at one point and just go get a job. I did my best to encourage Chris and was proud of his family for stepping up and helping him go on a trip with our team to play lacrosse in California.

Chris needed new cleats for the trip and his step dad reluctantly agreed to get him a pair and got them the day before the trip. In an attempt to save some money, the cleats he bought were quite stiff and not of the highest quality so the first day Chris wore them he got the most intense blisters and was unable to make it through the practice. Now here he was, in tears, on the phone with his stepdad who was now yelling at him for being soft when what Chris really needed to hear was, "It's going to be ok."

I took Chris to the drug store and we bought a ton of moleskin and bandages to get him wrapped up and ready to play for the next day. He'd been looking forward to this trip for so long and he was trying so hard to please everyone and wasn't really taking care of himself.

His first game was a disaster and he even got a penalty. That night I found him in the hotel lobby in tears. I explained to him that everyone on this team was really pulling for him and what he was taking as being picked on was really a level of love. I told him that his step-dad was out of line for picking on him about his cleats and that he needed to take 100% responsibility for not learning to wear an extra set of socks with the new cleats.

But I also talked to him about how his thoughts were really pulling him into this downward spiral. How he was completely creating in his game the negative thoughts that he was thinking about. He was expecting to drop the ball and miss passes. He was expecting not to be as good as the other kids who had been playing longer than him. But I knew that Chris had talent, and most importantly that he really "wanted" it to happen for him.

I shared with Chris how what he was thinking about was coming about and that in order for him to get better he would need to change what he was thinking about. He needed to see himself snagging ground balls and making great passes. We shared some tears and a hug because I really believed in Chris and I wanted him to believe in himself, too.

The next morning we taped up Chris's feet and he went out and scored two goals and had an assist. Our team won the game and Chris was a completely different player after that.

Now the ball was bouncing for him and not against him. He was getting the ground balls and making the passes. Instead of focusing on the bad things that could happen, he was believing in himself and that the game, and the people around him, weren't trying to make things hard on him, they were actually trying to help him. There was one particular play that I remember Chris making that completely shifted his game. Not the game he was playing in but his personal game. He snagged a loose ball by the sideline and in one complete motion he grabbed the ball, pivoted, switched hands and in this incredible stretched-out lunge, he took off, beating the defender and rifling a pass down to the attack man who scored. It was an amazing play that will be forever engrained in my head and his.

Today Chris plays lacrosse in college where he's studying Engineering. By shifting his focus to what he wants versus what he doesn't want any more he's able to attract into his life and his game things that support him.

It All Started With Albert Einstein

In 1935 Albert Einstein was studying this phenomenon when he started to work with Quantum Mechanics. (Stay with me here.) What he was discovering was that your thoughts have energy and they can attract into your life things of equal energy.

What that means is; what you think about, you bring about.

If you are thinking about being great in your sport but then you think about blowing a play or missing a move, guess what, that's exactly what's going to happen. You can work your tail off in practice but anticipate making a mistake in a game and that's exactly what you'll get.

As I mentioned at the beginning of the chapter, in sport we tend to get really focused on the idea of "more'. If we work harder. Shoot more pucks. Take more runs. Do more pullups. If we do all that THEN we'll get better.

But what I'm talking about is an overall mentality that good things are going to come your way. Here's an example of how NOT to do it:

- "I never get the good breaks."
- "Hopefully I'll win the next one."
- "I always get stressed for the big games."
- "I never perform on game day like I do in practice."
- "My coach hates me."

Here's some examples of good ways of thinking:

- "Good things always come my way."
- "I always get the breaks."
- "My best game always comes out on game day."
- "I'm always improving and learning from past experiences."
- "My hard work will give me opportunities to show my skills."
- "The ball always bounces in my favor."

Think Of What You Want and Not What You Don't Want

In order to be able to apply this type of thinking to your game you need to focus on what you want and not on what you don't want. It sounds easy but it can be a challenge. The tendency is to think about what you've done in the past and what your mistakes were. Think of the goalie who missed a save or a skier who missed a gate. We tend to review these situations and dwell on them negatively with comments like, "I really sucked on that play." or ,"I really blew it." This negative self talk only reinforces the negative feelings that are already in your head and all that you're doing is reinforcing negative.

Replace a Negative With a Positive

It's ok to look back on past performance as a way to create improved performance the next time around. As a goalie I would use a technique that really made the refs work harder than they wanted to. If I let in a goal I wouldn't fish the ball out of the back of the net, I would think about the shot I just missed and then visualized myself making the save I should have made and will make the next time around. By doing this I was replacing the negative picture in my head (the goal) with a positive image (the save) and I was able to build on that again and again.

For most athletes you're not really aware of the thoughts you're thinking and the way they are making you feel. From a coach and fan perspective you sometimes can see it with athletes sitting on a bench. Let's say a bad goal goes in and the team is down one goal with a minute to play. If the players are on the bench thinking, "This sucks. We're going to have to work really hard to score now and we haven't been able to score all game." Guess what is most likely going to happen? That's right, no goals. But if the coach and the players can think and behave positively and optimistically then they have a better chance of scoring and having a better performance overall.

What This Might Look Like For You?

Here are some examples of how this plays out for athletes in different sport performance situations:

- A ball takes a funny bounce past an outfielder resulting in a run being scored for your team.

- A player gets sick at the last minute giving you an opportunity to play in the game that you might normally not have gotten.

- The sun shining on the course revealing a bump that wasn't seen during the course inspection.

- The wind blowing a stray golf ball back into the fairway where it would have otherwise ended up in the hazard.

- An equipment breakage for an opponent that seemed "unlucky" at the time.

- I can go on and on with things like this but you get my point.

Use Words That Attract What You Want

I was emailing a mom in Ohio today whose daughter was about to compete for the state title. The mom wrote me and said, "Mia won the semifinal today and the next game we play is the team we lost to during the season. Hopefully this time around we will win."

I wrote her back and said , "There is no hopefully, Jedi. Only Do" citing an old Star Wars reference. The point I was making was that if you use the world "hopefully" you totally give out bad energy. By even referring to the loss in the last game then you're already putting energy on the negative outcome of the game they lost. Instead, I told her to watch the vocab and start to say things like, "With great ground ball play and solid shooting we will win the next game." That's a better way to frame it.

Focus On How You Want It To Be

Let's say you currently struggle with a move. Say, your a figure skater and you're having trouble landing your triple-loop. Continuing to talk about how you struggle with your triple-loop currently only reinforces more difficulty. Talking about how you want it to be as if you already are doing it now is even more effective.

Focusing on your current level of performance only continues to reinforce that level. But if you want to improve you must envision yourself as the athlete you wish to be as if you were that athlete right now.

Tame Your Limiting Beliefs

It's hard to think about yourself as though your hopes and dreams have already come true. One of the main reasons for that is we are often caught by our limiting beliefs about ourselves. You can blame a lot of things for your limiting beliefs. You can blame your past performance, or even your parents. You can be limited by your beliefs in where you've come from or how fast you're progressing. Whatever your limiting beliefs about yourself are, you can destroy those beliefs by doing one thing and that's taking action.

If you believe you're too short and you don't even go out and try to improve your performance then you are never going to get past that limiting belief. But if you go out there and take just the smallest bit of action you will see that your limiting belief just isn't true.

To continue on with the "too short" limiting belief you can look to see other athletes who have overcome that limiting belief and succeeded. In the NHL, Martin St. Louis was once called "too short" now they call him "too old"! At 5'8" inches he's one of the shortest players in the NHL. But not only has he been one of the shortest he is now one of the oldest players at 39 years of age. Oh and he also makes $5 million a year playing for the New York rangers. He's won a Stanley Cup. Olympic Gold. And numerous All-star appearances. When he retired he was asked how he felt having had such a long and successful career to which he replied, "If I had listened to all of the people who told me I was too short when I was younger, none of this would have happened."

If Martin St. Louis was caught up in the limiting beliefs of being too small he would have never been able to fight the critics who call him too old! The challenges and the critics never cease.

Trust Your Gut

You have a very powerful guidance system inside you and it's called your "gut." That's the place deep within you where intuition resides. You know the feeling. Sometimes you'll have this strong feeling deep down that you just know something to be true. Or you'll know that something is wrong. When we are young we are more in touch with this deep seated center of ourselves and it can really speak loudly if we listen.

As an athlete we tend to turn off the message our body sends us because our brain is trying so hard to get us to make things happen. Our brain is saying, "Work harder! More practice! More shots!" But our body is the gauge that knows what is really going on. There will be times when you just "know" something. It may be as simple as knowing when to take a rest. Or it can be more complex like when to get on the phone to call a coach for some help.

I remember early on in my athletic career being in a university book store. Something in my gut told me to look down and I happened to be standing in the middle of the Sports Psychology section. I had been exposed to sports psychology but wasn't particularly thinking I needed anything. But I was instantly drawn to a book on the middle shelf so I picked it up. It was called **Thinking Body Dancing Mind** by Dr. Jerry Lynch. I bought the book and took it back to the house where I was staying. I read the entire book straight through from start to finish. At the end of the book there was the contact information for the author. Something inside me was screaming out to call the number listed there for Jerry so I called and left a message. The next day, Jerry called me back and we began working together.

Now if I hadn't listened to my body I would have never been in that aisle of the bookstore. I wouldn't have looked down and I wouldn't have bought the book. And when my gut told me to call the number. I acted on it and it turned out to be one of the most pivotal phone calls in my entire athletic career. What is your gut telling you?

Create Affirmations To Keep You On Track

When I was working with Dr. Jerry Lynch he taught me about keeping affirmations next to my bed at night and reading them multiple times throughout the day. What an affirmation is a statement that is written as if it is already happening. So for me it was something like, "I am proud to be an All-American lacrosse goalie." Or, "I am happily walking into the opening ceremonies at the Olympic games."

So let's say you're a lacrosse player and you are a faceoff specialist. Your affirmations might read like this:

"I am comfortably winning 70% of my faceoffs."

"I am the number one recruit in the state of New York"

Or…"Division one Universities from all over the country are sending me letters to come to their school."

Now it might seem a little weird to write these down because they are not true...yet. But by writing them down and reading them over and over again and really feeling the emotion that comes when you say those affirmations you are creating positive energy that will help you attract those goals into your life.

Now you can create some notes in your phone that have your affirmations on them, but I like to write them down on three by five index cards so I can feel my hand writing them down. There is something about the physical act of writing them down that will really help you wire it into your thinking, so start by experimenting and getting a couple of your affirmations down on paper, on index cards, or in your phone. A great way to do it is put them in your phone and set an alarm for three times a day, every day. That way you will have a reminder to do it. Take a few moments by yourself to read them and feel the feelings of knowing they are true. Use the phone to remind you but then take a moment and actually write them on paper. It's called a "smart" phone for a reason and now you're going to get smarter by using it.

But What If Nothing Is Happening?

When you start focusing on what you want versus what you don't want and really feeling the feelings you'll feel once you are living out your dreams you may find that they aren't coming true as fast as you would like. That's ok. Just know that good things are happening for you in the background. As Mark Victor Hansen says, "What you want wants you!" So stick with it and stay patient. What you want is coming to you.

Conclusion

As athletes we can get very focused on more reps, more practice, more games. It seems like it is all on us all the time, and that is simply not the case.

Whether you believe in God, Buddha, energy, or the Great Big Force in the Universe, there is energy at play that can help you if you just tap into it. By focusing on what you want and not what you don't want, and by replacing negative thoughts with positives thoughts you start to tap into that force that is there to help you. When you watch what you say both externally and internally, you start to attract those things to you that will help you reach your goals. People will come into your life. Resources of time, energy and money. Be patient while silent forces work in the background to help you reach your goals.

Watch This Video

www.AthleteSpecific.com/
law-of-attraction

Take Action With These Steps

- Take out your journal and start by writing a handful of negative thoughts or sayings you commonly use.

- Now rephrase those negative sayings in the positive. Be creative and don't worry if they sound silly or stupid.

- Write down what limiting beliefs you may have been using in the past.

- Now rephrase those limiting beliefs into positive, affirmative saying that help you focus on what you want and not what you don't want.

Chapter 20
Stay Inspired With Great Friends, Teammates and Stories

"Friendship is so weird...you just pick a human you've met and you're like 'yep, I like this one' and you just do stuff with them."

Bill Murray
is an American actor, comedian, and writer. Best known
for his roles in Caddyshack and Stripes as well as
Saturday Night Life where he won his first Emmy.

When the going gets tough, which it inevitably will, you will need to have a strong team around you who can help you through the tough patches to get you back to a level where you have been before. I often tell athletes that you need to have valleys to have peaks, so it's not a matter of "if" the valleys will happen, but "when, and "what" will you do when they happen.

The Two Types Of People Around You

When it comes to reaching your dreams there are only two types of people and they are people who will:

1) Help you reach your goals.

2) Those who won't.
   It's really that simple.

When you are in a slump it's important that you keep your

vision on the best version of you that you can see. Get back into your visualization routine and really wire into your head how you would look if you were performing at your highest level. When you get back to that, everything else should start to fall into place.

Avoid Toxic People and Teammates

It's hard enough to stay focused by yourself, let alone being around toxic people and teammates. Remember how "environment trumps willpower"? Well, now that concept is as important as ever.

Toxic people and teammates will rob you of your motivation. They will say things like, "You can have a doughnut, just this once. Live a little!" Or more obvious, "How do you think you could possibly make that team. You're just a (insert negative adjective/noun combo here)." Wherever they fall on the scale their comments are not there to help you. They are there to hurt you and keep you from reaching your potential. You can look at them as "enablers" of poor performance

Don't forget that your success makes those around you jealous, and worse, it makes them look lazy. What they say about you is their business and not yours so shed their comments off your back like a duck in the rain. The water just rolls right off.

Fill Your Mind With Inspiring Stories

You have a tremendous resource available to you that I really wish I had when I was a young athlete and that's the Internet. I'm going to sound like a dinosaur when I say that I remember the time when getting video of your training was a pain in the butt. Now everyone has a multi-megapixel camera in their pocket that rivals the best video cameras from ten years ago.

And with that technology you have the ability to record inspiring videos of yourself when you have competed at your best OR you can hop online and Google inspiring videos and/or stories of athletes who have achieved what you want to achieve.

And part of your recipe to success is to surround yourself with great stories of athletes doing what you want to do. A great habit to get into is to start to look for, and journal about, great inspiring athletic stores of athletes just like you. Even those who are in a worse situation than you, who have gone on to make big things happen in their sport can be valuable to you.

It doesn't even have to be your sport, although that can be helpful. No, it really just needs to be anything inspiring that helps keep you on track when it feels like those around you aren't all that supportive.

You Gotta Believe

It is rare that elite athletes have 100% belief in themselves. They all have doubt at one point or another. Belief grows and contracts but it never shatters. If you expect that it is like glass and can break into a million pieces you are setting yourself up for failure. I like to envision belief like it is putty that can be shaped and molded. In order to reach your goals and dreams you need to believe in yourself. I know that if you're reading this book that you believe in yourself, even if it's just a little bit.

I mean listen, if you didn't believe in yourself, you wouldn't even be looking for ways to get better. So right now, inside of you there is a level of belief that is going to help you reach your goals.

It Starts With Belief In Yourself

To be successful, belief has to start with you. It's like a little spark starting a forest fire. It starts out as a small spark, but there are no other fires around to help it grow. Nope. At first that small spark has to land in the right environment where it can keep burning. And then the right amount of wind needs to come by to keep it glowing and growing just enough, but not too much that it gets blown out.

The same is true with you. That spark of belief in you needs a place to glow and grow. It would be great if your family and your immediate environment was ripe and ready to light you on fire. For many athletes, their parents weren't there to really fan the flames. Most athletes come from families with run of the mill parents who are supportive but also really busy with work and family and other commitments and interests. If you're lucky to grow up in a family where mom and dad already knew how to do what you're trying to accomplish, great! But the truth is that most athletes come from 'standard" athletic families. Think of my upbringing. My parents both had their Masters Degree in Music Me...

not-so-much.

But the belief started with me. And it was my responsibility to fan the flame.

Build Your Own Confidence

We know from brain research today, that with belief in one's self and the right coaching and training that people can learn to do almost anything at the highest level and that applies to you, too. But understand that confidence comes first. "Well, Coach, if I was better at my sport I'd have more confidence." That's not totally true.

In his awesome book, "**The Happiness Advantage,**" author Shawn Achor from Harvard teaches us that success doesn't breed happiness, and I'll add confidence. It's that confidence comes first. Think of bungee jumping. You don't need any skill or talent to bungee jump. You first need the confidence to just lean forward. The same holds true for you. Just lean into it with a little bit of confidence and your belief will grow and your abilities will also grow.

Find Examples Of People Just Like You Who've Made It

A great way to build your belief in yourself is to find examples of people just like you who have a similar background and who have reached success in their sport. By finding people just like you, you can create that well-if-she-can-do-it-I-can-do-it mentality needed to move forward.

If you need some extra motivation just hop online and look for some inspirational stories of people who are knocking it out of the park who came from nothing or have some physical limitation. There is no shortage of inspiration to be found online.

Think of Justin Tuck, the professional football player who was recruited, by mistake, when the recruiters for a school just happened to get lost in his hometown in Alabama and got directed to his house instead. He went on to a tremendous professional career winning multiple super bowls and going to the Pro Bowl multiple times.

How about the professional speaker (and surfer!) Nick Vujicic who was born with no arms and no legs and now goes around the world motivating others to reach their dreams.

Or how about another surfer, Bethany Hamilton who reached professional surfing stardom and then got her arm bitten off by a shark! You may have seen her movie **Soul Surfer.** But did you know she didn't let losing an arm stop her. She went on to win, without an arm!

I could go on and on, but what do you think you can accomplish if you're in a better situation than any of those people?

Eliminate The Word Can't
From Your Vocabulary

"Whether you think you can, or can't - you're right!"

Henry Ford
American captain of industry and a business magnate, the founder of the
Ford Motor Company, and the sponsor of the development of the assembly
line technique of mass production

People are quick to list all of the reasons why they **can't** do something. But all too often they won't take the time to list all of the reasons why they **can** do something.

I remember sitting in the Women's start house in Igls, Austria before a training session on the luge world cup circuit. The luge track in Igls sits high up the side of an Austrian alp. It's a beautiful place and an amazing photo to send home but sometimes the weather can get a bit unpredictable. It was kind of raining and snowing at the same time and that mix of weather was wreaking havoc on the track. Everyone's sled was a little off for a day like that and the mood in the start house was, let's just say, a bit weird.

Not only did it smell like sweaty armpits but all the athletes were complaining. It went something like this, "I hate the rain, I'm always slow in the rain," Or. "I Hate the snow, I'm always slow in the snow."

But other athletes would say, "I love the snow!" or, "The rain gets my faceshield wet but once I'm up to speed I love the feeling and the sound on my visor and it makes me go fast."

Which one of those athletes is going to have the better day training?

I left that day thinking, if I could just take all of those beliefs and pick the one that's going to give me the best chance to succeed right now, I'll have a good time. It's an attitude I try to take wherever I go.

I'll be honest though, it can be really hard to do it day in and day out. There are going to be some days when you're tired and worn out, or sick or injured.

You're not going to want to train or compete in conditions that aren't optimal and that's ok. But you have to eliminate thinking that you can't succeed in conditions that aren't perfect. You need to get rid of the word "can't" and replace it with "How can I?".

Beware Of What People Around You Believe

Just like the seeds from genetically modified crops can float into organic fields and contaminate them, so goes the same for ideas floating in the air around you. If someone around you is talking negatively remove yourself from that environment or throw some headphones on. You need to protect your thoughts just like you protect your money at the bank. Protect your mind from what other people say or think and you will be able to let those hopes and dreams of yours grow just like that ember waiting to start the forest fire.

And when people start to attack your beliefs remember this…

What People Say About You Says More About Them Than It Does About You

Your goals and your dreams, your approach on how you are going to make your dreams and goals come true are yours and yours alone. Because of that they must be protected. But when people start talking about you and your beliefs remember that what they say about you says more about them than it does about you.

When people ask me what sport I did in the Olympics they normally tell me, "You're crazy!"

When I was young I used to get caught up in that a bit and think, "I'm crazy? Really? I'm crazy!" That wasn't a really good feeling that I wanted to continue. But then I realized that they just didn't know what I know. When they said, "You're crazy!" What they were really saying was, "I have no idea how to do what you do so therefore I think you're crazy." That's what it really boils down to.

I heard the same thing as a goalie in most sports I played. But really, when you boil it down, if they believed what I believed and had the same knowledge that I had then I'd be facing more competition! So I learned to like hearing from people when they said things like that because it made me realize that what I did made me all that more special. And it's the same for you, too.

If someone you know, like and trust starts to say things like, "You're nuts!" or, "I can't believe you do that!" Just smile and say to yourself, "They don't understand my dreams and my goals like I understand my dreams and my goals and that's ok."

What You Believe In Is Up To You

You have a choice. If it's raining, you can believe you're great in the rain. If you didn't get enough sleep you can believe that your body is going to pull out the stops and give you a great performance even though you're a bit tired. If you forgot your favourite underwear you can think that your underwear has been holding you back anyway and you've been meaning to make a change. You can make a change and choose to believe the thing that will give you the best chance to succeed.

Conclusion

There will be times when your belief in yourself, in your process, in your goals will all take a hit. That is the time when you really need to stay inspired with great friends, teammates, coaches and stories to keep you motivated.

A great friend and teammate will keep you up when you are down. Your coaches will help you, too. But it's up to you to seek out the right people. You need to fill your mind with great stories of other athletes just like you or worse, who have made it even when times got tough. By filling your mind with positive stories you will be able to find ways to stay inspired even when the times get tough.

Watch This Video

www.AthleteSpecific.com/stay-inspired

Take Action With These Steps

- Grab your journal and take a moment to write down the people in your life who are inspiring to you and keep yourself motivated and upbeat.

- Take a moment to write down the names of the people who are a little less than motivating. Do your best to reduce or eliminate the time you spend with those people.

- Get online and look up inspiring stories to keep you motivated during the toughest of times. Having a library of inspiring stories can keep you up when you're feeling down.

- What are some things people have said to describe you that says more about them than it does about you?

Section 4
Game Day

"All of my training has prepared me for this moment."

Rhino
From the Movie "Bolt"

Now is the day it all comes together.

You've done the work. You've put in the reps and taken care of your body. You have adopted new habits and improved all of your Three Key Abilities: The Physical, Technical, and Tactical. Because your Abilities have improved your Belief in yourself has improved as well as your ability to manage your life around your goals. And finally, you've managed your Resources to the best of your abilities to be ready to compete.

Chapter 21
Make It a Great Day

"Be so good they can't ignore you."

Steve Martin
An American actor, comedian,
writer, producer, and musician

It seems like a lot, but today is a great day. To many athletes, if they have trained properly, Game Day feels like a rest day. It feels easy in comparison to the amount of work they have put in during the week and you get to reap the rewards.

How I Used To Think About Game Day

When I was a young athlete I used to think of Game Day as the ultimate battle. It was a day when "my better" was going to beat "your better." And that's how many athletes and coaches look at it. If you're going to yell in warm up I'm going to yell louder. If you're going to do ten push ups I'm going to do eleven. If you sprint I'm going to sprint faster. It was a battle and whatever you're going to do to win I'm going to have to do more of it and do it better.

But what we know now is that is a really unsophisticated way to look at competing. Because the answer to winning is not to be able to do more, or better. No, it's something else. You're not looking for more competition, you're looking for…clarity.

Finding Clarity

Now that you have reached Game Day, it's time to win. Everything you have done up to today is meant to help you win. That's why you're here and that's why your competitors are here. They want to win too and the rest of the world likes to romanticize that the way to win on Game Day comes down to "who wants it more!?"

And while that's great and all, but it's not about who wants it more but who understands what it's going to take to win and who can apply that knowledge along with their Abilities. I know, I know, that's a long answer but that's what it is you are trying to do. If you need to hustle, then you need to hustle. If you need to shoot more, then you shoot more. If you need to endure more, then you endure more. We want to understand the game with as much clarity as possible so we know just what it is we need to do in order to win.

Let me explain this a bit more: Let's say that at the end of last season you worked all summer long to get stronger and you put on a lot of weight because of it. (That doesn't necessarily have to happen but in your case it did.) This extra weight made you super strong but now you're not as agile because you didn't focus on that in the summer months. Every day you hit the gym with your trainer and you worked hard. Like, really hard. Why? Because you really wanted it! There was no one who was going to outwork you this summer, and they didn't. If there was an award for working hard, you'd get the gold medal.

But was it the "right" work? New season starts and you're in your first big competition. You really, really want this. You've been working for this moment all summer. YOU WANT IT!!!!

And you get absolutely schooled. What happened? Well, you weren't clear. You weren't clear on what it was going to take to win today. Your lack of effort didn't get you, it was your understanding on what it was really going to take to win and the abilities you truly need.

Back in Chapter 5 I talked about the different Flight Levels that you're going to need to bounce between to really get this down. You need clarity at all of the flight levels. From the big picture at 50,000 feet all the way down to the runway. Well, on Game Day you are at runway level and here is where some of your most important clarity will come from. In order to win you have to be very clear about your opponent as well as the environment you are going to be in.

Understanding Your Opponent's Abilities

Just like you need to understand your own abilities, you need to understand your opponent's abilities to have the best chance to win

AND to conserve your energy. Bet you didn't think of that now did you? When you're an athlete and you're a competitor and you want to win you tend to focus on winning over just how much energy it's going to take to win. It doesn't make any sense to wear yourself out in a victory unless you are trying to impress a coach on the sideline.

Just like, you're opponent has a physical ability as well as a technical and a Tactical Ability. Your job is to understand what they are so that you can withstand the challenges from that opponent as well as maximize the opportunities your opponent gives you.

Great competitors in any sport do whatever they can to understand their competitors strengths and weaknesses. In individual sports like tennis or swimming an athlete might know when their competitor is strong or weak. Say they are really strong but if the match goes long the competitor will fade. If you have better endurance you might have a distinct advantage the longer the match goes on. Same with the swimmer whose competitor may be slow at the start but have a great finish.

In a team sport like basketball it would be incredibly important to know that the player you will be going up against has a tremendous jump shot that will cause you to defend them further away from the basket. That same player is reluctant to drive to the basket which would allow you to play some very aggressive defense. But if you didn't know that you might lay back expecting him to drive to the basket only to give up an easy shot for him.

I could give you plenty examples of abilities to identify but I hope you get my point. Without understanding your opponent's abilities you can be missing major opportunities to take advantage of. You might also get run over.

How To Learn Your Opponent's Abilities

Most coaches and players learn their opponents abilities by trying to watch them in warm up right before competition and with today's technology there is no excuse for this. With a little bit of research you can probably find some really good video footage of your opponents online. Heck, if you know you're going to compete against this athlete again, have your friend video them so you can study their tendencies and take advantage of them later.

Talking to your coach and teammates is also a great resource to learn more about your competitor's abilities and how to take advantage of the opportunities they will give you. But if you're going in cold, you're going to have to watch yourself to start as you learn a bit about your opponent. This is a much slower tactic than doing some research before hand, but you want to be careful as you first start to engage your opponent and then let 'er rip.

Prepare For The Environment

Athletes don't always think of their environment as an opponent but it can be. Whether it's sunny or rainy, grass or clay, hard ice or soft ice, your environment provides challenges and gives you opportunities just like an opponent would.

With that in mind, it's important to prepare for the environment you will be competing in just as you would for the opponents you're up against. You'll need to consider things like weather and lighting, humidity and dryness. Will it be early in the day or late in the day? Will you be competing in sunlight or artificial light? Is the weather supposed to change in the middle of the event? What will you do to prepare for that?

Well-trained athletes are ready to compete in any situation in any environment. They believe that they can compete because they are prepared for anything and there are no surprises.

Prepare For The Venue

I remember much of the conversation in our team meetings at the Olympics revolved around the logistics to get us to and from the track. Because of the increased traffic at an Olympic Games it was going to take us a tremendous amount of time to load up the team vans and sit in traffic to get to the venue. Why did this matte

Your routine prior to competing can have a dramatic affect on your performance. At the Olympic level athletes and coaches are extremely aware of routines and anything that can disrupt them. The conversations around the van ride to the track was important because they were going to add a lot of time to our day and this would affect everything from having to take a leak before we got in the van to making sure we had enough food for the ride. Preparing for the venue in this case was a very big deal.

If you head to your venue and you're not prepared for it to rain, how would that affect your performance? If you're going to be stuck out in the blazing sun between games how would that affect your performance? If you didn't have access to food between games how would that affect your performance? You have put in so much work to have it be derailed because of poor planning because you didn't prepare for the venue you were to compete at.

Conclusion

Making your Game Day a great day comes down to a few strategic actions. You've worked out. You've trained. You've prepared. But these last few steps can either make or break your game day.

By seeking clarity when it comes to your opponent you will have an advantage when you are ready to compete. Understanding your opponent's Abilities will give you the edge when it comes to performing well under pressure.

You will also be competing against an opponent in a certain environment. Your understanding of what that environment will be and how to be ready for it will also dictate how well you perform on Game Day. Don't skimp on your preparation for Game Day. Knowing as much as you can will give you the ability to be prepared and to eliminate all surprises.

Watch This Video

**www.AthleteSpecific.com/
make-game-day-a-great-day**

Take Action With These Steps

• Take your journal and write down three ways you look at Game Day. (i.e. You need to get 'up' for Game Day. You have to outwork your opponent. etc)

- Now write down three additional ways to look at Game Day that may give you a better understanding to win. (i.e. Understanding your opponents strengths and weaknesses.)

- Think about your next competition and where it will happen. What can you do to ensure you have your best Game Day by understanding more about the environment and the venue on Game Day.

Chapter 22
Visualize Your Way
To Success

"I like visualizing a lot, so the night before a competition and right before, I will visualize myself. I'll close my eyes, turn away from everybody, and just see myself doing exactly what I want to accomplish."

Kacy Canatanzaro
The smallest competitor to complete the American Ninja Warrior race. nicknamed Mighty Kacy, is an American professional wrestler, gymnast and athletics-based television personality, currently signed to WWE, training at their Performance Center.

Visualization is a powerful tool to help you take your game to the next level and one that a lot of athletes are never taught to do correctly. I was taught how to visualize when I was a young Olympic athlete and I was able to apply it to every other sport I played in and I still use it today, even in business settings.

Visualization is the art of creating vivid, emotionally charged pictures in your mind that replicate what you are looking to achieve in your sport.

Researchers today understand that the mind doesn't know the difference between what is happening in real life and what is being imagined in your head. Your brain goes through the same process as it would if what you were imagining in your head was real.

I first learned about this when I was competing in the sport of luge and was footing the bill to train in Europe on my own. I had shared with Dr. Jerry Lynch that I was concerned that I didn't have enough money to take the same amount of training runs as the National Team which would give them a distinct advantage over me.

Jerry reassured me that this wouldn't be a problem if I created a visualization routine and stuck to it religiously during the season. It was a way for me to increase my training volume without having to pay for the actual training runs. Jerry taught me that the mind doesn't know the difference between what is real and what is imagined...with feeling. What the "feeling" part means is that you really need to sense the entire experience. The weather. The crowd. Your equipment. Your heartbeat. Your competition. The venue. Everything. The more you can actually put yourself in the situation in your mind's eye the more effective the visualization would be.

How Visualization Works

The art of visualization helps you get ready for competing before you actually compete. Everyone agrees that it's easier to do something if you've done it before, and the more you can do something the better you'll get. That's where visualization comes in because it's designed to help you refine your skills by visualizing yourself doing things perfectly.

Step 1: The best way to do this is to find a quiet space where you can relax. Put in your earbuds and create some quiet music but realize that you most likely won't have music on when you're competing. It may be better to put your earbuds in and put on some White Noise using an app like the White Noise app.

Step 2: Now close your eyes and daydream about yourself performing flawlessly. See yourself competing and doing your best in a competitive environment.

That's it!

By visualizing yourself performing perfectly you are wiring into your mind and your body all of the neural pathways that are used to perform just as if you were actually performing.

Before Bed Can Be 7X As Effective

Whatever is in the forefront of your thinking before you go to bed can be replayed in your mind upwards of seven times so why not make the most of it? I used to visualize my perfect runs as part of my bedtime routine every night I was on the circuit. I would prep my sled and then get ready for bed. After brushing my teeth and having a big glass of water I'd lie down in bed and close my eyes. It was then that I would take three training runs of the track that I was about to go on the next day. It got to the point that I was so dialed into this bedtime routine that I would usually fall asleep during that third visualization of my training run.

By doing this visualization right before I went to bed my brain would then continue my "training" while I was sleeping. Turning the process over to my unconscious mind enabled me to wire in the process.

First Thing In The Morning Works Too

To be doubly effective I would also repeat my visualizations first thing when I woke up in the morning. When the brain is calm it is floating in Alpha waves which are considered a higher level of consciousness than the higher frequency beta-waves that we're in during the day. So first thing in the morning, I would usually tap the snooze button and take the next nine minutes to visualize my routine again.

No matter what your sport you can see how visualization can help you accelerate your learning and your achievement. I work with a lot of goalies who visualize themselves stopping more balls and pucks, reacting faster than they have in the past. By visualizing themselves moving properly they are wiring in the neural pathways that allow them to have the proper response once their eyes are able to decipher where the ball is going.

Grant Fuhr, one of the greatest hockey goalies in history, was well-known to do kick saves in his sleep as he visualized the games replaying in his head. He did it so much he actually forced his wife to sleep on the couch! Ouch!

Visualize Doing Imperfect...Perfectly

As I mentioned above, it's important to visualize yourself performing flawlessly, but...

Early on in my luge career I was taught to visualize, and I was only taught to visualize having the perfect run. This was a huge mistake in an athlete's development. It was a false idea that trying to attain some level of "perfect" was going to win races or get the gold. And it was the summer after the Olympics that this really hit home for me.

That summer I rented an apartment where I lived by myself. Not having enough money to pay for cable, all I had was a VCR and a TV (Kids, you may have to ask your parents what a VCR is.) I had three tapes to play in the VCR, one of which was the race footage from the Men's Singles Race from the 1994 Olympics which was one of the greatest races in Olympic history.

What I noticed watching that tape over and over again was that of the three medalists, all of them came down the track differently. None of them had a "perfect" run and it was then and there that I realized that sport (like life) wasn't about doing things perfectly, it was about dealing with the imperfect aspects of sport...perfectly.

This was a huge distinction for me and one that I hope will help you as well. You see, when all you do is visualize doing things perfectly you put yourself in position to feel really stressed out when things don't go as well as you visualized.

I had also been taught things like, "Really see yourself standing on the podium having that medal draped around your neck!" Well...that's all well and good if you're trying to stay motivated through something really difficult. But that doesn't do you any good when you're trying to navigate through a difficult situation in a game or event. That is why I suggest to athletes that, yes, start with visualizing things going perfectly for you. But also, **visualise yourself doing things perfectly through imperfect situations**. When I would go to bed at night, not only would I visualize three perfect runs, I would also visualize what I would do if I entered each curve on the left side, or the right side of the track. For it was here that races were really won as I noticed on that Olympic race footage. It wasn't just about having the perfect routine it was about how my body compensated if things were off slightly. How would I recover with perfect position if I was in THIS situation? How would I get through THAT situation if that happened?

You can even visualize other situations not to dwell on them and attract them to you, but to see yourself handling things calmly and effectively. Let's say you're an equestrian and you get mud in your eye. Can you visualize what you would do if that happened and how you would get through it with ease? Let's say you're Janet Jackson at the Super Bowl and you have an equipment malfunction. How would you handle THAT and still sing? Hmmm?

By taking time to visualize the imperfect situations that may arise you can wire your brain to stay calm, cool and collected and to get through it successfully without losing time or losing points. Here are some other examples:

A field goal kicker can visualize kicking the winning the field goal with a second left on the clock, but he can also visualize the opposing team's coach calling a timeout just as he is about to kick it.

A gymnast can visualize the perfect routine, but she can also visualize having to wait through an extended delay while the judges fix their computers.

A skateboarder can visualize the perfect run, but can also visualize noticing that his board is cracked right before his final run and having to get a replacement board and riding that instead.

With some creativity I'm sure you can come up with some scenarios for your sport and how you can visualize not just doing things perfectly, but also how to navigate the imperfect situations that come your way during your competition. By taking just a little bit of time to first, admit that things don't always go perfectly and second, see yourself navigating those situations effectively. You will guarantee yourself solid performances no matter what your sport.

Have All Your Equipment Ready The Night Before

A well prepared athlete is one who pays attention to all of the details and your equipment is one of those details. It doesn't matter if you are a hockey goalie with all sorts of equipment or a swimmer with nothing but a Speedo, equipment can malfunction and you don't want it to malfunction when you are trying to perform at your best. Take the time to go over all of your equipment the night before you compete so you can go to bed knowing that everything is perfect.

I worked with a Junior hockey player who was about to play in front of a very prominent professional scout in a game the very next day. This hockey player had a pre-game routine of using a heavier stick in practice and warm ups because it made his game stick feel lighter. In one of the biggest games of his potential career this player grabbed his game stick and took to the ice getting a breakaway on his very first shift. As he bore down on the goalie he went to shoot and his stick snapped in half with his stick going one way and the puck going the other. What could have been an incredible goal and an event that the scout would remember turned into a complete dud. Not only that, by missing out on this opportunity in front of the scout, this player had a horrible game from that point on.

While I would have liked to see this athlete bounce back from the broken stick and the missed opportunity and continue to have a great game, some athletes just don't have that skill yet. The sad part of all of this was that the stick was probably broken before the game. It probably cracked in the last game. A simple flex of the shaft would have broken the stick in the locker room with plenty of time to get a new stick and then the chance to score would have still been there. Instead the stick snaps, the opportunity is missed, and the game goes on.

Had this hockey player gone over all of his equipment the night before this situation of the broken stick would have never happened. Yet, I see it all the time. An athlete has an equipment malfunction just before or at the beginning of the game that could have been solved well in advance.

Forgotten Gear. No excuse.

In one of my first ever luge trips to a foreign track, one of the girls on our team forgot her face shield. Her face shield! This is probably one of the most important pieces of equipment a luge athlete needs to have. It would be like forgetting your baseball glove or maybe even your cleats. She didn't just forget it at the track one day, she forgot it at home. In the United States. And we were in Canada.

Because she forgot this vital piece of equipment at home she missed the first day of training. No worries she thought, her mom can just FedEx it overnight.

While that might seem simple it did cost a small fortune to send. Not to mention her mom sent it in a soft-sided bubble envelope. Now, that might not seem like much either but luge face shields are made out of soft plastic. They are pliable but they are brittle and the face shield arrived flat as a pancake and in a million pieces. She then missed the next day of training.

The bottom line with this story is that forgetting your equipment is unacceptable. You need to take full responsibility and take an inventory of your equipment prior to any trip, game, or practice. You also need to do it early enough so you have plenty of time to fix or replace anything if it's needed. That hockey player with the broken stick I told you about earlier? He also broke not one, but TWO skate laces prior to the game! Now skate laces don't all of a sudden fray and break. No, these laces had needed replacement for a really long time and it was only a matter of time before they snapped. By taking two minutes the day before the game this athlete could have replaced the laces that he was going to need to replace anyway. Instead he had to run around looking for laces five minutes before he was supposed to take the ice.

All Details Matter

I work with a lot of athletes, parents and coaches who have big dreams. They want to play in college and maybe even professionally. Some want to compete in the Olympics as well. They will all shrug off what seem like small responsibilities that they will learn to take care of "some day." As though little details like having all of your equipment prepared before Game Day isn't something worth worrying about. They will just "deal with it" as it happens.

As an elite athlete you have an incredible ability to withstand challenges and take advantage of opportunities but you also have a limited amount of bandwidth to deal with it all. With just a little bit of pro-active action you can save yourself a lot of wasted time and energy. It is true that, occasionally, things will come up; but let's keep that bandwidth available for dealing with those rare occurrences and not leave ourselves open to situations we have created.

By taking care of small details you will free yourself up mentally to higher levels of thinking in your sport. That may seem a little strange but it's true. Think about it this way: if you are spending thirty seconds struggling to find your socks that you just randomly tossed in your bag you could be spending that time visualizing a great performance, or studying your competition. Instead you're raising your heart rate because you're stressed that you left them at home. Had you folded them together and put them in the pocket of your bag dedicated to your clean gear for that day's practice or game you would have that bandwidth. Make sense?

Think about it this way, have you ever been around a professional team? Everything is pristine. The gear, the locker room, even the practices are run down to the smallest detail. They don't just show up and wing it. I love watching Formula One racing just to see how organized and precise everything is. The engineers build everything down to the smallest screw with the utmost precision and because of that you have the fastest cars, with the best drivers who are some of the highest paid athletes in the world. Now do you think they got that way and THEN they looked at the details or did they take care of the details first?

Why Talk About Equipment Here?

It might seem odd that in the Visualization chapter I'm talking about getting all of your equipment ready but it all ties together. Here's why:

When you go through your equipment looking to make sure it's all ok and that nothing is broken, what do you think you're doing?

Not only are you just inspecting your equipment, you are seeing yourself using it. You are using your mind to decide if this piece of equipment is going to do what you think it's going to do? To do that, your mind has to play through a series of visualizations naturally. Here are some examples:

- As a soccer player looks at her cleats to see if they are worn out, she is envisioning herself running in them, and then making a cut away from a defender.

- As a tennis player looks at the worn strings on his tennis racquet he is envisioning himself serving the ball for an ace, or making a forehand smash that hits just inside the baseline.

- As a football player inspects his gloves he's envisioning making the catch as he tippy-toes the sideline.

- And on, and on…

When an athlete tells me he is having a challenge with visualization I have him go through this equipment routine and see himself using the piece of equipment he is inspecting. Quite easily the athlete starts to visualize the piece of equipment on his body and using it in a game situation. It's a little trick that maximizes the mind's ability to imagine a successful outcome which is exactly what the athlete wants to see on Game Day.

Get It All Organized To Avoid Having To Think

While I just talked about getting your equipment ready, you really want to have as much of your life organized so you don't have to think about anything other than your best competition on Game Day.

The brain is an incredible organ in our body with incredible potential, but we know through science that it does have a limit to its decision making. That's why, if you're trying to avoid eating junk food, but it's the end of the day and you don't feel like looking for anything healthy in the fridge you go for the bag of chips in the cupboard. It's like you've used up your Decision Points during the day and have none left to make the right decision about the chips.

If you've got a big game but you've got a big interview or three exams on the same day, you're going into that Game already having used up some of those Decision Points. By having your equipment all sorted, and anything else for that matter, you are saving up as many Decision Points to use for Game Day.

Before you go to sleep have as much organized and ready for the next day as is humanly possibly. Think about what it is you need to have a successful day tomorrow. You can even create a checklist that you print off of your computer of all the things you need in your bag so that you don't have to rethink it every time you do it. You just go down the list. "Socks? Check. Mouthpiece? Check. Jersey? Check. Etc"

Having checklists can eliminate much of the thinking you need to do and by doing it before you go to bed you can sleep peacefully knowing that you have everything in place. You're not going to bed wondering if you're going to forget something in the morning.

Conclusion

Visualization is the often misunderstood and underused secret to elite athletes. When you understand that the mind doesn't know the difference between what is real and what is imagined, then you will know that the habit of visualizing is just as effective as real practice.

Using visualization before you go to bed and when you wake up in the morning can be 7X effective than doing it during the day.

A strange form of visualization occurs when you get your

equipment ready for practice and competition. By working on your equipment and getting it game ready you actually see yourself using it which is a form of visualization. By getting your equipment ready you actually accomplish two things while you prepare for Game Day.

Watch This Video

www.AthleteSpecific.com/
how-to-visualize

Take Action With These Steps

- Dedicate a few minutes before you fall asleep tonight to visualize your performance at tomorrow's practice. Your brain will play that positive visualization over and over while you sleep.

- Right when you wake up, and before you go to the wash room, take some time to visualize today's performance while your brain is still in a quiet state.

- Take some time today to go through all of your equipment to look for any tears, rips, cracks, or anything that is otherwise broken.

- Commit to repairing any piece of equipment that is sub standard. Visualize yourself using that piece of equipment effectively in your performance.

Chapter 23
Get To Peak State

---

*"A flower does not think of competing
to the flower next to it.
It just blooms"*

Zen Shin Talks
A book with Buddhist undertones,
yet appropriate for all backgrounds.

We covered Peak State in Chapter 6 so if you haven't read that chapter go back and read it now. Go ahead, I'll wait.

Ok, ready?

Everything you've worked on in training, and by working on your visualizations about your performance, has prepared you to reach Peak State for your competition. Now if you've just been practicing and not thinking too much about getting to Peak State then you're going to have trouble gauging what you need to do to get there for Game Day. If that's you, then you're wasting a lot of valuable time and energy.

Peak State is that window where everything comes together to have your best performance, but if you haven't been training for that in practice, and have just been going through the motions, you won't be able to get there on your most important day, Game Day.

You Can't Just Turn It On

Many athletes feel that they will be able to turn it on when Game Day comes. Their practices are lethargic at best as they grind it out day to day. Because the practice isn't inspired it is rare that the game time performance can be inspired either. Don't let that be you!

If you have been paying attention in your practices you will be able to adjust your warm ups so that you can get to Peak State efficiently. You will know that if you are cold you might need more time to get your body warm physically but you may also learn that on days when you have work, or tests, or other obligations you may need to take a nap to get energized and to help you get to Peak State later. Every athlete is different and only you can know what it takes to get you to Peak State.

Resist Turning To Outside Aids

I knew a hockey player who relied on four cups of coffee and two Red Bulls prior to every game he played. (I told him to see his Doctor) The problem was, he also had two Red Bulls before every practice. This athlete was relying so much on outside stimulants to get himself going that he didn't even know where his baseline really was.

Your goal is to first understand what your body needs naturally in order to perform at it's best. This usually starts with getting enough sleep and eating properly to make sure your body is rested and recovered each and every day. The tendency is to think that you need "more" in order to perform your best. This can mean more hype, more caffeine, more "amped", but the problem is all of that can blow you right by Peak State and ruin your performance.

The Test You Can't Cram For

Every athlete I have ever worked with has wished they had done more (something) before Game Day. You are probably like that as well. It can be more time in the weight room, or more time working on their equipment. It could be having more endurance and spending more time on sprints, etc. There is always something you feel you haven't spent enough time on, and I'm here to tell you that you're not going to be able to suddenly make up for it all the night and day before Game Day. Now is not the time to try and overcome all of the procrastinating you have done. You've probably spent plenty of time in your life "cramming" for a test. Maybe it was math, or spelling or calculus, it doesn't really matter but whatever it was you probably got away with it, to a point. While you may be able to cram your head full of information and pull off a solid performance on a test in school, your body doesn't work like that.

Your sport isn't like that either. It won't reward procrastination.

All of those training sessions you blew off or didn't take seriously will all look like missed opportunities on Game Day. Great performances come from lots of consistent work over a long period of time. Whatever you feel you have missed or haven't missed, let it go. You will have a better performance getting enough sleep the night before Game Day, than taking extra reps in the weight room or on the field.

Immature athletes will know that a big competition is coming up and then try to fill their days with extra training. Instead of three days a week in the weight room they will do five days in the weight room. They will stay up late and worry about their Game Day instead of visualizing and getting to sleep.

A mature athlete will know that in order to have their best performance they need to taper off their training and get lots of rest and nutrition. A mature athlete will actually do less before a big Game Day instead of trying to cram in more. Their body will be rested and recovered and this will give them the opportunity to have their best performance.

Play Like You Practice and Practice Like You Play

You may find that you practice better than you play. I ran into this problem in the sport of luge and also when I was playing lacrosse. I found that I tended to perform better in practice than on Game Day and that really frustrated me.

When I looked at why this might be happening I made a list of all the reasons that might be causing my performance on Game Day to be different than my performance in practice. It ended up being a really long list and I had two, one for lacrosse and one for luge that I will share with you here:

Lacrosse:

- Field: Different field (away games etc)
- Clothing: Wearing game day jersey, game shorts.
- My special underwear (Hey! Don't judge.)
- Putting too much pressure on myself to do more on Game Day than I do in practice.

- Seeing types of shots that I didn't see in practice that week.
- Coach standing on sidelines instead of on the field behind the cage where he likes to stand in practice.
- Girlfriend in stands. Not there in practice.
- Parents in stands. Not there in practice.
- Game day stick instead of practice stick.
- Wearing eye black on game day and not in practice.
- Routine for practice different than on Game Day. (bus ride etc, leave from last class, get dressed on bus, etc)

Luge:
- Ice typically in better shape in competition than in training.
- Wearing race suit on race day and not in training.
- Long breaks between runs on race day. Training runs typically one after the other. Feels like two first runs instead of first run then second run.
- Sled is taped for race day for aerodynamics and not training.
- Runners not polished to same standard as on race day.
- Race time early in morning, training typically later in the day.
- Second race run usually better than first race run.
- Race booties instead of comfortable training booties.
- Ride to track with men different than training runs done with whole team. Van ride is very different.
- Different music on training days than on race days. Van ride noisy. Usually quiet.

This is a partial list of what I noticed was different between training days and competition days in both those sports. And as I looked at those lists there were certain things I could control and other things I couldn't control. I was the same person from practice to Game Day. Nothing about me changed physically, but what did change were certain things that I could control so my goal was to make as many things in practice the same as they were on Game Day.

Here are some of the changes I made in each of my two sports:

Lacrosse:

- Visualize the night before and morning of Game Day. Specifically focus on the Game Day environment (Game Day Jersey and shorts, referees, coach on sidelines, girlfriend in stands,etc)

- Wear game day jersey and shorts in practice the day before game.

- Use Game Day stick in last half of practice on day before game.

- Skip wearing eye black on Game Day

- For away games, stretch and visualize on bus on way to field. Not enough time when we arrive.

Luge:

- Visualize race environment the night before and the day of race.

- Prepare runners the same as on race day. (Put duct tape on sled for aerodynamics to slow myself down)

- Wear race suit in the last training session prior to race.

- Listen to mellower music on race day.

I made additional tweaks to this list here and there but what you'll notice is that all of these changes revolved on how things made me feel on Game Day. I wanted to feel just as confident as I did in Practice as I did on Game Day and what these lists helped me uncover were all of the things that made me feel different.

For some athletes they can wear their special underwear on Game Day and be just fine. But for me, the answer was "consistency". In both lacrosse and luge I wanted to feel the same as I did in practice and that made all of the difference.

Over the years I've come across many athletes who don't perform on Game Day as they do in practices and for each of those games the recommendations I give fall into three distinct categories:

1) **Costume**: Just like an actor getting ready to play his part on stage, the costume can put the athletes mind in a very different space. It can be a jersey, a race suit, a special golf shirt. Whatever it is for you, wearing it so much that it becomes second nature and doesn't affect your performance can be a

critical change to your game. If you find that what you wear on Game Day affects you negatively, look to see how you can wear what you wear on Game Day in practice so that you can get comfortable performing at a high level while wearing it.

2. **Environment**: What can you do to prepare for the environment that you are about to compete in? Many sports allow training sessions on the same field of play that you will compete on. But even then, it's not always the actual field that makes the difference. While a golf course, or a football field, or a basketball court may be the same, what surrounds it often changes. There may be packed stands and music. There may be bright sun or bright lights. It might be pouring rain or snowing. And while you can't always affect the environment you can do everything you can to visualize the environment the best you can. Your goal is to do what you can so that there are no surprises and that it feels like you've been there before even though you haven't.

3. **Body**: What can you do to be ready for *how your body is going to feel* come Game Day? Is it going to be hot out and therefore you are going to feel hot? Will you be coming from a stressful environment? Will the ride to the event be longer than usual? All of these scenarios can affect how you are going to feel and it is your job to replicate those feelings in practice so that they won't be a surprise on Game Day. I knew on Game Day that I was going to wake up in the morning and my body was going to be pretty close to getting ready to go. If I continued with the same warm up I did in practice then I was going to be over-ready. I was not going to be in Peak State because I would have over-cooked myself. (I explain this more in Chapter 6) What I needed to do was actually tone my warm up down in order to get to my Peak State.

Conclusion

Getting to Peak State is a process that gets refined the more experience you have as an athlete. No matter how you wake up each morning, you will develop the awareness to get to Peak State no matter how you feel.

You can't expect to play better on Game Day than you do in

practice. If you do, you can probably up your intensity in practice and have even better performances on Game Day. Your mantra should be, "Play like you practice and practice like you play." Everyday.

With steady, consistent practice you will get yourself to your Peak State everyday and will be well on your way to steady, consistent improvement.

Watch This Video

**www.AthleteSpecific.com/
getting-to-peak-state**

Take Action With These Steps

- Grab your journal and make a list of the consistent steps you take to be ready on Game Day.
- Now make a list of the consistent steps you take to be ready for your practice sessions.
- Compare each list and see where you can improve by adding or reducing steps to have the best Game Day possible.

Section 5

Get Results. Review Those Results. Keep The Lessons. Try Again.

"You will fall. And when you fall, the winner always gets up, and the loser stays down."

Arnold Schwarzenegger
Austrian bodybuilder. Actor. Former Governor of California

So how did it go? Did you win? Did you lose? Would it surprise you if I told you that it doesn't really matter if you win or lose? Just because you won or lost today has no bearing on your long term success. In this section we are going to explain just why that is the case and how you can avoid making rash decisions based on short-term results.

Chapter 24
How To Learn
From Losing

---

*"I never played a round where I didn't learn
something new about the game."*

Ben Hogan
An American professional golfer, generally considered one
of the greatest players in the history of the game.

You will lose more than you win. It's just a fact. And while the ratio of how many wins to losses you experience varies on your sport, just know that one of the most critical aspects of your training is learning how to deal with losing.

Losing, and specifically how you learn from losing is extremely important. The truth is, most people are very sore losers. They get angry and upset. They get burned out and frustrated. But a result is neither good or bad. It's just a result. A win. A loss. A fast time. A slow time. A high score or a low score. The results aren't good or bad but how you think about them makes them so.

E+R=O

You may have seen this formula before. It stands for Event, plus your Response equals your Outcome. It means that the Event has no meaning other than what your response is to it. Have you ever seen someone win a race only to be disappointed in the result? Ever seen someone lose a game and go so far off the deep end, ranting and raging that you thought, "Dude. Settle down."

An event is exactly that...and event. It's not good or bad. Right or wrong. It just...is. But how you react to it gives it a feeling. The win or loss is now good or bad. But it doesn't have to be the case.

If you don't like the Outcome of your Event, just change your Response. It's really that easy. There is no need for excess emotion just a change in your Response. Here's an example:

Event: You kick the ball and miss the goal.
Response: You tell yourself you suck and you should quit.
Outcome: You're upset and have a negative experience.

Event: You kick the ball and miss the goal.
Response: You think about how you struck the ball and make the appropriate adjustments for the next time you get a shot at the goal.
Outcome: You now have better awareness and ability to make the most of the next opportunity you get.

You have control over three things in your life. They are the thoughts that you think, the images you visualize in your head, and the actions you take. How you decide to use those three things will determine everything you experience in your life. If you don't like you Outcomes just change your Response. Think a different thought. See yourself doing it better. And then change your actions the next time around. Simple really.

Obedience To Your Goals

It is after bad performances in competition (and sometimes practice) when your faith in your goals and belief in yourself can be really tested. As we will cover in this section it's important not to make rash decisions while you are in an emotional state after a tough loss. It is here where you start to doubt the goals you set and if they are ever going to come true. It is here where your obedience to your goals is so important. If you've ever seen dog behaviourist Cesar Milan on TV you might know a thing or two about obedience already but I doubt you've thought about how it pertains to your goals. Just as a dog is loyal to the Alpha in a pack, you must be loyal to the Alpha that is your goals. Let me explain:

When a dog is in a pack situation (a pack can be a dog and it's Owner by the way) the dog is obedient to the Alpha, just because he or she is the Alpha. They don't think about it. They don't have a bad day and say, "Nope, I'm not obedient to you today because the ball had grass on it." They are obedient, period. And that is how you need to be with your goals. You are going to have up and down days, months, possibly even years. But just like that dog, you must remain obedient even when your faith in your goals is lacking which it will some days.

The Highs Aren't So High and The Lows Aren't so Low

You love your sport. It's fun, for the most part. And a bad day doing your sport is still a much better day than doing your homework or getting a job.

If you can understand this one thing, you're entire career in your sport will be waaaay better. It doesn't matter if you're in it for a couple years, or for life. Here's what I need you to understand:

...you are going to be doing this for a long time.

"But Coach, I don't think I"m going to be doing this too long. It all seems too hard. It's why I'm reading this book. I'm trying to decide if I want to keep going or not."

That's ok. I get it. (We will get to your goals in a bit) But the key is this: you have to have a longer-term look at things and have both feet in. The more you can think like that...that you are committed to this trip for the long-term...the more stable your thinking will be and the more success you will probably have. Athletes who can only think short-term ride a roller coaster of emotions that causes them to make abrupt decisions.

I understand you may have some short-term pressure situations that may be coming up. Don't worry, it happens to every athlete. If you can wrap your head around the fact that this is going to be a long journey and it's not going to end tomorrow, you're going to be much better off than if you think the end of the world is coming tomorrow.

With that in mind, I want to share with you some of the best advice I ever received as an athlete.

I was at a race in Sigulda, Latvia. We had just had a pretty solid finish in one of our first races. Life was good! We were excited. On

Cloud 9 really.

And then our coach pulled us aside.

We weren't in trouble but we were in a pretty interesting head space to receive a message that would last us for the rest of our career. He said...

"Listen, guys. Life is good right now. You've had a great result today. But someday you're going to have a bad result. And it's important to know that...the highs aren't so high and the lows aren't so low."

What incredible advice to receive at just that moment. The highs aren't so high and the lows aren't so low. We got it. It made sense. It took us, gently, from this peak of the great result and knocked us down just a little bit. It took the edge off the peak. Instead of having this exaggerated high, we had a more professional approach that we were solid, but still had more work to do.. By keeping the high from becoming too high, what our coach was doing was preparing us for the lows that would inevitably come some, and even greater results that would come another day.

Athletes who focus on short-term results have incredible highs and incredible lows. I had the honour of coaching a very talented female athlete who was in tears every time she didn't win. I also had the opportunity to work with a male athlete in the sport of football who would want to quit for about forty-eight hours after every loss. It didn't matter if he lost by a point or twenty. Mentally, he was "done". But after a few days he'd be back. Just imagine where this athlete could have been if he wasn't on such a roller coaster.

If you understand that you need to limit your "highs", your lows won't be so low. And even if you think they might be low, they probably aren't. It was the perfect advice.

You Win Some You Learn Some

There is no good or bad. It just is. That is why you can't have a good experience or a bad experience. You just learn how to do or not do things. If you don't like the result, just change your action next time around and see what that gets you. By taking the emotion out of the result you are always in learning mode. And when you are always in learning mode you are constantly in "get better" mode. You aren't stuck in the dead space between good and bad you are in a more positive space of learning. Always.

It's important to recognize that if you take a very short-term view of your time in your sport then you will tend to succumb to these roller coasters of emotion. With a longer view of the time in your sport you will tend to chalk up bad results as not a big deal and just part of the longer road ahead.

What I'd really like for you to take away from this section however is that there is no "good" or "bad" when it comes to your results. Your results are just experiences that you can learn from and apply to your overall development. When you have a bad result it's not some personal affront to your well being. You don't need to take it personally. When bad results happen, and they will, it is your time to ask, "How did I make that happen and what can I do differently next time to fix it?"

Bad results can be broken down into categories related to your Key Abilities (See Chapter 8) Your goal is to identify what it is you need to improve to do it better and how to fix it. That's it. Here are some scenarios that you can probably relate to and how you need to focus to fix them:

Not performing as well on game/race day.	Need to step up the intensity in practice to recreate game/race day environment. (See Tactical Ability)
Getting outmuscled in one on one play.	Might be a weight room issue. Could just be a developmental/age issue. (See Physical Ability)
Over excited the day of competition.	Athlete may be over excited naturally on day of competition. May want to tone down warm up and down-regulate everything. Watch caffeine intake day of and sleep the night before.
Stupid mistakes on race/ game day.	May need to create a warm up environment that ups the mental tension prior to competition.

Does well in training and not on game/race day.	Possible training competitors not difficult enough, and giving athlete false hope. May need to handicap oneself further in training to work harder.

These are just a few examples of what can go wrong and what you can do to improve. The key is to not lose it after a mistake happens. There is no right or wrong, you are just taking the outcome of your competition and figuring out what abilities you need to improve to have a better outcome the next time around.

The Five Stages of Loss and Grief

It may seem pretty strange to be talking about Loss and Grief when it comes to athletics but it's really not. As athletes we are constantly putting ourselves in situations where we may lose. It's why we have a win/loss column in some sports. It's why we give out medals. I win, you lose. I feel good, you may (potentially) feel bad. When you win, I feel really bad. How bad? Well that depends. It might be somewhere between, "This pizza tastes bad." To, "You just ran over my cat." To, "My sister just died from cancer." Bad. And while we just talked about how to stay out of this negative headspace, you're probably going to have moments when you grieve over a loss and that's ok for now.

When you lose you must remember that feeling bad about it is completely personal. Each athlete goes through it differently and there is no one right way to do it. What is true for each athlete is that they do go through the same five stages. Here they are:

Stage 1: Denial

"That did NOT just happen!"
"I did not just screw that up."
"They don't deserve to win, I do."

I remember crashing in a race that I was destined to win. I just needed to get the sled down the hill and the race was mine. But going into the final curve I relaxed just a bit too much and entered the final curve just a little bit early. My sled flipped like a pancake and before I could do anything I was sliding on my face in perfect position. I didn't even have time to get my hands out and protect my face. I was sliding on my face in perfect position with my sled on top of me. It even took me a few seconds to process what was going on. I was feeling good a second before and now the whole front side of my body was on fire as the heat from the friction of the ice burned through my suit and into my skin.

As I slid to a stop I thought to myself, "That did not just happen!" I gathered my sled and dragged myself out of the track and waited for the track truck to come get me. As I pulled up to the finish I didn't want to see or talk to anyone. I grabbed my gear and hid in the corner. I didn't even stay for the awards ceremony. This is a good example of Denial and Isolation.

Stage 2: Anger

In phase two, after we stop hiding from what just happened we get really ticked off. This is usually where we lash out at our friends and family. I've seen athletes kick things and break bones AFTER the actual event because they took their anger out on some inanimate object like a wall, a piece of their equipment, or someone else.

After a missed goal, a fall, a bad race, we will direct that anger on something else. If you've ever been around an athlete in this stage and they say something mad at you just know, they aren't mad at you they are mad at what just happened through you. Give them time.

I've been mad at referees and race officials. I crashed once and was mad at the ice chief because I swear there was a bump in the track that made me crash. (There wasn't.) During the Anger stage you don't want to try and figure too much out. Things are too raw to process what just happened so give yourself some time to cool. There are still a couple of stages to go through.

Stage 3: Bargaining

In stage 3 the feelings of helplessness really start to kick in. As you grasp to regain some sort of control over what just happened you may start to think all of the "if only's":

• If only I had trained harder.

- If only that ref didn't call that penalty.
- If only I was taller/faster/skinnier/wore a better suit/played better music. Etc.

The "if" only's are plentiful and you might even start to bargain with God for a different outcome. Many of the "if only's" are directed at things outside of our control which can only make us feel worse. It is in this stage where an athlete can start to be critical of themselves and look for things to improve. This is a critical time and can start the improvement process. It's not necessarily a process that feels that great but it is where an athlete can start to make some "ah-ha" moments on what they can do to improve.

Stage 4: Depression

There are two types of depression that athletes go through depending on where they are in their career. The first type of depression is a mourning. The athlete is coming to grips with how this result will affect their season, or perhaps next season. There are a lot of worries that an athlete will go through at this point. They may worry if they will make the team next year or if their team is in or out of the playoffs. They might worry that, because they messed up, their coach may get fired. They may worry that the sacrifices their family has made for them was all for nothing.

The second type of depression lies much deeper and isn't as straight-forward. It's a very private depression that revolves around the reality that you might actually be done with the sport altogether. Sometimes in this stage trying to analyze what went wrong is unnecessary and all the athlete really needs is a hug and some kind words.

Stage 5: Acceptance

In the Acceptance stage an athlete starts to withdraw from the situation. They aren't happy but they are able to assess the situation that just happened and learn from it. As coaches we want our athletes to get to this stage pretty quickly but ultimately it's up to each individual athlete to move through these five phases at their own pace.

You might be thinking, "Sheesh, Jonathan, that was really heavy. It's like someone died or something." Well, you'd be right. To some athletes a bad result is like someone died and that's what I'm trying to temper by sharing with you all of these stages. The truth is that sport isn't life or death. It's just that some athletes and parents and coaches treat it like that. No one should have that type of pressure on them. We ultimately want sport to be fun and interesting. A learning environment that teaches us lessons not just for the sport itself but about life.

When I see an athlete crying after an event or even just a practice I think to myself, that athlete really cares. Sometimes I think to myself that athlete really, really, REALLY cares! And sometimes you can care too much.

Feel The Emotions And Work Through Them

I've been guilty of coming to an athlete when they were full of emotions and wanting to help them shrug it off quickly and move on. This is the wrong approach because some athletes are just plain emotional. If you are an athlete that is extremely emotional and you want to cry, find a place to cry and let loose. Seriously. Just let it all out.

It's important to not bottle it up because that just increases the tension in your body. Your body is looking for a release and that is why you want to just well up and cry. Just let it go.

When I was left off my first Olympic team in what was supposed to be a slam dunk of making the team I went back to my room in the Olympic Training Center and just bawled my eyes out. I was a wet mess. My face was red and I got so sweaty. I was sad and angry at the same time. As a young athlete I didn't understand what I'm about to tell you. But the best thing I did at the time was get to a private space and let it out. Let it ALL out.

When you have a result that really hits you, you will go through the typical stages of mourning. I just want to help you go through them a little faster by understanding just what is going on and why.

Dealing With In-Game Emotion

Alright, it's Game Day and you're jacked up! Ok, well, maybe not. You're ready to go and you followed the "Peak State" advice I gave you back in Chapter 23.

But what about "in game" emotion. When something happens, either the game isn't going as well as you wanted it to, or someone "wronged" you and the ref didn't catch it. These small examples can get your blood boiling.

We've all seen the ref miss a call only to have the player who is now offended "retaliate" and get a penalty for the retaliation. A soccer player who gets schooled comes back and tackles the player with the ball only to get a yellow card. You have probably had this happen to you if you've been playing long enough..

So there is good emotion and negative emotion. It's ok to get emotional and have that emotion help you. It's all good if it's helping you get to, and stay in, Peak State. But when emotion gets too high it can have a negative effect on your game. You can "lose your cool" and do things that put you in bad situations all because you let those in game emotions take advantage of you.

"But Jonathan, If I didn't hit that guy back he'd think he got the best of me and think I'm soft." Really? Would you rather be right in that situation or would you rather win?

I know you'd rather win.

In the moment is where you have to keep your cool. Other competitors are going to want to get you off your game. And you can't let them. Some of the best examples of this is in the sport of professional hockey. Two Captains, Sidney Crosby and Connor McDavid are fantastic at NOT letting their opponents get the best of them. I can imagine what they are saying to themselves during some of the games I've seen them play. I can hear them say, "Oh, yes. Thank you. I really appreciate your glove in my face. And I really appreciate your stick between my legs. Oh yes, that feels lovely. Please wait a moment while I GO STICK THIS PUCK IN THE NET!"

Both of those captains show a tremendous ability to not let their opponents get under their skin. They stay above it all and are motivated by their opponents efforts. **They stay focused and they raise and lower their emotions based on the task at hand which is to do what is necessary to win.** It is extremely rare that you see them lose their cool and take an unnecessary penalty. They lead with a certain confidence about themselves and they do what they are there for...to win.

Being Challenged By Your Most Powerful Opponent...You.

You will be challenged all of the time. Sometimes you will be challenged by other opponents, but you will also be challenged by probably your biggest competitor...yourself.

We can be our toughest critic and for a lot of high performing athletes the voice inside your own head can be relentless. No matter what you do or how well you perform there is often a voice that says, "You could have done that better. You're not trying enough. You're not good enough. Etc."

While positive self-talk is great, it doesn't hurt to have bit of negative self-talk. For some athletes negative self-talk can be motivating and is the catalyst to drive you forward. One of my favourite athletes, Mikaela Shiffrin of the US Ski Team is pretty hard on herself. Check out her instagram post:

69,421 views

- *@Mikaelashiffrin Sometimes, you have to be negative. Sure, positive self talk is important, but honestly, sometimes the only thing that get's me through a workout is the voice in my head that says "you **can't** do this". Those words, screaming in my mind, relentlessly with each set. Each rep. Each interval. Each second. I yell that at myself. I can't. I can't. I can't. I can't. But I push anyway. I can't. I push. I can't. But I still push. And at the end of my workout, after I have told myself "I can't" at least a million times, I realize two things.*
- *1)I can*
- *2)I did.*

That's a pretty motivating approach to negative thinking. Mikaela has a proven track record that her mental and physical approach works for her although I'm sure a lot of coaches (and her MOM!) would say, "Mikaela don't be so hard on yourself."

Dealing With Your
Automatic Negative Thoughts

Negative self-talk can be motivating, to a point. It works like a bell-curve. Depending on the athlete, negative comments can create an "I'll-show-you" approach to training and competition that creates momentum and helps get you to Peak State. But if that negative thinking gets too intense, or continues for too long, it will take you away from Peak State.

There is a saying that goes, "If I talked to you like you talk to you, we wouldn't be friends for very long." It's true. You can be tougher on yourself than anyone else out there. Tougher than your coach, your parents, your teammates. But even the best athletes have Automatic Negative Thoughts. (ANT's for short). They start out small and simple, but then they can get out of control to the point where you "disasterize" the whole thing. What is "disasterizing"? It's making something seem worse than what it really is. You're turning a simple negative thought into a disaster and you don't have to do that.

These Automatic Negative Thoughts pop into everyone's head, but you don't have to listen to every one of them. Dr. Daniel Amen of www.AmenClinics.com describes a fantastic technique to dealing with your ANT's. It's important to understand that ANT's come in nine types:

ANT Types:

1. All or nothing" thinking: thoughts that are all good or all bad.

2. "Always" thinking: thinking in words like "always, never, no one, ever, etc."

3. Focusing on the negative: only seeing the bad in a situation.

4. Fortune telling: predicting the worst possible outcome in a situation with little or no evidence for it.

5. Mind reading: believing that you know what another person is thinking even if they haven't told you.

6. Thinking with your feelings: believing negative feelings without ever questioning them.

7. Labeling: attaching a negative label to yourself or someone else.

8. Blaming: blaming someone else for the problems that you have.

So now that you know the different types of ANT thinking you can now apply the two techniques to kill your ANT's:

1. When an automatic negative thought enters your mind, train yourself to first recognize the type of negative thought it is AND THEN WRITE IT DOWN. (By writing down the thought you immediately get it out of your head.

2. Talk back to your ANT: When you talk back to your ANT just like you were talking back to another person you take away it's power and can regain control of your mood and feel better.

Here are some examples:

Automatic Negative Thought (ANT)	Type of ANT	How to Kill the ANT
There is no way to win against this guy/girl.	"All or nothing"	There are lots of ways to beat them if I think a little more strategically.
I never win when it's raining.	"Always" thinking.	I have just as much chance to win when it rains as I do when it's sunny.
The coach doesn't like me.	Mind reading.	I don't know if that's true. Maybe she's having a bad day just like I do sometimes.
The whole stadium will laugh at me.	Fortune Telling	I don't know that.
I'm so stupid.	Labeling	Sometimes I do things that aren't too smart, but I'm not stupid.
It's the ref's fault.	Blame	I need to look at what I could have done differently to keep the ref from being in that position.

Remove The Emotion

As athletes we put ourselves in situations that can create a lot of emotion. The way we describe "big" games or "tough" competition can put a frame around the picture. But just like a picture frame that surrounds a picture, we can remove that frame and just see the photo. That's what we are trying to do here as well.

After a tough loss, or even a great victory, it's important that we do what we can to remove the emotion from the situation. This is really hard, but it is possible.

A great technique for taking the emotion out of the situation is to rise up to that 50,000 foot level that we explained in Chapter 5 and try and view your performance as you might when watching a game that you didn't have any interest in. Just the other day I was watching a hockey game on TV that had two teams from Europe playing that I had never even heard of. (I was having a late night snack, ok?) I watched that game with no real interest other than just watching two teams play. I could watch the game unfold and players play without any emotion on my part. But when I watched my home team play in the playoffs I could feel my emotions start to rise because I really wanted them to win. When the other team scored I found myself yelling at the screen! But when I flipped channels to watch those two other teams play I was just watching a hockey game. No emotions.

That's how we want you to be able to look at your own performance. Just like you were watching a game that you had no interest in. You can watch and see productive performances and non-productive performances. You can see what needs to be done better and how to improve it without throwing a layer of emotion over it that clouds your view.

When you can start to look at your game without emotion you start to really apply your personal power to the situation. You can look critically but with no judgement. A bad play or a good play isn't a personal attack on your psyche, it just is.

Was The Competition Appropriate?

All competitive situations basically fall into three categories.

1. Too Easy: Not challenging enough. (Waste of time)
2. Just Right: Great balance of challenge. (A good use of time)
3. Too Hard: Too much challenge. (Also a waste of time)

Obviously there is a bit of overlap between the three categories but for the most part, you end up feeling that your competition was either a good use of resources or that it was a waste of time. What you are looking for is a an opportunity that allows you to challenge your physical, Technical, and Tactical abilities just enough so that you can improve and see further improvement, without getting demotivated.

While each game you play will be different in its own way, you want to have a mix of competitive events so that you can start to experience a variety of challenges. For example, if you play in a soccer game where you never get to see the ball or each time you get it you are quickly stripped of it by an opposing player, that's not a productive event and not a great use of time. But a game where your abilities allow you to see a play unfold and then make it happen, that's a great learning experience.

A swimmer can benefit from a race that is against extremely talented swimmers too. They may lose by an incredible amount of time yet they can see progress in their own times and swim a Personal Best time under official conditions which can be incredibly rewarding despite losing by a bunch. This is where being very sophisticated in how you look at winning and losing comes into play. You can still learn a lot when you lose.

Care Less For Big Breakthroughs

In my first season in the sport of luge we had an International Invitational race in Lake Placid. The old Lake Placid track was a roller coaster perched on a moving mountain with bumps and twists and turns like no other track in the world. It was rare that foreign countries came to Lake Placid because the track was so bad. But to us it was home and I was excited to race against some international foes.

The format for this race was pretty cool. On the first day we would have a full race with the men getting three runs, the women's race would be three runs, and then the doubles would have a race. On the second day, the top two sleds from each country would race in a team competition, but I didn't expect to race in the team competition as we had some pretty experienced sliders racing on the US team. I was coming along pretty quickly in my development but I didn't expect I'd be in the top two finishers.

Much to my surprise, I finished fourth in the men's singles race.

Second overall of the Americans. I was in the team competition the next day! But the morning of the race I woke up with a horrible cold so bad that I don't think I've had a cold like it since. I went to bed feeling fine and woke up in the morning coughing, sneezing, and overall just feeling horrible. But today was the race I was looking forward to! I was bummed because there was no way I was going to be at my best.

The team competition is a one run race for each athlete. The times from each athlete for each country would be added together and the team with the fastest total time would win. I was racing with Dan Ray. Dan was a lumberjack (literally) and was strong as an ox. As a Junior he was already on the Senior National Team traveling on the World Cup circuit over in Europe. I had no idea what he was doing at home at the time but he was super fast and had easily won the men's singles race the day before.

The old Lake Placid track was really short so there's not a lot of track to make up for lost time. Dan was super strong and way stronger than I was physically. He could tear the start handles off and consistently broke the 39 second barrier on the track. I had never gone less than 39 seconds and was bummed because the track was going to be fast and I was so sick there was no way I was going to have a fast start.

When the race started I was a nose-dripping mess with no energy. Perfect. What a wasted opportunity I thought. I did my warm up, got dressed, and got my sled ready. When the race started I was sweating but I was freezing cold. My fever was ramping up and I was sweating into my helmet. Dan was one of the earlier sleds and I would come down after him. His time? A 38.84. A very fast track. Darn.

When I got out to the handles I had already given up on the race. I felt loose but had very little energy. Maybe someone else should have raced? I felt the pressure to do well but in my head I had given up. Today was not going to be my day.

The track announcer came over the loudspeaker, "The track is clear for Jon Edwards." With that the green start light came on and the countdown timer started to go. I pulled my face shield down and did a couple of rocks in the start handles. Not...feeling...good. I thought. I went into compression and pulled off. When I settled a bead of sweat ran down my face and tickled my cheek. "Can't do anything about that now." I thought as it annoyingly ran down my face, behind my ear, and down my neck.

The run was solid, but the start had to have been slow. I felt no snap. No energy. But I slid well and had one of my better runs. Going through the big omega turns I had a pounding headache and the pressure in my head was messing with my proprioception and balance. I drove by the numbers and not with a whole lot of feeling and sensitivity. As I made it through the tough eleven-twelve curve transition all I could think of was, "get...me...off...this...thing!" With two curves to go I just couldn't wait for it to be over so I could get out of this helmet.

When I came up the short outrun I was slow to sit up and break so I slammed against this big six by six foot foam block at the end of the outrun. BOOM! I slumped down in my sled a little sick to my stomach and with a massive headache. The track announcer came over the loudspeaker and said, "Finish time for Jon Edwards...38.86!"

I had just broken my personal best time by over a half a second! OMG.

But why? I was baffled. In some ways I went through the five stages of grief but after a good result! I was in denial. "How the heck did that just happen?" I was angry. "You should have pulled harder!" I was Bargaining. "Why couldn't I have been sick tomorrow?" I was depressed. "What a wasted opportunity." And then finally, acceptance.

Only later did I find out just why this all happened and why I had a good result. As an athlete sometimes we want things so badly. We do all of the physical and technical things really well and we strive to do them tactically perfect. But we are trying so hard that there is no flow to it. It's like the icing that makes the cake so good. The oil in the engine. There is a point where we care so much we can't reach Peak State because we are just trying too hard.

That day, because I was sick, I just let it all go. I had a "here goes nothing" attitude. I was going to do what I knew I could do, but because I felt I had no chance to win I just didn't care about the result.

I was so happy after that day that I had gotten sick. It had opened me up to a new experience of caring but not caring. In my mind I knew what to do and had this feeling of, "Well, this result is really out of my control. Let's just have a good run and see what happens." The result spoke for itself.

Can you replicate getting sick all the time? Definitely not. But you can replicate the attitude of doing everything possible in training to let it go on game day.

Dr. Jerry Lynch had taught me the concept of **Thinking Body, Dancing Mind** which was the title of his book.. This concept of working really hard in training. Analyzing. Improving. Analyzing. Improving. And then on the day of competition letting your brain take a break and let your body do what you know it can do naturally. It was a tremendous feeling and it's a skill I teach every athlete I work with to this day.

You can really over think things on the day of your competition. You can blow right through your Peak State and make stupid mistakes that you wouldn't normally make. You can also come into your day of competition and be so relaxed, as I was that day, that you sail into your Peak State with no effort whatsoever.

I believe that you can care less to have a big breakthrough. As you work hard you begin to fight for your results. But sometimes you just need to let go and let it happen on it's own. Here's where things can get spiritual for some. Some athletes will give the credit to God, or a higher power, or a collective conscious. The bottom line is that if you feel that all of your results are totally up to you and you alone, it can get really stressful.

Grading Your Win's...and Losses

I developed a concept to help coaches work with goalies in any sport after the goalie had let in a goal. The concept was that you should grade each goal that went in on the goalie or any save that the goalie made just like you would grade a math test.. Originally, it was a way to help young goalies remain confident even though they might be letting in a lot of goals.

For example, to be a great goalie in any sport, you need to be successful at three things:

1. You must see the ball/puck.
2. You must know where it's going.
3. You must move in front of the ball/puck.

These three things have to happen to make any save, so if you let a goal in it's not like you got an F on that test. There were probably some things the goalie did right. So let's say the goalie saw the ball, knew where it was going, but moved to it a bit slow. Let's make that grade a 75 out of a possible 100, or something like that.

Goalies are notoriously hard on themselves. They are the only athlete on a field that has their "grade" shown on the scoreboard the whole game. Think about it, what's the first thing you think about when you see a score of 6-0 on a game that isn't football? Man that goalie must really stink! You never hear, "Wow, their penalty kill must be really horrible today." It just doesn't happen and that's why most goalies get really down on themselves when they lose and feel good when they win. The grading system I implement with them helps a goalie to stabilize the good and the bad. If you remember my section on **The Highs Aren't So High And The Lows Aren't So Low** earlier in this chapter, you'll remember the importance of maintaining a level of stability in one's emotions. This grading system can help you do that.

No matter what sport you play you can look for ways to grade your performance off certain measurables than just winning and losing. This way, if you win you can feel good about the win but can also walk away with important things to work on, and if you lose you can hold your head high knowing there were certain aspects of your game that you did very well. We aren't just comparing the goals for or the goals against, but on the game as a whole.

When I competed in the sport of luge, a timed event, you were trying to be the fastest athlete to the bottom of the hill. But if you only looked at the finish time, you could put yourself in a pretty bad mental space. What my coach taught me early on was how to look at a time sheet. I could then see that within certain sections of the track I did well and others not so well. This averaged out to the time at the bottom. But I could feel good about the sections of the track where I did well, and could then strategize for ways to improve the sections where I didn't. And that's what I want you to do.

For my goalies, we break down every goal and see just what it is that they need to work on. We can make it very granular. Maybe they need to work on shots from players who are running from left to right and the shot goes between their legs. Maybe it's on shots from 17 yards away that are time and room shots at high velocity. Whatever it is, we can break it down and improve.

You can have that exact same experience in your sport. You can break down the game within the game and see just what you are good at and what you need to improve.

Here's the key, you will always find something to improve. The best athletes always do. And that is awesome! It means you are in a situation for lifelong learning which keeps you engaged. It's the basis of life and you're getting to experience it right now. So relax. Have fun and enjoy the moment that even though you may have lost today, when you compare yourself to the other athletes around you, you've got some good things going for you and some things you need to work on. That's it. That's all. Now go home, have a great dinner and get some sleep. Tomorrow is a new day.

Dealing With Injuries

Injuries suck. They hurt. They cost time, energy and money. They keep you from doing what you love. There is nothing good that ever comes from being injured!

Or is there?

I've had my fair share of injuries. Actually, I've had so many that they have affected my body well after I retired from competitive sports. Many of my Olympic friends still deal with injuries that they sustained when they were competing many years ago. At the time, the injury was a nuisance that had to be overcome quickly in order to compete.

When I look back on competing with injuries I sometimes cringe. I wish I had taken better care of certain things than I did, but hindsight is 20/20 and I did the best with what I knew, then. I also did the best according to the guidance that I had at the time. Athletic trainers, physical therapists, and coaches all had an influence on how I treated my injuries and when you combine that with the pressure to compete you wonder if the advice had been different if the pressure hadn't been so high.

Regardless of the environment the injury happens in, I have learned something very important over the years about injuries and that is…

…injuries are the body's way of finding an excuse to rest.

What?

Yes. Injuries are a way for the body to finally rest.

I talked about how as an athlete is basically like a bathtub with multiple taps of water coming into it. The taps represent stress in your life and they can be school, work, family money, food, etc. All those stress points are in addition to the stress we associate with The Primal Triad that I spoke about in Chapter 11. While all of these factors affect you as an athlete, when you get injured you will typically focus on the mechanism that caused the injury. You sprain your ankle and you think about the other player's foot you stepped on or the slippery surface that you slipped on. A torn hamstring results in a focus on the warm up that day or the change in stride length that caused it. A concussion gets attributed only to the offending player that hit you.

Coaches and medical professionals don't help this either by focusing completely on only what caused the injury. They want to understand this just as quickly and easily as you do and want to put your injury into a little box that they can understand. When you get injured you're going to go through the Five Stages of Loss and Grief that I outlined earlier in this chapter, but what many athletes don't understand is that your coaches and support team will go through it too, and they will all want to get you back to playing and competing as fast as possible because they think, as you will, that an athlete who is playing will be happier than an athlete who is not playing.

But here is where I feel most athletes and their support staff miss the real purpose behind the injury: **it's a reason for the body to rest.** And during that resting phase the athlete now has a reason for introspection on their overall stressors on their life and how it is affecting their body.

Now, you might be like a lot of people who doubt this level of thinking so let me give you a few examples of athletes I have dealt with personally to show you how it all panned out:

Concussed: I work with a lot of goalies and on three separate occasions I assisted parents and coaches help these athletes get back on the field. At first, a concussion just looks like a very simple reaction to trauma to the head, but the symptoms that follow can tell a larger story. With these three goalies the trauma to their head all came from different mechanisms; one was a body check that resulted in a shoulder to the head. The second was a shot to the facemask on a rather simple play from ten yards away. The third was also a shot but this time to the side of the head from a missed pass in warm up that the goalie didn't see coming.

For the player who got checked, at first glance it was a shoulder to the head which was unfortunate. However, the time the athlete spent on the sideline ended up giving him time to rest a sore knee as well as to watch a few practices and a game which he was normally never able to do. The act of standing on the sideline, while frustrating at the time, was actually a blessing that allowed this goalie to rest his sore knee. Of even greater benefit was the fact that this goalie was able to watch his team play against a team that they would eventually play in the semi-finals of their state championship. The time on the sideline allowed this goalie to see some shooter tendencies that he was able to take advantage of in that semi-final game. This goalie would never have been able to uncover this flaw in the shooter by being in the cage as it was the perspective only from the bench that allowed him to figure it out. The concussion was therefore an opportunity.

The second player who was hit in the mask by the ball was really looking for an opportunity not to play in the cage anymore and the ball to the mask was an opportunity for her to step back and evaluate her game. Her parents, who were huge fans and who were there every step of the way were also able to realize that their daughter was unbelievably happy now that she didn't have to play in the cage. This was a revelation since their daughter had been a goalie since she was nine years old. The concussion now gave them a forced rest that allowed all of them to gain new perspective. Ultimately, this goalie went back to her team but switched to offense. Her understanding of the challenges most goalies face allowed her to be an incredibly accurate and effective shooter resulting in her leagues scoring title. The rest allowed this player to truly find her passion and to come back stronger than ever in a position she wouldn't have considered otherwise.

The third goalie who was hit in the side of the helmet was the most interesting story of all. In this case the goalie was hit right in the temple resulting in a very serious concussion that knocked her to the ground for a minute. It was a scary scene but she eventually came to and was able to walk to the bench on her own. Out for two weeks she decided to step away from the game. This very dedicated athlete had been taking a protein drink supplement as part of her training that had been recommended by her mother. While the protein shake tasted ok this athlete suffered from very bad gas and stomach issues. Since she wasn't able to play, she ditched the shakes for two weeks and found her stomach issues went away completely. Her allergies to the natural grass field her team practiced on also cleared up which was an added bonus. While it's hard to think that a concussion solved her allergy and stomach issues, the more I coach the more I see these added benefits that come from the rest caused by an injury.

The most incredible example I had heard of was of an injured hockey player who was forced to stay off their team bus for the next road trip. That bus crashed killing a handful of teammates who were sitting where this athlete normally sits on the bus. Now you might say, that can't be related at all, but the injury in question forced this athlete to stay at home and rest which ultimately saved his life.

Running Out Of Gas Or Blowing A Tire?

You can call these examples extreme, however, as I mentioned earlier the more I am around sport the more I see these sorts of things happen. The body always finds a way to rest whether we like it or not. We like to refer to athletes as a car, that somehow slowly runs out of gas at times and just needs a fill up to get going again. I like to think of it as a blown tire, or a broken axle, either one forces the athlete to pull over and get some repairs while the traffic continues on down the road. An immature athlete and their support staff will rush an athlete back into traffic for fear that the other cars will be too far down the road and that they might never catch up. When in fact, if the athlete stays on the sideline they will come back better than before and with a better system to navigate the traffic down the road.

Getting Sick

Getting sick is a lot like getting injured. It's a nuisance but it can also be a great excuse to rest. I know a lot of athletes who, when they got sick, were actually excited to have an excuse to stay in bed. This is a sure sign of not managing their training and recovery because a rested athlete is a happy athlete.

Getting sick is not "unlucky". It's not some unfortunate event that has picked you randomly and left others ok. You don't "have" to get sick. It's not a annual or bi-annual requirement of life. Getting sick is not normal contrary to what the marketing folks from the flu vaccine manufacturers would like you to think. I laugh every year when I hear people say, "I get the flu every year like clockwork." This does not have to be. I like to tell people, "Hey, it's not flu season. It's called winter."

When I was an athlete did I get sick? You bet. It was common that a bug would go around the team and we'd all get sick to a degree. But I look back on those times knowing that it didn't have to happen. A well rested, well nourished, well hydrated athlete is able to defend itself from the common bugs that we are exposed to. As a well-rested, healthy adult I rarely get sick. In fact, I can't remember the last time I got sick and that's because I: 1) Don't expect to get sick. 2) Am rested. Happy.

And healthy. 3) Have minimized my exposure to other sick people.

If you are well rested and keep your nutrition high quality and stay hydrated getting sick for you should also be a rare occurrence.

Getting Sick When The Off Season Comes

Have you ever noticed that you get sick when you finally have some time off? This is not uncommon at all. Personally, when I was high school age, I would get a cold pretty much every holiday break that we had. At the end of a tough season of training I would go home, sleep for twelve hours and then quickly develop a cold that put me in bed for days. All I would want to do is sleep. It was like my body said, "Hey…. yeah...so we've been waiting for you to stop training and competing. We just want you to know that we need some rest and lots of it. Good night."

I would crave all sorts of my favourite foods. I would binge eat pizza and drink cans of coke like they were about to get discontinued at the grocery store. I would then sleep for twelve hours and take naps. It was awesome! In about four or five days I'd be back to normal and ready to start training again.

I encourage all of the athletes I work with to look forward to taking time off when the season allows it, but not to expect to get sick. I look back on my time and realize that I looked forward to getting sick when I had time off just like people anticipate having the flu every winter. It doesn't need to happen.

Injuries Shouldn't Be Part of The Plan

I believe that most injuries are preventable and I'm often surprised at most athletes acceptance of injuries as part of playing. Sure, when you are competing on the edge of your best performance things can go sideways, but with proper planning and physical preparation injuries can be 100% avoidable.

Living in Canada I've seen my share of box lacrosse games which are played in hockey rinks when they are drained in the spring. If you've ever wondered what is under that flat sheet of ice, it's a big 'ol flat sheet of concrete and I'm not sure if you know this, but running on concrete isn't good for...anyone. But athletes like to play lacrosse and why not play indoors, right?

It's not uncommon to see a lot of young athletes with shin splints at the age of ten in this sport! I watched a group of sixteen year olds playing and 20% of them had a pre game and practice ritual of seeing the athletic trainer to get their shins wrapped. Um...wrapped might not be the best word there, it was more like a cast on their lower leg to help them relieve the pain from running on that rock hard floor. Any runner will tell you that running on a hard surface is not a great idea yet when we are in the heat of competition and competitive training we will often overlook what looks really obvious to the outside observer. As a coach and consultant, I come into groups and see these types of situations all the time and it's often a surprise when I point it out. Or, it's met with a, "What are you going to do? We've got a game to win this weekend and he's our top player."

An injury like a shin splint is the combination of a number of things that all athletes should understand. We've got a combination of lack of physical ability coupled with an unforgiving surface and a lack of recovery time for the body to adapt. In the box lacrosse example many of these kids transition from playing ice hockey which is a completely different motion for the lower leg. It is very low impact compared to the high impact of running on concrete. But you don't have to be playing box lacrosse to have a similar scenario where your body isn't ready for the forces that your sport requires.

So what do you do for keeping yourself from getting injured?

Understand Progression: I had a strength coach who told me that if you place a ten pound plate on your foot, no problem; but if you drop a ten pound weight on your foot from six feet up, that's a problem. The truth is that everything is possible with proper progression. Start slow and work up to fast. Use lighter weights and then progress to heavier weights. Shorter runs to longer runs. You get the idea.

Strength Throughout Range Of Motion: While most coaches and parents focus on the world "flexibility" what you are really looking for is the ability for your body to withstand forces over a large range of motion. Personally, the most injury-free I ever was was when I was a hockey goalie. I started every practice working on what, I thought, was flexibility, but what I was really working on was being strong over as wide a range of motion as I possibly could. It was no good if I could get into the splits and not get out of them, and it wasn't any good if I could reach with my glove and not be able to hold on to a puck. What you are looking for is not just being able to bend your body over a wide range of motion, you are looking for strength over the widest range possible.

Protection: Protection can be a helmet, a shin guard, or a shock absorbing shoe. These are all examples of protection but most athletes fail to realize that protection serves two purposes: 1) To protect you from external trauma. And 2) give you confidence to make you more aggressive in your play making.

Conclusion

There's a lot to talk about in this chapter and it can all be boiled down to your emotions and how you related to your wins and losses. You're going to win, and you're going to lose, but how you respond to those wins and losses is most important. Ideally you get to a point where every win and loss is a learning experience with little to no emotion involved. You don't need to get riled up or upset about a loss, and on the flip side you don't need to get overly excited when you win. By keeping a neutral position you will always be in learning mode no matter what the result.

While I want you to get to a point where the emotion of your wins and losses is tempered and is almost nothing, it's going to take you a bit to get there. In the meantime you need to understand that you're going to go through the phases of Denial, Anger, Bargaining, Depression and Acceptance. The faster you can move through these stages, the better. For you, your teammates, your coaches, and your family.

Go back and read this chapter again because it is just that important. And then watch the video…

Watch This Video

**www.AthleteSpecific.com/
you-win-some-you-learn-some**

Take Action With These Steps

- Take your journal and write down a time when you had a bad reaction to what you felt was a bad result.

- After you got over your negative reaction, what were some of the things you thought to do next time around so you had a better result.

- Looking back on your reaction to that result, do you think you wasted time by spending so much time in an upset state?

- How would you treat that experience differently knowing what you know now?

Chapter 25
Tools of Your Trade: Equipment For Skill Acquisition and Protection

---

"It isn't hard to practice finishing. You can do it on your own: just take a couple of touches and shoot at goal. You can do it with whatever equipment you have."

Harry Kane
An English professional footballer who plays as a forward for Premier League club Tottenham Hotspur and the England national team

---

$700 hockey skates. $200 sneakers. $300 lacrosse sticks. You name it and equipment for...everything...is getting pretty expensive. It doesn't matter what sport you play, there is a piece of equipment you will want or need to compete at a higher level. But how do you decide?

There is an endless number of choices you can make for your equipment needs. I have a couple of criteria when it comes to purchasing equipment but first and foremost, your equipment choices will be dictated by your resources in priority to your immediate needs. My recommendations won't always fit every athlete but this is a general rule of thumb.

How NOT To Make Equipment Choices

Let's start with how NOT to make equipment decisions: If you are basing equipment decisions on what is cool and what your buddy has, you're probably not going to make the right choice for you. Now that's not always the case, I get it, but for the most part just wanting to buy a piece of equipment because an athlete you admire has it is not the best decision making. That's called marketing.

I was confronted by a hockey mom in the hallway outside of one of my talks and she said, "Coach, I can't stand it. My son wants every expensive stick out there. I just can't afford all of this stuff!" I told her that I understood and asked if she'd be comfortable if the three of us had a conversation about it. She agreed and after the rest of the parents and athletes cleared out we grabbed a seat in the locker room. Now this athlete was pretty big for his age. He was stronger than his age group and already had a pretty decent stick. (This was his third of the season by the way.) I backed the conversation up a bit and asked what part of his game really needed to improve and to my surprise it wasn't his shot or his stick handling ability. It was his skating.

With limited resources and taking the "Athlete as CEO" approach we needed to look at where we could allocate dollars, if there were any, to improve his game. When he mentioned skating his mom was a bit surprised. She had already bought him skates early in the season but his feet and ankles hurt which he hadn't shared with his mom. He knew that she had already spent a lot and he didn't want to disappoint her that the money she spent wasn't spent on the correct things. But I noticed these were some top of the line skates and they weren't too short or too long. It turns out this athlete just didn't have any arches!

My recommendation was to invest $75 in a pair of footbeds for the skates which made this player extremely happy. I said, "Listen, spending money on a stick isn't going to improve your game as much as fixing how your feet feel in those skates. The skates are decent so spend the money there and you'll have a bigger bang for your buck."

Sure enough, the change in the footbed changed this athlete's skating ability incredibly. Instead of his foot sliding around in the skate he was now "locked in" and his edgework improved so much he actually found himself getting open quicker and his ability to make passes with the same stick he already had improved. We actually recommended changing sticks to a cheaper model that didn't break as much in favor of a plan to invest in some power skating lessons which would increase this athlete's ability even more. As I like to say, "If you can't get open you won't have a chance to pass the puck."

This is just one example of how wanting to buy the latest equipment may not be the best purchase for you. It doesn't make the biggest bang for the buck. What will make the biggest bang for the buck for you in your sport? Is it new skates? New shoes? A new piece of equipment?

How Equipment Improves Your Abilities

We live in an incredible time when technology has made advances in equipment incredibly fast. That has done two things: 1) driven the cost of some equipment down 2) driven the availability of expensive equipment higher.

Just this last week I heard a parent lamenting, "OMG a $300 hockey stick!? $1000 skates? You've got to be kidding me!"

But there is more to understand because the question should be, "How would a $300 hockey stick help me?" And, "How would $1000 skates help me?"

Now I know you would agree that there are some pieces of equipment out there that wouldn't help you despite the high price but there are others that might. The question to ask is this:

Will this piece of equipment help me acquire skills and abilities faster than I currently do and/or will it allow me to showcase my skills and abilities better than I currently do?

Let me give you an example: I work with a lot of goalies and the discussion around equipment usually revolves around how bulky it is and how heavy it feels. That's all well and good but the rules are the rules and there is certain equipment that is just mandatory to wear so there is no option NOT to wear it.

But here is where an interesting discussion begins. For an athlete who is really good, investing in lighter equipment may allow that athlete to move faster and make more saves. That would be a pretty solid investment as long as the lighter equipment didn't put the goalie in a position where they might get hurt.

But let's say the goalie is new and is still learning. A young/new goalie might have a fear of getting hit and getting hurt in the process. If they are wearing old and outdated equipment they may be limiting their development of their abilities because they have a fear of getting hit. But investing in new gear would probably eliminate their fear and allow them to focus on making the save and not worry getting hurt.

When it comes to sport EVERY single one of them has this discussion. From skiers to soccer players there will always be the opportunity to invest in new equipment but the discussion should always revolve around these two points:

1. Will it allow you to showcase your existing skills better than you currently do?

2. Will it allow you to learn more quickly because you are able to focus on the skill you are trying to learn and not worry about getting hurt?

The Best Lesson I Learned From Playing Golf

I love to golf and rarely get to play nowadays, but when I started I made the best decision I could possibly make to learn this incredibly difficult sport. I said to myself, "Listen, golf is hard enough as it is, I want to start with a set of golf clubs that are as forgiving as possible." I knew that you're trying to hit this little tiny ball with this tiny club face, I didn't want one that was going to be really hard to hit. Now people don't usually think about that sort of thing so when I went to the store to buy my first set of clubs the sales guy was a little upset when I started out by saying, "I want the most forgiving set of clubs you've got." Turned out it was a much cheaper set than this guy wanted to sell me, but I stuck to my plan and after I bought that set and went and played I was happy. I enjoyed the game and was able to learn quicker than if I had bought a more advanced set that was harder to hit.

In these examples the equipment choice ends up allowing the athlete to learn quicker and perform better. It is the biggest bang for the buck.

There was a year I was competing in the sport of luge and the speedsuit technology and aerodynamics changed. I had an old speedsuit that was super-slow compared to the other suits on the market so I arranged to buy a $600 speed suit from the Japanese team that at least put me on the same playing field as my competitors. If I had spent that money on a training week in Europe it would have been money flushed down the drain. It doesn't matter how good I was, without that speedsuit it would be like dragging a parachute in a 100 yard dash.

How Saving Money Can Hold You Back

One last story: I worked with a skier once who lacked the ability to make quick turns on her skis. Her coaches recommended that her parents send her to a strength and conditioning coach to get her lower body strong so she could work the skis back and forth and be able to slalom effectively. It turned out that she was really slow compared to other girls her age.

After a couple of sessions I could see that this athlete was incredibly strong for her age. In fact she was one of the strongest athletes I had seen at her age. Turns out that she also loved Parkour, that sport where athletes run and jump around a downtown using ramps, and ledges and rails as obstacles. She had been in gymnastics when she was young but didn't like the environment so she continued with Parkour . After a few discussions with her parents about her advanced strength, I asked about her equipment. "What size skis are you currently using?" She was on 160cm skis.

160 cm skis are what World Cup skiers use and the typical female slalom skier uses skis even shorter than that. A longer ski is harder to turn and takes much more strength to get the ski to move. This athlete was 16, and while incredibly small the skis were holding her back. I asked why she was on those skis and the dad said that they were hand me downs from her older brother who used them two years prior!

In this case this family didn't need to invest in strength and conditioning sessions for their daughter. They needed to take that same amount of money and invest it in skis that fit. This was not the place to invest cheaply as the ski length is incredibly important to the performance of the skier. They were already investing a small fortune for her to train and compete and yet in one of the most important places (her skis) they weren't investing enough. Once they made the change this athlete quickly become one of the top racers on the team. Her confidence went through the roof and she is well on her way to reaching her goals of making the national team.

How Technology Makes You Want More

Your equipment is there to help you get to the next level, whatever that is for you. With today's technology the ability to create new equipment is incredibly easy. What used to take years to improve now takes days with the introduction of supercomputers, artificial intelligence and 3D printing. Sports equipment companies are in the business of selling equipment so coming up with something new and wrapping a cool title on it is designed to make you feel like you aren't enough if you don't have it.

I worked with a Golf Professional who once told me a story about the marketing director of one of the top Golf Equipment manufacturers in the world. He said, "There hasn't been much new in golf in twenty years. It's just marketing and how we tell the story. In the end you still have a ball, a club, and the athlete. What that athlete does with the club is the real story. The rest is just wrapping paper."

There will always be some new whizbang piece of equipment available to you because technology is improving at an exponential rate and we will always be looking to improve. But how that equipment applies to you and if it is the right piece to improve your game, only you will know. Your job is not to be jealous of others who have the latest and greatest. Investing in new equipment is solely based on how it can improve your game and the resources you have. You put yourself in a bad place if you feel that because you don't have a certain piece of equipment you are lacking and are at a disadvantage.

Conclusion

Your equipment is critical to how you learn your sport and it's easy to lament the fact that equipment can be expensive. Your love of your sport will dictate how you invest in your sport and what equipment you buy. But now is not a time to lament the fact you may not have all of the resources you wish you had to afford better equipment, it's time to go out and do something about it because you understand that better equipment can help you learn faster and develop the skills you need at a faster rate.

Watch This Video

www.AthleteSpecific.com/equipment

Take Action With These Steps

- Think of the last equipment purchase you made and how it affected your performance, if at all. Did you fall prey to good marketing and buy something you didn't need? Or did it give you a boost in energy and confidence that helped you perform better.

- Write down all of the actual performance improvements your last equipment purchase actually made for you.

- What is the next piece of equipment you would like to invest in? Why?

- What piece of equipment could you invest in that would accelerate your performance?

- What equipment does your coach recommend you invest in to improve your performance? Why?

Chapter 26
Learning How To Win

"First they ignore you.
Then they laugh at you.
Then they fight you.
Then you win."

Mahatma Gandhi
Mahātmā Mohandas Karamchand Gandhi was the leader of the Indian
independence movement against British rule.

A critical aspect of learning how to become an elite athlete is learning how to win. Some may call this "finishing". I call it "owning it." However you describe it, the idea is that you must learn how to win.

In order to "win" you may have to stick a landing, dig deep for a final kick, focus your energy to finish a lift, or a block. You may have to take the last shot, or help your team position themselves for better defense. You may have to relax harder (sounds contradictory) than you ever have before or you may have to impose your will over your competitor.

Whatever it is, there is a benefit to having winning experiences as you develop. There is something about finally experiencing how to cross that finish line, score the winning goal, stand on the podium. Whatever your sport. You must learn how to win. And I'm not talking about getting a participation medal. That's not winning and young athletes know that. You know when you've lost and it's critical to be able to develop the mental muscles to get over that experience. Whether you are on a team or you are in an individual sport, bouncing back from a loss and finishing to win is a skill set that all great athletes possess.

Canada Vs. USA: A Battle of "Nice"

Leading up to the 2010 Winter Olympics in Vancouver, Canada, Canada's 13 winter National Sport Organizations, the Canadian Olympic Committee, Canadian Paralympic Committee, Sport Canada, WinSport Canada and VANOC met to develop a plan that would become known as Own the Podium. It was a program to help funnel additional government money to the athletes who had the best chance at winning a medal at the Olympics. I had the opportunity to sit in on a meeting where Own the Podium presented some very interesting facts to the sports organizations of Canada.

Own the Podium had done some very interesting research and found that of all the countries in the world, Canada had the worst results when it came to having an athlete who was in the top three in the World leading up to the games, who then came through and finished in the top three at the Games. What this basically said was, Canada was winning medals all year long and then was "choking" at the Games.

The flip side to that example was the United States. They had the BEST results when it came to having athletes who were outside the top three in the World during the year, who would then earn a medal at the games. These athletes were stepping up and "finding another gear" and taking advantage of other athletes faltering and taking Olympic medals that others felt weren't really theirs to take.

So why was that? Why were the American's winning medals when the Canadians should have been, but weren't? The Canadian government looked at it and thought, "Let's put money to our best athletes so they can have all the resources they need to win." As you know, resources can help an athlete, but not always. There was more to this Own the Podium thing than just money: it was an attitude.

You Need To "Own" It

The word "Own" in Own the Podium means that it's yours. There is this idea of "possession." What Canada was saying (and what was unusual for them) was that, "This whole podium thing? Yeah. That's ours. Not yours. Ours. So we're going to take it and you're not."

As an American living in Canada, Canadians are "nice". I've been living in Canada since 2001 and have spent many other days in this great country. I'm proud to call it home and love living in a place that many others around the world love to come and visit. It's a beautiful country full of very nice people who are friendly, welcoming, and say "sorry" a lot. True, if you're playing hockey with them and you do something wrong they will gladly punch you in the face, but outside of that, they are really nice people. And while I use the term "they" I can really say "we" because I have spent so much time here. My wife is Canadian, and so are my kids.

As American's though, we tend to be cocky and brash. To the world, American's are perceived as clueless on some levels and disrespectful in others. We have an air about us as we live in the greatest country in the world. We are God Bless America and Apple Pie. We are college football and NFL crazed. We are also home to some of the most amazing innovations in the world, and people from around this world want to come to the United States to study and to work. To be part of that opportunity and to take advantage of the freedoms that we have to offer.

When it comes to sport, American's are some of the best in the world at harnessing that bravado and dominating. Sometimes we fail, but as the Own The Podium group saw in their research, more often than not, we get athletes to perform at the highest level when it counts the most.

So while the resources from the government were important, it was this American attitude that the Canadians were really trying to cultivate. They wanted to "own" that podium. Did it work?

Well, while the goal was to be "the number one nation" at the Olympic Games, this goal turned out to be a little vague. How do you measure that? Medals? Overall results? In Canada's case, they finished in the top three on the overall medal count. You might think that's a failure, especially when they finished behind the Germans AND the Americans. However, they did win the most Gold medals of any nation. In fact, they tied the most gold medals ever won by a nation dating back to 1980 when the Russians won 13 gold medals in Lake Placid. (The Norwegians also won 13 gold medals in 2002 in Salt Lake City)

So was it a success? I believe so. Why? It wasn't just about the medals, it was about an attitude. It was about, "Alright we are a winter nation and we should be winning these medals! They are ours." The following Olympics, the Canadians finished fourth overall in the medal count, but still won 10 gold medals (one more than the American's).

And an interesting point to the Canadian's performance: they won more medals across more sports, than any other nation. The Russians and the Norwegians and the Germans are typically very good in the cross country skiing events where one dominant athlete could win multiple medals. Same was true for the Austrians in skiing. While many nations showed dominance in one sport, Canada was able to shine across multiple sports.

So what can you learn from the Canadians? There is a point where you are going to need to say to yourself, "I deserve this just as much as anyone. I have proven to myself and to others, that I can do this!" Sport is designed to have winners and losers. It's just the way it is. Ultimately, you need to win and feel great about winning. Some of the best athletes in the world seem brash and cocky and while we may not like how they go about it, we respect their ability to win and win often.

One of the ways to learn how to "own" it, is to play "up" within your sport. Playing up can expose you to tougher competition so that when you come back down to your age/ability level things seem easier. In this next section we're going to talk about some of the benefits, and some of the pitfalls of playing up.

Playing Up

At some point in your athletic career you will have the chance to "play up.' This usually means playing with older kids whose Physical, Technical and Tactical Abilities are better than yours. There are many reasons why you'll get called to play up. Some are in your best interest and others aren't. Here's a list of some of the reasons why you might get called up:

- You are head and shoulders above your age group and playing up is the best option for you to have competition that is more competitive for your skill level.

- The team or group above your age bracket is desperately short players. They are playing the best team in the league and they really need you to play because they won't have enough players to play.

- Your coach wants you to get some experience with the older group. You won't play, but you'll get a chance to do warm ups and to dress with the team. If the team is winning by a bunch you may see some game time.

These are just a few of the possible reasons that you would get the chance to play up. Depending on your position, these decisions to play up can either help you or hurt you. So how do you know if playing up is a good decision for you?

Understand that playing up is rarely in the best interest of the player. There are times when it is a strategic decision, but many times it's for the benefit of the program. Sure, there are times when it works out but the chances of getting hurt or demoralized is pretty high. Whenever I consult with an athlete or their family and the possibility of playing up comes into the equation my first question is, "Will the athlete be safe?" Let me explain with a couple of examples:

A Good Example of Playing Up

There was a really big lacrosse league that played all summer long in my home state of Massachusetts. I really wanted to play but as a goalie it was hard to break in if you weren't already associated with a team. I registered and to my surprise I was put on a team as a free agent. I was the only goalie.

Did I mention I was still in eighth grade?

I was put on a senior men's team called the Flantim's who had won the year before. These guys were all in their twenties and early thirties and I was...fourteen.

As you can imagine when I showed up the older guys were like, "Who the heck is this kid?" Until I played. As you can imagine I was pretty nervous getting shot on by these much older guys, and a lot of the balls went whizzing by my head in that first game. When the second game came around, the shots weren't that fast because I was slowly adjusting to the speed of the shots. It was an incredible experience and luckily I was never injured by a shot hitting me somewhere on my body. That summer was one of the best lacrosse experiences of my life and one that was critical to my development. I was able to play up in a safe environment and can you imagine what it was like getting shot on when I went back to school for my freshman year? My brain was so used to the faster shots from those older players that I felt so confident when I went back to school.

This was a pretty extreme age jump. Going from 8th grade shots to the shots of college age players was a pretty big leap, but I managed to keep myself protected and was able to play at a really high level. The guys were great to me, too. Once they could see that I could play, they were quick to mentor me and help me get better in all aspects of the game, not just stopping the ball. A funny side note: My Mom would drive me to the games as I was too young to drive and the guys would usually end up at a local player's house for beers after the game. Guess who got invited??

The key to the success of that experience was that my physical ability was pretty close to the players I was playing against. My only real fear was getting checked by a much larger player if I ventured outside of the crease. I knew the shots would be more accurate so the chances of me getting hit were low, but I wore extra protection just to make sure I didn't get stung by a ball and could keep my confidence high. The speed of the shots were obviously going to be much faster but I knew that once my brain adjusted to the speed of the ball that my body would soon follow. This was an example of a great experience.

Playing Up With a Bad Outcome

Many years later I was working with a soccer player who was a freshman in high school at fourteen years old. He had the opportunity to play in a men's league and was doing great. His Technical Ability with the ball was fantastic and mentally this kid acted much older than fourteen. I was not really excited for him to play up because physically he was pretty slight. He had not "filled out" as some would say and I was reluctant and feared that he would get pushed around by the older guys.

Now in our city there is a story of a very famous professional soccer player who played in England. He grew up playing in the men's league in our city because he was so much better than all of the other kids in his age group. You can see how the parents of the athlete I was working with might think that their son might be the next professional following in his footsteps. Unfortunately, the experience for this athlete didn't go so well. In his first game with the men's team, after making a rather bold move with the ball through the legs of one of the defenders, that same defender came back and made a hard tackle, boots first, breaking the ankle of this fourteen year old soccer player. Obviously, not a great experience "playing up" for this athlete.

Another Playing Up Example
To Learn From

Sometimes playing "up" is just a natural byproduct of the team that you play on or the league that you play in. Many years ago I was watching a Junior A hockey game in Calgary where I live. There were two brothers playing on the same team one of whom plays in the NHL today. At the time, the younger brother was quite small for his age but had the same tenacity and Technical Ability as his older brother. Since their earliest years playing hockey, the two brother played on the same team as soon as the younger brother was in the age category. They were a "package deal" from some people's perspective.

Tenacity is a great attribute to have. Coaches love tenacity and in the hockey world, people love that hard-working, blue-collar trait. But tenacity can also put a small athlete into trouble against his larger competitors no matter what the sport. That "put me in coach" mentality is oftentimes rewarded in all sports yet it can end up resulting in some unfortunate circumstances.

In Junior A hockey, the age range between the youngest and the oldest athletes is five years. From seventeen years old to twenty-one years old. That is a huge age difference! So many mental, emotional and physical changes happen in athletes over those ages. The Physical, Technical, and Tactical abilities vary widely and the Psychological and Biological Ages of those athletes are incredibly varied.

There was a particular play in this game where there was a loose puck at center ice. Player A (the younger of the two brothers, aged 17) turned at the blue line and skated in a diagonal to center ice to get the puck. He was skating full-speed while at the same time one of the opposing team's players made an identical move at the opposite blue line. It was like they were opposite sides of a four leaf clover. He too was skating full speed however he was twenty years old, about fifty pounds heavier, and his skating ability was quite a bit stronger than Player A. (When you start applying some physics here you'll start to understand where this is headed.)

As the two players headed to center ice they both had their head down focused on the puck. At the last second Player B looked up, brought his hands to his chest and got ready to level Player A (the younger player). Player A, never got his head up.

Have you ever seen any Bugs Bunny and Roadrunner cartoons? Remember when Wile-e-Coyote would be running full-tilt and then run into a huge boulder, or a freight train, or a car that he didn't see till the last second. Remember how his arms and legs would just wrap around it and he'd be frozen like that?

Yeah, that's exactly what happened to Player A. When he collided with the much larger Player B his arms shot out straight ahead. Like his hands were flying forward while his body just stopped. Player B ran right over Player A who was knocked unconscious immediately. As Player A fell to his back (as Player B went over him) Player A's arms stayed straight, pointing straight to the sky as he remained motionless on the ice. It was an incredibly scary sight to see and I have to say I wouldn't want that to happen to any of my players. Unfortunately, this is an all too common occurrence in hockey, and other sports with such large age gaps. Playing up in this instance wasn't the best option for Player A, whether his brother plays with him or not.

How Do You Know If Playing Up Is Right For You?

This isn't always a clear decision. While playing up may seem like a good thing, there are a lot of options to consider. These are some of the questions I ask:

- Barring any unlikely circumstances, will the athlete be safe and able to avoid injury. (As a strength coach, I often told the parents of the athletes that I worked with that getting stronger, if anything, would help their athlete get out of the way of getting hit or injured.)

- Is the level of play slightly more complex than what they are playing now but not too complex? (If it's going to be too big of a jump it's probably not worth it.

- Will the athlete be exposing him/herself to coaches who may then select this athlete for future teams? (The answer to this question is often "yes" but chasing coaches who you want to impress often leads to disappointment.)

- Will this experience fatigue the athlete for other events that may be more important? (While I don't always recommend saving one's self for a particular event there are often events that hold more weight for an athlete's performance i.e. Nationals)

- Is the athlete rested/healed enough from prior injury so that this experience won't set them back further? (Playing injured is rarely a good idea unless there is a long structured break after the event)

These are fluid decisions that don't always come with black and white answers. Here it is vital to have unbiased advice from someone like myself, or a coach who you can really trust. An experienced, objective parent or relative can also be helpful here.

Threatening Coaches: Play Up Or Else

Your coaches might not always have your best interest in mind. I don't make a lot of friends saying this but, Coaches who put gas in their car with the hopes and dreams of young athletes often compromise their advice in order to keep their programs alive.

One of the bits of advice coaches spew to athletes is that they should play up for a variety of reasons. The problem is that their reasons are for the benefit of their program and not for the athlete. I see this happen a lot with goalies, but it can happen at any sport at any position.

On many occasions I have consulted with families who have been given an ultimatum by a coach, "Play in this event/tournament/extra practice and I will give you a chance next season with (enter team name/tournament/event) next year." This is horrible advice and falls in the same category of coaches saying that you should specialize in only one sport and that you should specialize with them in their program.

My initial reaction to coaches who say that you should play up, or else, is...if you are that good to play up now, you will most likely be better later and be worthy of the same opportunity. It is rare when I see a coach truly hold a grudge against an athlete. Most coaches, when given a choice, will field a roster with the best players they can get their hands on. If you're good, you're good. And your goal is to be so darned good that they have to pick you.

In the city where I live there is a very prominent sports program, with a very prominent former professional athlete at the helm. His promise to parents is that if you pay him the $6000-7000 dollars to go on this one trip to a showcase event he will get your kid a scholarship to play in college.

It's a lie.

Over the years I have mentored a number of families about the realities and the cost/benefits of being involved with the program. I have even seen the head of this program strategically bash athletes who are not in his program to other college coaches. On more than one occasion I have had to defend athletes who were in no need of defense just because of the slander spewed by this guy. This kind of behavior makes me sick.

There is more than one way to get to your goals. You are never stuck on one path. Ever! Whenever you feel you are in a situation like that you need to take a step back from your sport, relax a little, and your mind will come up with other options to help you reach your result. It's that simple. There is always another option.

How Always Playing 'Up" Can Help/Hurt You

A situation that I find incredibly interesting is with athletes who always play up. Typically this means "up" in age, but it can also mean up in ability regardless of age. These athletes are rarely in a position to win because they are typically deficient in one or more of the Three Key Abilities to be able to win. This is particularly true of individual sports where you are finishing by place. Even in team sports, an athlete playing up is rarely a part of the team that does the winning. While they may celebrate after the win, they didn't really create any activity to make the win happen. While it's nice to be part of the celebration, what we really want to develop is an experience of actually doing the winning. We aren't looking to win for "win's" sake. We want to learn how to finish. How to bring it home. How to not succumb to the stress of landing it.

More often than not, athletes who play up will lose. The idea is that if you play up you'll get exposed to tougher competition and learn "what it's going to take to get to the next level." This is great if the level is appropriate. You can play up and lose by a little, or play up and lose by a lot. One can be motivating, the other can be so demoralizing you want to quit. In both situations you need to be protected mentally from the outcome. You have to go into the competition with the understanding that you will probably lose overall, but within the competition there will be moments where you will see glimpses of hope in your abilities and that is what will be truly inspiring.

There is value to having a bedroom full of medals and ribbons that are earned. It helps to develop winning "inertia". A momentum of success that can be looked back on when times get tough, and times will be tough someday. Athletes need to add to their Toolbox an inventory of experiences where they have a wide spectrum of wins and losses. Times where they dominated, or came from behind. Where they won under ideal circumstances and where they won under not-so-ideal circumstances. We don't always have all of those experiences in our Toolbox, but having a selection of other winning experiences allows an athlete to draw on past successful experiences.

Failing Early

When I started coaching in a sport like luge we would often get worried about kids who moved up the track but who had not yet had a crash. Kind of like a goalie who has yet to learn how to take a shot from a player that stings. Learning to crash is important to the overall development of an athlete because if all they experience is success, that first crash could happen at a much higher speed and be a really bad crash. We wanted athletes to crash and have trouble while they were developing because we want them to get the experience of crashing and getting back on the sled and going again. You may have heard the term, "get back on the horse." Well, that's exactly what we want to happen. We want that athlete to get "bucked off" and then develop the character to get back on and try again.

While non-athletes would look at crashing as a negative experience it's really a positive learning experience that pays big dividends later. Just like in any sport, an athlete who only has successes can be unprepared for the inevitable challenges that come later on in a career.

An Important Lesson About Losing

I will share another story here keeping the names and the sport changed to protect the innocent. This was a pretty painful story to watch happen in real life but it's lessons are too important not to share.

Madison was a prodigy by all definitions of the term. She came into her sport with an innate talent created by years involved in other sports. She'd been a gymnast and played soccer as well as a number of sports. An all-around athlete, she came into her new sport and rose quickly up the ranks winning everything domestically. She even won internationally.

As a junior she was four-time Junior World Champion in her sport. Winning came easy and when the time came for her first real shot at an Olympic team it seemed like a no brainer.

She wasn't going to be the best from her country but making the team was supposed to come as easy as all of her other victories. It was a given that she would make the team and her friends and family had bought tickets to fly to see her compete in the Olympics. It takes time to plan for those things and it's not uncommon for families to buy tickets well before the team is picked. There would be a big entourage supporting Madison at the Olympics.

Unfortunately, it didn't come so easily. In a race that she wasn't expected to win, but should do well enough to make the Olympic team, Madison finished well off the pace. In fact, she was so far back that she was left off the Olympic team all together. Madison was still a Junior, and while Junior athletes occasionally make their respective Olympic team, Madison was beaten by Senior aged athletes. Many of these athletes had been competing for a full decade longer than Madison and to the outside observer, beating them would have been the exception and not the rule.

But to Madison it was supposed to happen. She was expecting it. Her friends and family were expecting it because they loved her and were supporting her and they wanted it to happen just as bad as Madison did.

Unfortunately, Madison's coaches didn't help her with this at all. **They allowed her to develop an expectation of winning and not appreciate her wins.** There is a difference. It's one thing to train and compete and win all the time. If you don't lose every once in awhile you become so used to winning that when you lose it can be unusually traumatizing.

And for Madison it was the worst trauma of all.

What did Madison do after that first big, heart-breaking loss?

You might expect that she would be upset. She might need a break. Some time off. She'd be down for a while but she'd get back on the horse and ride again. You'd expect that after a big loss. So, what did Madison do?

She quit.

Completely. Done. Over. Turned in her gear and left her sport, the one she dominated for so many years. For good. A year later she was the shell of the person (not just the athlete) she had become.

Now this is a very extreme example, but it's a true story nonetheless. You might think well, that's really weird and it would never happen to me. You would be surprised. It's important to understand that you can't protect an athlete by avoiding the possibility of losing. In Madison's case, the effort to protect her never sufficiently addressed one of the most important aspects of winning which is appreciation.

We spoke earlier in Chapter 16 about focusing on what you want and not on what you don't want. People may read this example about Madison and think, "Why would you want to teach her about losing when she's winning so much? Wouldn't that put a negative in her head?" I don't necessarily believe it would but what I would rather teach is an understanding of, and an appreciation for, everything that goes into winning. Because when you appreciate winning you realize that it is something you worked hard for against others who are also working equally as hard. When it happens, it is the culmination of hard work. But to an athlete who is winning all of the time it doesn't really feel all that hard. There is "work" but it doesn't feel like work. Because it doesn't feel like work, an athlete can develop an unhealthy expectation of what work really feels like. It comes easy and the idea of now having to "work" for it seems too much. So they quit.

In the case of Madison this is an example of a great athlete wasted. It shows an uncovered flaw in the athlete but it also shows a major flaw in the coaches and the supporting cast of characters around her. Their inability to help her understand a sense of appreciation for her wins while preparing for losses is a sad case. It is important to celebrate your victories. You've worked hard for those victories no matter how large or small. But they can give you a false sense of hope or an unrealistic expectation that can hurt you later when the inevitable losses come.

You Don't Always Learn From Your Victories

Winning feels great! Don't get me wrong. Winning is a fantastic feeling. All of your work has come together, and today, you have beaten your opponent. That feels awesome.

But winning can also give you a false sense of hope. While it is important to win, it is even more important to look at *how* you won.

Hopefully your coach comes in after the game/competition and says, "Great game. We did some great things today that helped us win. But..." and here's the most important job of your coach, "we need to work on a couple of things if we are going to stay on top."

In Olympic level sports where events are timed, an athlete will get a timesheet after every training session and after every race. You could see how you stood against your competitors from the start all of the way to the finish. If you were losing, you could see all of these places where you were deficient and how you could make up time.

But if you were the fastest athlete in the session it wasn't as easy to tell what you needed to work on. If you lost the race you would pour over the time sheets trying to find the time that you lost and the errors you made that lost that time. When you won...well...you didn't look at the time sheets that closely.

Winning can make you lazy like that. I mean really, you won! Who cares what your mistakes were, right?

Wrong.

When you win and how you win feels great in relationship to your competition and what your goals are. If you win a local regional competition that's great. But what is your goal? Is it to just win the regionals? Or are you on your way to win Nationals?

If your goal is to win Regionals, celebrate your tail off. You have won! You reached your goal and that's awesome. Celebrate and party and put the plaque on your wall.

But if your goal is to win Nationals, or go to the Olympics, celebrate but look closely at how you won. Dissect your performance and look critically at what you need to do to improve.

Developing Character

All of this winning and losing is what competing is all about. Learning to win and learning to lose develops character and it tests you and challenges you to quit, every day. You've heard me say that an athlete puts himself in a position to be embarrassed every day and then promises to never let it happen again. It takes guts to get up when you've been knocked down. It takes courage to make mistakes and try again expecting a different result. It takes perseverance to keep trying when past results have been poor. And it takes many other qualities that all add up to character.

It has been said that character is a combination of traits that you would show even when no one is looking. When you're running laps in an area that the coach can't see, do you cut the corner? When the ref isn't looking do you trip the other player? When it's Sunday, and you should really be eating healthy, do you grab the pizza instead? All of the decisions you make, make up your character.

All that being said, I've seen some great athletes with really bad character traits. Just because someone is a "good" person doesn't mean they will win, and just because someone is a "bad" person doesn't mean they will lose. I will say this however, "character" catches up with you. It may not be tomorrow, and it may not be next week, but bad character traits eventually catch up to every athlete. Even in retirement.

"Just "Testing". Thanks"

In chapter 24 we talked about taking the emotion out of the process of winning and losing and I will remind you again here, as you go through all of the inevitable ups and downs of training and competing you can look at them positively or negatively, or you can take them as a challenge to your character. They are just "tests." Some are small and some are large, but all-in-all they are just tests of your character. Did you have a challenging practice today? How are you going to rebound and come back from it? Are you going to get all tied up in a knot about it? Or are you going to soldier on knowing that you are greater than ANY test you will come across.

My friend is one of the top snowboarders in the country. When she comes down the halfpipe and throws a new trick and misses it, she always says, "Just testing!" It's a fun little way to turn what most people would call a "fail" into a positive spin that keeps her mind in a positive state. She doesn't get down on herself for not landing the trick. She just realizes that what she just tried didn't work, so she'll try something else the next time. This was a test. It is only a test.

Conclusion

Just as an athlete needs to learn how to lose and deal with the inevitable setbacks that come from sport, an athlete also needs to learn how to win. How to "finish" and get the ball across the goal line. There is a level of confidence and authority that must be developed for an athlete to take possession of the victory.

By failing early and staying positive an athlete can learn how to deal with adversity and to keep going, but learning how to win is also a skill that must be learned. If an athlete constantly plays "up" and is never in a chance to win they never learn that ever important skill of winning.

Watch This Video

www.AthleteSpecific.com/
learning-how-to-win

Take Action With These Steps

- Take your journal and write down a time when you had a chance to win but didn't. Why did that happen?

- What could you have done to make that victory happen?

- What did you do to ensure you won the next time you were in a similar situation?

- Think of a time that you played "up". What did you learn from playing in that situation? How did you apply that knowledge to future events?

- Think of a time that you "failed". Now instead of thinking of it as a "fail" think of it as "testing". How does that make you feel? What can you learn know that you view it as a test and not a failure?

Chapter 27
Is It All Worth It

"I wanted a perfect ending. Now I've learned, the hard way, that some poems don't rhyme, and some stories don't have a clear beginning, middle, and end. Life is about NOT knowing. Having to change, taking the moment and making the best of it. Without knowing what's going to happen next.

Gilda Radner
Was an American comedian, actress, and one of seven original cast members of the NBC sketch comedy show Saturday Night Live.

If you have read this far, congratulations. If you jumped right to this chapter because you read the directions in the introduction then... congratulations. I have high hopes for you.

This was an epic book that has taken me the better part of nine months to complete. To say I'm not a little fatigued by the whole thing is an understatement. But if this book helps just one person, then I have done my job. (But I really hope it helps many more than that.)

As I edited this book, i debated what to leave out. They say you don't write a book, you edit one. But when it came to writing this book I didn't want to eliminate things that I felt could help you right now. I wanted the odds to be very high that you could pick up this book and get an answer to your question right now.

And that was especially true with this chapter. Some people told me that it was a bit of a downer to end on. Others told me that this chapter was, quite possibly, the most important chapter in the book. So what I was about to cut out, has made the cut and stayed in the book.

You're Going To Live a Very Long Life

I get an email every Friday from a guy by the name of Peter

Diamandis. I highly suggest you subscribe to his email by going to **www. Diamandis.com/subscribe** because what you will find is a discussion of where the convergence of technology, and our lives, are headed. Why have included a discussion about where our lives are going in a book dedicated to success in sports? Because the title also includes "life" and our time in sports is directly connected to our success in the rest of our lives.

It's important to understand that we are going to live a very long time. With the help of advances in technology the people at the forefront of those fields are saying that if we can just live until 2032 that we will have the potential to live through just about anything.

But the question then becomes, if we are going to live such a long time, what is our quality of life going to be?

Why does this matter now? Well, because you are going to probably risk a lot for your sport. I know I did. There will be opportunities to play where "Your coach/team needs you." And you'll play through a quad tear, or a shoulder strain, or a neck injury. You name it, you'll play through it, in the name of sport. For the short term. But your body is going to be with you forever.

From Performance To Preservation

I interviewed Steve Maxwell, an incredibly gifted athlete who, in his 70's, has the body to rival most Olympic athletes. You can listen to my interview by clicking here: http://thebusinesscalledyou.com/steve-maxwell In our discussion Steve and I talked about the problem most athletes go through and that is deciding when it is time to shift from a life of performance in sport to a lifetime of preservation. As I write this I feel like my warranty has expired. I have two hips that need replacing and two shoulders not too far behind it. My neck has had the equivalent of a hundred car accidents and my left quad has a tear that never healed resulting in countless ankle sprains and a messed up pelvis.

But I went to the Olympics.

The question then arises, "Was it all worth it?"

And my answer would be to you, "I'm not always sure."

I don't share this to scare you, not at all, many athletes come through their athletic career with flying colors. Others suffer the physical consequences of trading their health for their sport.

The Exciting Problem of Sports

Athletes have an interesting problem and that most people aren't athletes. With obesity rates climbing and couch-potato status being assigned to billions of people around the world, having an athletic physique is something to be revered. And if your athletic physique gets you on TV, look out, the attention is even greater.

That is why competing in sports is so special. It's unique. It makes you stand out. And ironically it doesn't matter if you are in the Olympics or make it to The Biggest Loser, you tend to get similar attention.

But with this attention comes a bit of a problem. A sense of, "Nothing is better than this." In fact, that's what people say to you when you make it to the Olympics. They say things like, "Oh, man, the rest of your life is going to be boring compared to this." And it doesn't even have to be the Olympics. It can be your High school championship, or your college sports experience, or anything else for that matter. People will envy you, and if you drink that Koolaid you'll believe it.

Many athletes work their entire life for an athletic opportunity and one of two things happen;

1. They make it.
2. They don't.

And you can be cursed either way if you don't understand this simple statement:

This is going to be one small goal in a lifetime of goals for you.

Let me say that again. Whether it's the Olympics, or anything else you are pouring your heart into, when it's over, it feels like it's going to be hard to replace it.

In some ways, that's true. Hear me when I tell you, the sport part of you never leaves and it will be something you need to feed for the rest of your life. But for the "achievement part" of your life, there will be other goals to go after. Your job will be to find what's next.

Protect Your Brain

It's the only one you've got. And as I write this book we are learning more and more about brain health every day. Check out Dr. Daniel Amen's books to learn about your brain and how to protect it and how important it is.

I debated long and hard as to whether I should talk about tis in this book, but alas, it may be what you need to hear so here it is.

I want you to be safe, happy, and healthy for a very long time. And understanding that your quality of life after you compete in sports is paramount you need to make sure you're protected while you play.

Protect Your Joints

We've got one set of joints, although I'm looking forward to being bionic personally. But there are many things I would have done differently looking back on my training, namely taking care that I was more flexible and that my joints were more ready for Gameday. This would have involved more warm-up time. More time taken for flexibility and strengthening of the supporting joints. Would this have solved how I feel today? Most likely. But the bottom line is we do the best with what we know at the time. And at the time I did what I thought was right. And I regret I didn't know more at the time about how my training would have affected my body later in my life. And I can tell you that many of my athletic friends who have nagging injuries later in their life would agree with me.

He Who Chases Two Rabbits Loses Both

This ancient quote is paraphrased from Confucius and basically mans that if you're trying to go after two goals at the same time, you're not going to get either one.

Now sometimes you have to do two things at once. Go to school and compete. Train and have a job to earn money. I get it, because I did all of that. But the bottom line is the more you can allocate your resources to your athletic goals, the greater the odds of them coming true. If you are stealing resources from your athletic goals (time, energy, money, etc) to do something else then your odds go way down.

But as you come to the end, or you reach the end of your athletic endeavours, you need to immediately immerse yourself in your next big goal. Because if you don't, you will fall back into your sport because you haven't found somewhere else to put your energy and this isn't healthy. You need to understand that your sporting experience is just one of an amazing number of experiences that you are going to have in your life. What are those experiences going to be? I don't know. But YOU now have amazing tools to go out there and make them happen.

Give It All You've Got

This isn't the "Rah. Rah" part of the book. I'm not telling you to go out there and risk your health and your happiness in exchange for athletic greatness. I know too many athletes who have done that and look back with a bit of regret. What I am telling you is to master all of the habits to be great. I've laid out a lot in this book and the truth is that all of the steps you master to be successful in sports you can apply to everything else in your life. Don't, how you say, "half-ass" it.

The lessons you will learn through sport are too important to not take seriously. Give it all you've got. Your results don't matter. Your effort does.

About Olympian Jonathan Edwards

Jonathan Edwards is a US Olympian, an entrepreneur, author and a speaker who lives in Calgary, Alberta Canada with his wife Michelle and his two kids, Quinn and Makena. He speaks internationally on the topic of high performance to sports groups as well as corporate groups with a fun and engaging style. There are a number of ways to connect with Jonathan. He is available for speaking, consulting, training, and if you have something creative in mind he is always open to new ideas to collaborate!

Connect with Jonathan:

www.AthleteSpecific.com: This website is where Jonathan posts weekly blog posts on topics relevant to athletes, parents and coaches. You can also find products and online courses to improve your athletic success.

www.TheHighPerformanceYou.com: Here you can find resources to improve self esteem, have more success, and increase productivity in your life. With a number of courses around a variety of topics you are sure to find a resource for you. Jonathan also provides corporate training and keynote speaking to organizations across North America.

www.TheBusinessCalledYou.com: As a way to give back, Jonathan regularly coaches and mentors other speakers, authors and leaders with their business to help share their message. Jonathan believes that "we are at our finest when we are sharing what we know with people who know like and trust us." The world needs more of us at our finest.

Instagram: @olympicjonathan
Facebook: @olympicjonathan
Twitter: @olympicjonathan

Acknowledgements

This book wasn't created in a vacuum. It's a lifetime of inputs from some of the best coaches out there, distilled into three hundred pages of wisdom. Good coaches. Some bad coaches. And a lot of people in between got me to where I am today and I thank them all.

You only get one chance to thank those people in a book like this, so here it goes. As complete a list as I can possibly make without forgetting anyone.

To Mom and Dad. Seriously. Who knew classically trained musicians could create an Olympian.

To Coach Winslow who asked a bunch of clueless fifth graders, "So who wants to be our goalie?" To Coach Blecharczyk who called us all "nimrod's" but got me to love playing lacrosse and to Coach Ide who helped me get really good at a young age. To Coach Huntington who was the catalyst for me to leaving Thayer Academy and to Coach Snow who brought me to Lawrence Academy and all the athletes I played with there who helped me become an All American.

To all the guys I ever played with on the Flantim's at the Baggataway Summer Lacrosse League at Babson College and to specifically Hal Bean who took a flyer on a free-agent, eighth grade lacrosse goalie. Those hot summer nights helped me to grow up fast and become a better athlete.

To all of the influencers at Camp Dudley in Westport, NY. For five summers I was immersed in a variety of sports and some wacky activities that shaped who I am today. Specifically, Andy Bisselle, Willie Schmidt, Ben Nelson, Carl Koenig, Mark Davenport, and to Lin Hancock and Steve Luke who introduced me to the sport of luge. And to Bob Goodwin who helped make some of that dream come true.

To all of the lacrosse coaches who impacted my game and my mentality to sports in general. Roy Simmons, Dom Starsia, Ted and Dick Garber, Pete Lasagna, Tony Manzelli, Jeff Snow, Ned Ide, and to Coach Corrigan at the University of Notre Dame who was right, "Not coming back to play college lacrosse will be your greatest regret." So true. I know I could have brought you an NCAA title way back then.

In the sport of luge I have so many people to thank. Mark Grimmette for being a great doubles partner. Chris Thorpe and Gordy

Sheer for being great teammates. And to all of the other teammates and competitors in such a great time in my life: Duncan Kennedy, Wendel Suckow, Bill Tavares, Joe Barile and Steve Maher. Erin Warren. Cammy Myler, Bethany Calcaterra, Maryann Baribault, Paul Baribault. Renee Myers, Brendy Reeves. Bonny Warner. Dawn Peterson. Kitty Manning. Cynthia Wight. Zianabeth Shattuck-Owen. Larry Dolan. Adam Heidt. And to the many coaches who helped that dream come true: Lin Hancock for the perfect introduction. Dmitry Feld for that one phone call, "Hey! Jonny E! You wanna do some doubles?" John Fee. "Bullet" Bob Hughes. Ron Rossi. Beverly Detweiler. Amy Chapin. And to Claire Sherred, Hans Sparber, Karl Brunner, Miro Zajonc, Fred Zimny, Jeff Scheuer, and to the myriad support staff, medical
personnel, sponsors, etc. Thank you.

To my now, fellow Canadian friends, competitors, and teammates. To Walter Corey, thank you. To Karen Hall for developing my "love" in/of the sport. Clay Ives, Harry Salmon, Steve Harris, Bob Gasper, Andre Benoit and so many others.

To Mary Dumont who was as competitive as I am and to Robin Soloway (Farmanfarmaian) who is an inspiration just to be around.

For coaches and athletes who have inspired me along the way: Wolfgang Schaedler, Paul Schimoler, Wolfgang Staudinger, Larry Quinn, Quint Kessenich, Georg Hackl, Markus Prock, Charles Poliquin, Charles Staley, Alwyn Cosgrove, Gray Cook, Mike Boyle, Mark Verstegen, Dave Tate, Louis Simmons, Thomas Incledon, Eric Cressey, Richard Way, Jerry Lynch, and so many others, too many to mention here.

And lastly, in regards to this book, I'd like to thank a handful of people who were so helpful in getting it done: To Mom, seriously, for being a great proofreader. I love you. Ruben Gonzalez at www.TheLugeMan.com for reading and helping to keep it on track. To my readers and input-givers: Owen Taylor, Alisa Marino, Jordan Levy, Brian Burkard, Joshua Fischer, Todd Wickstrom, Rom Elwell, Christopher Hurtgen, Pete Terech, Kim Maggi, I thank you all.

And to those I have forgotten, it's not out of malice. Probably the hardest thing to write in a book is not the book itself, but the "thank yous" to everyone along the way. To those I have missed, a sincere 'thank you'.

References and Resources

Page 118: The book "Getting Things Done" by David Allen is a fantastic book about productivity and time management.

Page 119: The Aura Sleep Sensor by Nokia can be found here: https://www.withings.com/ca/en/products/aura/sleep-sensor-accessory

Page 119: The Sleep Time app by Azumio is a great app for your phone that keeps track of your sleep and will wake you up when you are in a light sleep cycle: http://www.azumio.com/s/sleeptime/index.html

Page 119: For a list of White Noise devices to help create a silent sleep environment go here: http://www.nosleeplessnights.com/best-white-noise-machine-reviews/

Page 119: For darkeness in any room try this over-ear sleep mask: https://www.amazon.ca/Sleep-Master-smblu01-Mask/dp/B0015NZ6FK

Page 120: For a list of humidifiers for your room go here: https://www.amazon.ca/b?ie=UTF8&node=2224061011

Page 120: For the ultimate in duvets, pillows and featherbeds check out The Great Canadian Down Company: https://greatcanadiandowncompany.com/collections/duvets-and-comforters

Page 125: Research on tap water and how to find out if your tap water is ok https://www.ewg.org/tapwater/#.WbUuotOGN3I

Page 134: The story of Dale Begg Smith of Canada and then Australia. Olympic Champion in freestyle skiing: https://en.wikipedia.org/wiki/Dale_Begg-Smith

Page 135: My friend Vickie Saunders in Australia runs a global company teaching athletes how to get sponsorships for their athletic pursuits: http://www.thesponsorshipconsultants.com/our-team/

Page 206: If you've ever wondered where the whole "10,000 Hour

Rule" got started. Check out this website and read it for yourself: https://graphics8.nytimes.com/images/blogs/freakonomics/pdf/ DeliberatePractice(PsychologicalReview).pdf

Page 264: A great book by Harvard educated Shawn Achor: The Happiness Advantage.

Page 264: Justin Tuck is a former professional football player who played for the New York Giants. https://en.wikipedia.org/wiki/Justin_Tuck

Page 264: Bethany Hamilton is a professional surfer from Hawaii. She had her left arm bitten off by a shark and then proceeded to recover, and then win a professional surfing event. The movie Soul Surfer is an adaptation of her biography: https://en.wikipedia.org/wiki/Bethany_Hamilton

Page 278: The White Noise App can be found here: https://itunes.apple.com/us/app/white-noise-free-sounds-for-sleep-and-relaxation/id292987597?mt=8. And for Android can be found here: https://play.google.com/store/apps/details?id=com.tmsoft.whitenoise.lite&hl=en

Page 297: Cesar Milan of TV Dog Training Fame has a website and you can find it here: https://www.cesarsway.com/

Page 306: Dr. Daniel Amen is one of the top brain Doctors on the planet. With numerous bestselling books and courses, you can find his work at www.AmenClinics.com

More Book Bonuses!

I appreciate you taking the time to invest in this book. And as a thank you I've put together twenty-seven videos (one for each chapter) just for people who have purchased this book.

These videos are only available to readers of this book and can not be found anywhere else. In these videos I take a deeper dive into each of the twenty-seven chapters and add some additional concepts I was not able to cover within the pages of this book.

To access these videos head on over to: www.AthleteSpecific.com/athlete-guide-video-bonuses and get access today.

Did Someone Lend This Book To You?

I've got a video just for you! Seriously. I know what it's like when someone who loves you lends you a book like this and I have a special message just for you.

To get access to that video head on over to: www.AthleteSpecific.com/someone-loves-you

Don't Be Afraid To Reach Out!

Did you know, that as a buyer of this book, I don't always get to know who you are or where you are from? That's especially true if you bought the book on Amazon or as a Kindle. So no matter if you bought it through one of those retailers, or got it digitally, or if you stole it off the shelf somewhere...I want to hear from you!

Take a moment to send me an email and let me know what you thought of the book. You can do that easily by emailing me at coachedwards@athletespecific.com

55958999R00191

Made in the USA
Columbia, SC
18 April 2019